THE
DIARIES OF
NIKOLAY PUNIN
1904–1953

 ARRY RANSOM
UMANITIES
RESEARCH CENTER

Harry Ransom Humanities Research Center Imprint Series
Published from the collections of the HRHRC

Reflections on James Joyce: Stuart Gilbert's Paris Journal,
edited by Thomas F. Staley and Randolph Lewis

The Letters of Ezra Pound to Alice Corbin Henderson,
edited by Ira B. Nadel

THE
DIARIES OF
NIKOLAY PUNIN

1904–1953

EDITED BY *Sidney Monas*
AND *Jennifer Greene Krupala*

TRANSLATED BY *Jennifer Greene Krupala*

UNIVERSITY OF TEXAS PRESS
Austin

The publication of this book has been aided by a subsidy from the Center for Russian, East European and Eurasian Studies at the University of Texas at Austin.

The publication of this book was assisted by a University Cooperative Society Subvention Grant awarded by the University of Texas at Austin.

First edition, 1999

Requests for permission to reproduce material from this work should be sent to Permissions, University of Texas Press, Box 7819, Austin, TX 78713-7819.

⊗ The paper used in this book meets the minimum requirements of ANSI/NISO Z39.48-1992 (R1997) (Permanence of Paper).

LIBRARY OF CONGRESS CATALOGING-IN-PUBLICATION DATA

Punin, N. N. (Nikolai Nikolaevich)
  [Diaries. English]
  The diaries of Nikolay Punin : 1904–1953 / edited by Sidney Monas and Jennifer Greene Krupala ; translated by Jennifer Greene Krupala. — 1st ed.
     p.   cm. — (Harry Ransom Humanities Research Center imprint series)
  Includes index.
  ISBN 0-292-76589-4 (hardcover : alk. paper)
  1. Punin, N. N. (Nikolai Nikolaevich)—Diaries.   2. Art critics—Russia (Federation)—Diaries.   I. Monas, Sidney.   II. Krupala, Jennifer Greene, 1967–   III. Title.   IV. Series.
  N7483.P86 A3   1999
    947.084′092 —DC21
    [B]

                                      98-58095

To Konstantin Kuzminsky,

Irina Nikolaevna Punina,

Anna Kaminskaya,

and Leonid Zykov,

who helped make this book possible

CONTENTS

ACKNOWLEDGMENTS

This translation was a labor of love and would have been impossible without the love and support of Gary and Claire.

We would also like to acknowledge the indispensable help and support of Irina Nikolaevna Punina, Anna Kaminskaya, Leonid Zykov, Elena Lifschitz, Marian Schwartz, Leslie O'Bell, Vadim Rossman, Tatiana Karmanova, Irina Yanova, Phillip Herring, Robin Bradford, and the entire staff at the Department of Slavic Languages and Rare Manuscripts Department of the Harry Ransom Humanities Research Center at the University of Texas at Austin. And we owe a special debt to Thomas Staley, whose initiative started publication rolling.

Sidney
Monas

INTRODUCTORY ESSAY

Nikolay Punin and Russian Futurism

The avant-garde movement in the arts that became Futurism took shape between 1908 and 1913, first in Italy and then in Russia, achieving international prominence, even notoriety, and its greatest influence in the years immediately following the First World War. Closely related to Vorticism in England, Cubism in France, and some aspects of German Expressionism, in tone Futurism was antitraditional, anticanonical, and extremely antibourgeois. There was some affinity with radical political movements, with the new government in Russia, and with fascism in Italy, although it would be a mistake to characterize Futurism as either bolshevik or fascist. In the long run these (always tenuous) political associations served Futurism most unhappily.

Nikolay Nikolaevich Punin (1888–1953), art historian and critic, was probably the most respected voice of Russian Futurism in the visual arts. As a critic he was as important to the painting and sculpture of his time as the better-known Formalists were to literature. His lifetime spanned the old regime, all three twentieth-century Russian revolutions, the scrambled world of the New Economic Policy (NEP), and the Stalin years. A talented writer deeply involved in a dynamic cultural milieu, Punin brings that world and its inhabitants to life in his diaries.

In spite of the current "postmodernist" groundswell against the "modernist" hegemony over the arts of the 1920's, we are becoming increasingly aware of the expressive greatness, the variety, the innovativeness of those *anni mirabiles,* as well as the many follies, above all their arrogant tendency to overreach and outdo themselves. We have discovered new virtues in previously "rejected" writers like Wyndham Lewis, Blaise Cendrars, Djuna Barnes, Andrey Platonov, and Marina Tsvetaeva* as well as half-accepted painters like James Ensor and René Magritte and deepened our understanding of the "giants"—James Joyce, T. S. Eliot, Ezra Pound, Osip Mandelshtam,* Boris Pasternak, Anna Akhmatova, Pablo Picasso, Wassily Kandinsky, Kazimir Malevich*— I make no attempt to name them all; they are numerous. What seems to be going on in postmodernism is a rejection in the arts of what some call the megalomaniacal or "totalitarian" aspects of the putative modernist aspiration to change the world or make the whole world into a work of art and at the same time a scholarly-critical appreciation of the vitality, energy, originality, variety, cosmopolitanism, and revolutionary spirit of the intensely intercommunicative arts of the 1920's and continued exploratory use of many of the artistic devices they pioneered.[1]

Among these arts, self-styled Futurism had a distinctive place. It emerged in the visual arts out of its predecessor, Cubism, and involved both a continuing abstraction of forms and a hypostatization of the machine. To the Futurists all life either resembled a machine in its power and efficiency or fairly cried out to be refashioned in that mode. Ironically perhaps, the movement arose in the two least industrialized and least mechanized countries of Europe—Italy and Russia. Perhaps, as some writers have suggested, this was because Italy and Russia, still at an early stage of industrialization, could regard the modern city as a place of hope and the machine as a kind of savior.[2] Perhaps it was merely a reaction against the prevailing artistic language in the process of degenerating into sentimentality and vagueness, grown stale and remote from daily usage.

There was much about Futurism that was transient and ephemeral: its strident tone was bound to grow hoarse, its cocksureness to falter, its contempt for tradition and convention to be seen as a figleaf disguising the insecurity of raw ambition. Nevertheless, it was a movement that changed artistic practice and understanding forever. Nikolay Punin was quick to grasp its vitality and its relevance to modernity. He became its most eloquent spokesman and most persuasive critic.

Yet he was never "merely" a Futurist critic. Like all great critics, he was too sensitive, too intelligent, too erudite to be the man of one school only. His deeper commitments were to art and the expansion of human horizons. Many contemporary artists whom he was the first to appreciate were far removed from Futurism. He was a pioneer in the renaissance of interest in the old Russian icon. He thought the realist nineteenth-century Russian school of art known as the Wanderers* (Peredvizhniki) underappreciated. He brought Japanese and Oriental art into the Russian art scene. He was a formidable scholar of the European art of the Renaissance.

Turn-of-the-century Symbolists, whose modes dominated the arts and at whom the Futurists took aim, tended to link poetry and music, but the Futurists saw the most vital connection as between poetry and the visual arts. Throughout the nineteenth century there had been an intensive exploration of the relationship among the arts and a symbiosis among them. Friedrich Nietzsche's *Birth of Tragedy from the Spirit of Music* had an enormous impact on the Symbolists, as did Richard Wagner's concept of the *Gesamtkunstwerk*.

The Futurists by no means abandoned the link to music or the search for a "total" work of art, but they derived their fundamental inspiration from Paul Cézanne's reordering of space and spatial forms, as well as from the latest philosophical and scientific theories of the relationship between space and time.[3] The Cubist tendency to include bits of the real world in artworks—newspaper clippings, bits of objects, etc. (collage)—continued into Futurism and beyond into its offshoots in Russia, such as Constructivism. Constructivism (and its prime mover, Vladimir Tatlin)* tended more and more to smear the boundary between life and art, to take art out of the "musey-rooms" and into the streets, to abolish the necessity of "the esthetic gaze," and to create instead the art of "materiality," to make life into art, while the Suprematists (Malevich here) sought to refocus the esthetic gaze on primordial forms, primitive perceptions of shape, color, and texture.[4]

Futurist poets, who were generally also painters, tried to develop what they called a "metalogical" language (*zaum*)* that transcended ordinary sense and made full use of the expressive qualities of the sound and rhythms of language, the deep inner impulse of words to dance. Vladimir Mayakovsky,* Velemir Khlebnikov,* and Aleksey Kruchenykh also paid minute and meticulous attention to how words looked on the page, to the art of the book. Sound, sight, and sense were intricately interwoven.[5]

Russian Futurists were prolific with manifestos. Indeed, they turned the manifesto into an art form, using typographical devices, distortions of conventional line-spacing, capital letters, different typefaces, especially italics, drawings—many of the eye-catching devices that nineteenth-century radical pamphleteering had pioneered to catch the eye of newly and crudely literate readers. They used street-theater and performance art to attract attention, bizarre costumes to distinguish themselves from the more genteel Symbolists. The Futurists were outsiders, as against the established canonical artists and styles. They were hooligans who felt a natural sympathy with radical revolutionary political movements, but were not reliable members of underground organizations. Leon Trotsky saw them as bohemians making a bid for public notice with their *bizarrerie*.[6] Lenin (Vladimir Ulyanov) viewed them with puzzled distaste. At the revolutionary moment, however, the bolsheviks accepted whatever intelligentsia support they could get, whether from the wild Futurists or from a great, weary Symbolist like Aleksandr Blok.*

As a movement in the arts and as an artistic language Symbolism had no doubt grown tired. In a 1922 essay the poet Osip Mandelshtam wrote:

> *The Russian Symbolists discovered . . . the primal figurative nature of the word. They put a seal on all words, all images, designating them exclusively for liturgical use. This has very uncom-*

fortable results—you can't get by or get up or sit down. Impossible to light a fire, because it might signify something that would make you unhappy.

Man was no longer master in his own house; it would turn out he was living in a church or in a sacred druidic grove. Man's domestic eye had no place to relax, nothing on which to rest. All utensils were in revolt. The broom asked holiday, the cooking pot no longer wanted to cook but demanded for itself an absolute significance (as if cooking were not an absolute significance). They had driven the master from his home and he no longer dared to enter there.[7]

One thinks of Gertrude Stein and "A rose is a rose is a rose."

Nevertheless, Mandelshtam also and rightly characterized the Symbolist movement as *leonine.* Both Futurist and Acmeist practice were dependent on it, like the biblical honeycomb in the dead lion.[8] One could argue that Symbolism, in spite of its respect for the past and the canon, was the first avant-garde movement in Russia. It is on the border of modernism, though which side of the border might be disputed.[9] It is fair to say that Futurism derived as much from Symbolism as from Cubism, but this is a historical nicety, removed from the clatter and brouhaha of artistic conflict.

In any case no Russian poet or artist of the period between 1900 and 1925 would have agreed with W. H. Auden's dictum that "poetry makes nothing happen." Auden was of course reacting against the Romantic notion of poets as "unacknowledged legislators" and the social pressures of the 1930's and 1940's pushing poetry in the direction of social commitment. There was, however, a kind of "Futurist Moment" between 1913 and 1923, in which it appeared to many that poetry might make almost anything happen, a sense that enormous changes were imminent and that the right word needed only to be said for them to happen.[10]

That was certainly the atmosphere of the avant-garde in the arts everywhere across Europe, whether it called itself Futurist, Vorticist, Surrealist, Expressionist, Dadaist, Absurdist, or whatever. Most of these movements began well before the First World War, but the war no doubt intensified and complicated matters. It gave a ferocious impetus to both the creative and destructive aspects of the avant-garde, introduced a heightened cynicism, and increased contempt for sentimentality, hypocrisy, and untruthfulness. A stalemated war of attrition helped polish the metaphor of an "avant-garde" with its implied daring, resourcefulness, and mobility. While it contributed to the awe over the power of the machine, it cast a shadow of doubt over the machine's presumed benevolence. Traditional authority was discredited, and not only in the arts. In Russia, a revolutionary government came to power and, as it withstood the assaults of traditional authority upon it, attracted to itself avant-gardist sympathies in general.

The attraction of a new world rising on the ruins of a discredited tradition (Ezra Pound's "old bitch gone in the teeth") was a powerful one. Few artists indeed had had much to do with the bolsheviks in Russia before the revolution, and the Russian intelligentsia as a whole refused to cooperate with them in their first months of power. But the bolsheviks dangled that tempting opportunity called "a new world" before the eager intellectuals. Nikolay Gumilev,* a talented poet and even more talented critic and impresario, had always been a convinced monarchist and hated the bolsheviks, who shot him in a trumped-up treason case in 1921. But in 1919 and 1920 he ran a workshop for aspiring proletarian poets.[11]

Even traditionalists or retrospectivists like Gumilev or Anna Akhmatova were antibourgeois; it was part of the intellectual mind-set of the time, and not only in Russia. While Futurists wanted to throw the canon and its icons like Aleksandr Pushkin or Dante Alighieri "overboard from the ship of modernity"—i.e., refused to regard them as any longer canonic—the Acmeists and others more retrospectively inclined wanted to "make it new" (Pound's phrase again), insisting that tradition to remain alive had constantly to be renewed—a position not unlike T. S. Eliot's in his essay "Tradition and the Individual Talent." It is a mistake to exclude retrospectivists like Mandelshtam and Akhmatova and Eliot from the avant-garde.

The Russian Futurists, it is true, were mightily obsessed with the machine, in both the literary and visual arts. This made a gritty paradox: on the one hand, maximum impact on the audience, ambition to change the world; on the other, depersonalization, withdrawal from any interest in the nuance and detail of individual psychology, abandonment of both the individualized subject and the claim of the artist to hieratic mediation; on the one hand, a passionate charge of lyrical hyperbole, on the other, a condescension, a literal down-putting of merely personal emotion or precedence of lyrical feeling, whether of subject or artist. Nikolay Punin lived at the heart of this Futurist paradox.

Punin identified himself with the Futurist rejection of sentimentality, of obsession with the nuances of individual psychology (à la Anton Chekhov), of Symbolist mysticism and overemphasis on mood and tone, and of Symbolist neo-romantic hostility to intellection as stifling of passion and spontaneity. And yet he did not wish to lose his soul. He was aware of a certain conflict between mechanical abstraction and the spontaneity of feeling that was characteristically human, that he sometimes feared as deficient within himself, and that he struggled to retain.

Punin's career might well be called meteoric. By 1913, in his late twenties, he was a prominent figure in the Russian art world. By the 1920's, he was known abroad. After 1923, he began to encounter obstacles and his activities were restricted. From 1929 to 1949, he was known largely as a university teacher and the author of the standard textbook on the history of West European art. By the time of his final imprisonment in 1949, he was largely forgotten, both at home and abroad.

Until recently, Punin was almost unknown abroad except as a name attached to better-known figures, especially to Anna Akhmatova. And even his importance in her life and work has been grossly underestimated.[12] During the heyday of his career, he championed artists like Vladimir Tatlin and Kazimir Malevich. The range and depth of Punin's artistic taste and knowledge were truly great and enabled him to recognize, appreciate, and articulate diverse talents, from the fierce expressionism of Vasily Chekrygin* to the restrained impressionism of Nikolay Tyrsa* and the more conservative style of Vladimir Favorsky,* yet for all this he was but dimly appreciated.

At home, his memory fared only slightly better than it did abroad. In 1949, an enemy of his discovered indignantly that one of his books was still in print, and that was quickly remedied. A long generation after his death, in 1976, a book of his more conventional and conservative essays was republished with articles on icon-painting, various nineteenth-century Russian painters, Japanese art, and Picasso.[13] Only in the last three years have some of Punin's most characteristic essays on the revolutionary art of the 1920's begun to appear, largely through the work of his daughter, Irina Nikolaevna Punina, and members of her family.[14] From among these we include in the present volume a fragment, "Apartment No. Five," as edited by Leonid Zykov. The full text was published in *Panorama iskusstv* (Panorama of the Arts), volume 12, by the Sovetskii Khudozhnik press (Moscow, 1989). For reasons of space it cannot be included here, but it is certainly worthy of translation as a whole. In 1930, Punin was commissioned by the State Publishing House (Gosizdat) to write his memoirs. Between 1930 and 1932, he wrote a work in twelve chapters, about two hundred typed pages describing the situation of the arts and cultural politics from 1916 to May 1917. The publishers rejected what he had written, no doubt for political reasons. We do not know whether Punin intended to continue or whether he considered it done. This was the book to be called *Art and Revolution.* Zykov informs me that he and Irina Nikolaevna plan to publish it in Russian soon. From about 1916 until his death, Punin was arguably one of the three or four most talented art critics and historians writing in Russian. During the 1920's, he was undoubtedly the most influential.

Anatoly Lunacharsky,* Lenin's commissar of education (or enlightenment), appointed Punin head of the Petrograd regional visual arts section of the commissariat in 1919. The section was abolished in 1921; that was his only job within a government structure. His prestige and influence and importance did not depend on any official government appointment. His work in organizing the Petrograd museums, his teaching at the university, and his job on the board of the State Porcelain Factory,* though prestigious and not without government connections, came to him on the basis of his professional merits. He was certainly no apparatchik, and not by character a commissar. As an editor of *Iskusstvo kommuny* (Art of the Commune) he was an important voice of Futurism and the avant-garde. He was the only self-proclaimed Futurist who had anything like an ecumenical education in art history.

Far from a powerful egotist, Punin was a man constantly torn by self-doubt, frequently troubled and even self-denigrating. He deeply envied Akhmatova her poetic creativity, but envy (so destructive in some lovers) drove him not to attempt to destroy her, but to love, cherish, and even depend on her. Above all, he was torn by the Futurist paradox, the struggle between deeply charged personal emotion on the one hand and the ideal of intellectual control and aggressive mechanomorphic abstraction on the other. He tried to combine the words "thought" (*mysl'*) and "feeling" (*chuvstvo*) into a hyphenated thought-feeling or feeling-thought, but what T. S. Eliot called the "dissociation of sensibility" in literature, the reciprocal distancing of thought from feeling that Eliot considered so debilitating, Punin never entirely escaped.

At this point I should say something about how the diaries came to Austin. The story, which has its own pleasures, also bears on the larger picture.

While living in Leningrad in 1974, researching a book on the cultural significance of St. Petersburg, I became acquainted with the city's literary "semiunderground." It was the time of Leonid Brezhnev; Stalinist terror was a thing of the past, but life was far from comfortable for writers and artists whose works did not conform to the crumbling but still enforced standards of Socialist Realism. Brushes with the KGB, arrests, and threats of arrest were common. It was the time of Aleksandr Solzhenitsyn's expulsion from the Soviet Union. Publication and exhibition were denied and, above all, the wish almost all artists share to be "known," to have a "public," was denied them, except on official conditions that most refused to accept.

It was the time of clandestine poetry readings and art exhibits in private apartments. "Art" had become a way of life and gathered to itself an extraordinary array of vivid, intense, dedicated personalities. Some were talented, some not very; and the narcissism of these occasions did not altogether pass me by, though as long as a sinister knock on the door followed by arrests and confiscations remained a real possibility, these gatherings had their charm and excitement. This was the world of Andrey Sinyavsky, under his pseudonym Avram Tertz, described so vividly in his story "Graphomaniacs." In this world, Futurism, while not the only presence, was a powerful one. But it was a Futurism curiously detached from conscious politics, a purely "art for art's sake" Futurism!

Most of those who attended knew each other, read each other's works, and commented at length with free and easy spontaneity on each other's pictures. They all claimed to be fed up with any kind of politics, for or against the regime. Of course, that was in itself a political stance, and all knew it would so be regarded by the authorities.

In this milieu I became acquainted with Konstantin Kuzminsky, a figure of notorious eccentricity. In his early thirties at the time, he had a full beard, a paunch, red hair, blue eyes a little dimmed by drink; dressed in old leather; and was easily engaged, with a disposition toward extreme statement and a striking appearance that called to mind the anarchist Mikhail Bakunin or a number of Russian saints. Kuzminsky was a Leningrad poet of the same generation as Joseph Brodsky. He had run afoul of the regime, had refused to give way to it, and continued to act in a flamboyant, nonconforming manner.[15]

Kuzminsky had a flair for public drama. One morning, for example, he stretched himself full-length on Nevsky Prospect, the busiest street in Leningrad, forcing traffic to move around him. (To this very day I regard his confidence that traffic *would* move around him as a remarkable act of faith, worthy of his resemblance to the saints!) His own writing dwindled. He enjoyed reading passages from his own and others' samples of *zaum* and the spluttering reaction of much more genteel members of an older generation who would accuse him of being, as he put it, "A Fu-fu-fu-fu-futurist!"

Kostya became an impresario of "unofficial" Leningrad poetry and painting. He compiled vast typewritten anthologies and attended innumerable exhibits. His father had been a well-known, conventional Socialist Realist painter, a member of the academy, but however strained relations might have been between Kuzminsky and the old man, Kostya did learn a thing or two about painting from his father. Talented painters respected his opinion of their work. He knew vast amounts of poetry by heart and would recite at great length. He also took a certain pleasure in discomfiting me by long quotations from English poets I had little taste for, like Rudyard Kipling and Algernon Charles Swinburne.

Kuzminsky militantly aligned himself and his own writing with the Futurism of the years 1908 to 1922, and with Cubo-Futurist painting, but as an impresario he remained refreshingly eclectic. Writers of all schools brought their works to him. He even pirated some. His aim was to collect all poetry that could not officially be published. Intellectuals, Russian and foreign, who spent any time in Leningrad gravitated toward Kuzminsky, putting him at the hub of what was, to be sure, a rather small universe. It was big enough, however, to prompt the regime to make life increasingly uncomfortable for him. He applied to emigrate, and the authorities let him go.

Kostya had important "connections," who worried about him, and everyone knew the first weeks in America were hard for an immigrant. Martha Golubeva,* Punin's last wife (referred to in the diaries as "Tika"), had once been Kuzminsky's mother-in-law. Punin had entrusted most of his archive to his daughter, Irina Nikolaevna, but part, including the Punin-Akhmatova correspondence, to Golubeva, under the not unrealistic apprehension that if they came into Akhmatova's possession she might censor them. Golubeva died in 1963. After her death, her daughter, Nika Kazimirova, returned some, but not all of the archive to Irina Nikolaevna and her family (including Leonid Zykov). Nika was charmed by Kuzminsky and married him. By 1974, when I arrived on the scene, they were divorced; Kuzminsky had remarried and so had Nika, yet she retained considerable affection and concern for him. She offered to sell an important part of Punin's diary to my university for his benefit. A check was immediately forthcoming to ease Kostya's early days in expensive, hurly-burly America.

The most important result of Kuzminsky's first years in America was a massive anthology, in many volumes, of unofficial Russian poetry.[16] It does not reflect the taste of his own writing, but a genial and generous eclecticism. It is rather Punin-like in this respect. It is dedicated to the ongoing life of poetry as such, not to Futurism.

The notion, much bruited about recently, that Russian Futurism as the heart of the avant-garde nourished rather than opposed the principles of Socialist Realism, while it may contain a grain of bitter truth, is fundamentally belied not only by the generous taste of the "too late"

Futurist Konstantin Kuzminsky, but also by the all-embracing toler-
ance of Futurism's chief ideologue when it was in its prime, Nikolay
Punin.[17]

Thanks to Irina Nikolaevna Punina and Leonid Zykov there has
been a recent revival of interest in Punin. She has generously provided
us with portions of her father's diary, letters, newspaper clippings, and
other documents from his archive. In this volume we have included
all of our original purchase (1915–1936), while editing, with current
American interests in mind, the remainder. Konstantin Kuzminsky
has, in the meantime, established himself in the United States and is
now holding court in rural New York clad in his accustomed Oblo-
movian robe. He travels little (due largely to the American ban on
smoking in airplanes), writes a column for the New York Russian newspaper *Novoe Russkoe Slovo,* and remains a Futurist. His multivolume
anthology of unofficial Russian poetry of the 1960's and 1970's stands as
a unique work, a monument for the perusals of scholar and prosodist,
an exotic maze for the more casual Russian reader.

While Punin might well have been capable of echoing Emilio
Marinetti's encomium to "la macchina," his more considered opinion
would have been that the roaring car and the winged victory were
both beautiful.[18] ("The form is the same; the content changes . . .")
Although his rhetoric was rather better, he might well have echoed
Kazimir Malevich:

> *The new life of iron and the machine, the roar of motor cars, the
> brilliance of electric lights, the growling of propellers, have awak-
> ened the soul which was suffering in the catacombs of old reason
> and has now emerged at the intersection of the paths of heaven
> and earth.*[19]

Punin's writings of the period were not immune to that exultant,
apocalyptic, cosmic tone, but the diary on the whole strikes a rather
different note, generally more moderate and more easily available to
common human experience and sympathy.

In literature it is well known that Russian Formalist literary criticism
arose as a defense of Russian Futurism. Its key concept, "defamiliariza-
tion" (*ostranenie*), "making it strange," or "making it new," justified the
aggressive Futurist assault on generic boundaries. The expression of
areas of human life and experience exhausted by the generic resources
of conventionalized high art could be freshened by drawing on previ-

ously despised or ignored genres or unexpected perspectives. This seemed to the Formalist critics a key to the process of literary history, which at the same time justified literary study as an autonomous discipline, relatively independent of social and political shifts.[20] Although the Formalists had been influenced by two notable German theorists of art of the period between the turn of the century and 1914, Heinrich Wölfflin and Wilhelm Worringer, as had Punin himself, and although the Formalists were among the first to take a serious theoretical interest in the new art of the cinema, they contributed nothing directly to criticism of the other visual arts.[21]

Reasons for keeping a diary can be varied and complex. From 1934 to 1953, merely writing a diary in the Soviet Union was a risky business. Punin himself razored out a number of pages. Nika Kazimirova razored out the entries for October 1917. Even after Punin's death in 1953 there was a risk attached to the diary, and the family showed courage in keeping it intact. The diary omits mention of Punin's meetings with many of the cultural luminaries of the period, so it is doubtful that its primary purpose was mnemonic. It was primarily an exploration of his own inner self, a dialogue with his soul, one might say, except that Punin had a certain distaste for such language. What is expressed in these pages is not a powerful ego or some megalomaniacal need to change the world, but a deep need to be in tune with the changes that are taking place, to be alive in his time. In spite of the fact that he takes pains to show the diary to a select few—to women only, as it turns out; Akhmatova particularly, with whom he even maintains a "conversation book" (the phrase is Zykov's), but also (select passages) to Galya, Tika, and Irina—it is fundamentally a private document. Self-doubt is one of its most prominent motifs. Yet I think that he wanted posterity to read it. At the same time, he allowed it to pass through the filter of the women who loved him the most. In part, he kept a diary to test the adequacy or inadequacy of words in relation to his thoughts and feelings, or "thought-feelings" as he put it; in other words, because he was a writer.

He begins the diary at the age of sixteen, writing in the somewhat stilted literary language he later attacks as having no relation to contemporary life. He searches his memory of the past ten years for "significant" events, one of the most vivid of which is the death of his mother, his reaction to it, and the interpretation laid on that reaction by other members of his large family. His siblings thought him cold and unfeeling. One cannot help thinking of the episode of the mother's death in Leo Tolstoy's early novel *Childhood,* and there is something of the flavor of a literary set-piece. Yet the analogy is apt. Like Tolstoy, Punin tries to distinguish between what one is supposed to feel on such occasions (and the temptation to act out what is expected of one) and the complex, dense obscurity of what one really feels.

Like other men who have lost a tender, loving mother in childhood, Punin always felt the powerful need for a woman's love and approval, and no single love, no single source of feminine affection, could ever be quite enough. He needed a woman who regarded him as central to her life. He could temporarily tolerate (with some pain) shared affection for "sibling" rivals, but the sense of his own centrality had constantly to be renewed. The diary notes two or three passionate love affairs and some minor infatuations. There is the Turgenev-like (*First Love*) unconsummated "triangle" with Lida Leonteva ("Dama Luni")* and the student Evgeny Fedorov. There is his wife, Galya Ahrens,* who in the long run, he says, was the "only one" who remained loyal to him. There is the beautiful, dazzled young student N. There is the notorious glamour-girl of the art-world of his time, Lilya Brik,* who lived in a ménage-à-trois with her husband and the poet Vladimir Mayakovsky and whose sensual delights haunt Punin, along with her "impossible" opinions. There are two or three others. But above all there is his long, deep, unstable yet remarkably persistent involvement with Anna Akhmatova, one of the great poets of her time, a towering beauty in a world of small women.[22] The diary makes clear that their relationship was deeper and had a far greater influence on both their lives than is commonly assumed.

Punin came from a large, warm, conservative, upper-middle-class family. His father was a doctor who had served in a military hospital in Helsinki where Nikolay, or Kolya, was born and later a prosperous practitioner in Pavlovsk and Tsarskoe Selo.* The doctor was traditionally religious and in Nikolay's earlier years a rather stern taskmaster, though more tolerant later. When Nikolay tried to shy away from what he feared would be a difficult Greek exam, featuring Plato, the old man insisted he take it; the later Platonist who repeated in his art criticism that "it is the content that changes; the form remains the same" fondly kept the old man's letter in the same notebook as his own diary. Both his mother and his stepmother were traditional Christians, and conventional religion was part of the family atmosphere. As an adolescent in touch with the ideologies of his time, Punin lost his Christian beliefs. Later, as a Futurist ideologue himself, he saw religion as part of that world of sentiment and feeling that the Futurists thought needed to be brought under the control of superior consciousness and precise knowledge, that in a sense needed to receive instruction from the world of the machine. Yet he never entirely managed to repress what were undoubtedly religious needs. Instructively, he later noted in his diary: "The way to God is woman."

Punin was a precocious reader, and his notes on Immanuel Kant and Arthur Schopenhauer were quite sophisticated for his age. Later he discovered Nietzsche, with whom the diary continues a love-hate affair almost to the end. In general his comments on philosophers are acute and articulate but not markedly original, with one exception. Although he never had more than moments of enthusiasm for Marxism, a brief flirtation really, he did note that while Marxism was a weak philosophy, it nevertheless provided a credal system out of which a "real" philosophy "might grow."

From an early age, Punin admired Germany—indeed, he was an enthusiastic Germanophile and hated England. Germany was the heart of Europe, the most advanced country, homeland of philosophy, music, and the machine. And the homeland of socialism—especially of a kind of socialism that was as much aristocratic and monarchical as democratic; that was indeed somewhat resistant to democracy, about which young Punin, as a Nietzschean, had mixed feelings. Even with the outbreak of war, even with the death of his brother in the war and the overflow of youthful patriotic Russian emotion, he retained his admiration. Rather than turning anti-German, he continued to see Germany as the model Russia should emulate. In 1918, with his friend Evgeny Poletaev,* he published a book called *Against Civilization,* fundamentally an attack on the Anglo-French liberal tradition and an encomium of Germany and German "state capitalism" that some have seen as "proto-fascist," though in the diary he expresses mixed feelings about the book.

Later, during the period of the Second World War and the terrible nine-hundred-day Siege of Leningrad, his admiration seems to have drained away, but a certain awe remained. In the early days of the siege, he refused evacuation to Samarkand (later he accepted), because that would have meant moving with the academy and he preferred solitude under siege, "chasing windmills," as he put it. His disillusionment with the regime was nearly complete by then, and he believed the bolsheviks, alas, would not seriously fight. In the streets, he noted the "sheepishly submissive faces of the passersby." He compared the atmosphere of the city under siege with that of the Ezhovshchina* in 1937, the most terrible year of the great purge. He took only casual note of the horrors like the severed hand lying in the snow after a German bombing. Yet on October 11, 1941, he noted a change of atmosphere and mood in the city, a turn in the tide, the feeling that the city would survive the siege. He had long abandoned Germany as a touchstone.

In the early diary entries England served as Germany's antipode. In the 1920's, when Ramsey MacDonald's emergent Labor Party was having its ups and downs, in no small measure dependent on the British public's association of "socialism" with the newly created USSR, Punin's Anglophobia found nourishment in the daily newspapers. In 1925–1926, and especially during the British General Strike, diplomatic relations between Britain and the USSR were very tense and were indeed for a time suspended. Punin was certainly not alone in England-bashing at the time of the forged so-called Zinovev Letter, but his call for war with Britain over the seizure of the Aland Islands dominating the Gulf of Finland was not widely echoed.[23] It would be my conjecture that Akhmatova, who loved English literature and read it avidly, softened his attitude in later years.

Punin's dialogue with himself in the diary intensified and matured with the years. Although he noted at one point that "there is not a single contradiction in me," he made no attempt to fuzz over the many quite obvious contradictions that leap to the eye.

The Platonist who insisted that in art it was "the content that changes; the form remains the same" wrote with equal insistence that "beauty is not canonical." The cynic who called prostitutes "the only women brave enough to be sincere" boasted of Akhmatova's praise that "you can write like the tenderest of angels"; the "ladies' man" capable of carrying on three affairs simultaneously could also more or less sincerely reproach Akhmatova's infidelities: "It is characteristic of *love* that it relies on *one* person." The tender lover who called Akhmatova "Olen" (deer) and delighted in her nickname for him, "Kotik" (pussycat) or "Kotik Murr" (a cat story by E. T. A. Hoffmann), wrote on another page, "There is no wonder in my soul," and even denied that he had a soul at all. The realist who scoffed at superstition could not help seeing an earthquake that rocked Japan in the 1920's as a kind of cosmic revenge for the Russian defeat at Tsushima. The "spokesman" for Russian art who could in the early 1920's compare Picasso unfavorably with Tatlin could also write later, "Picasso is time, life itself." The Futurist, charmed by the power, efficiency, and beauty of machines, who could note, "I live like a well-organized machine," also resisted the encroachments of the cold steel of rationality upon the warmth of the human soul. "I have sworn not to become just a technical apparatus."

When Punin met Anatoly Lunacharsky for the first time in late November 1917, the new bolshevik commissar of education was socially isolated and ostracized and happy to greet any friend he could find from among the intelligentsia.[24] Their temperaments were congenial. Lunacharsky, far from being a fanatic, had a certain reputation among the Party's core of being a political lightweight, indeed even frivolous. He called himself "an intellectual among the bolsheviks and a bolshevik among the intellectuals," which was a bit of a brag since he did not seem to have been very deeply committed either way. Punin knew that Lunacharsky was a poor critic and a terrible playwright, but they got along. Lunacharsky was a bon-viveur, expansive, generous, and amiable. He was sincerely enthusiastic about the arts and sciences and recognized the importance of maintaining their autonomy from political interference if their services to the ideals of the revolution were to be sustained. He appointed Punin as well as Punin's friend the avant-garde composer Arthur Lourie,* Malevich, and Tatlin and even Evgeny Poletaev to important positions in the commissariat. For some reason both Lenin and Nadezhda Krupskaya admired him; when Punin was arrested for the first time in 1921, for suspicions roused by his roots in the old regime, Lunacharsky came to his rescue. Unfortunately, when Punin was rearrested in 1936 and 1949, his old comrade was no longer among the living.

In his brief sketch "Apartment No. 5," Punin has captured some of the élan and enthusiasm engendered by that swashbuckling ex-sailor Vladimir Tatlin and early Constructivism. The dominant music here features the breakdown of boundaries between art and life, between the esthetic gaze and utilitarian reality, between the museum, the gallery, and the "musey-rooms" on the one hand and the streets, the boulevards, the squares, the factories, and the mills on the other. Tatlin was working on a model for his never-to-be-built monumental tower to the Third International. The conception was grandiose. It was to be of immense size, spiral in shape (the shape of revolution, Tatlin insisted), constantly in motion, containing offices, planning rooms, a landing pad, all twisting and turning, with an owl-like command of the entire cityscape. One knowledgeable and astute observer at least has compared Tatlin's conception of the tower to the Dome of the Rock in Jerusalem, which Tatlin must have seen in his sailoring days, the oldest surviving example of Moslem architecture, built in the days when Islam was a revolutionary, not a reactionary movement.[25] Tatlin's disciples were assembling the model from a variety of materials and were talking passionately about the quality of materials, and Tatlin was urging them on with a barrage of curses, blessings, and (by no means a trivial item in the hungry days of War Communism, 1918–1921) a pot of stew.

Before Tatlin, Punin was awestruck. He was a man of action, which

Punin was not; a man capable of "materializing" his passions. The clothes Tatlin designed for himself, to my eyes somewhat absurd, roused Punin's enthusiasm. Both Punin and Tatlin played an important role, however, in engaging accomplished artists to design clothes, as well as other items of mass consumption, for the people. Punin was on the managerial board of the porcelain factory that produced china designed by Futurist artists.[26]

While Punin as a critic defended both Tatlin and Kazimir Malevich, his deeper sympathies would seem to have been with Tatlin. For even the Suprematist Malevich, with his insistence on a return to primordial shapes, depended on the esthetic gaze to be seen as art. It was still "easel painting," whether the famous black square or the *White on White,* in which a white square painted on a background of a different shade of white melts imperceptibly at one of its nether edges into the background.

Tatlin, on the other hand, worked in the hubbub of daily life with the materials that daily life offered. He did not so much want to change the world as to bring out its true nature. In defending the design of his aircraft, the "Letatlin" (in Russian *letat'* means to fly)—a kind of one-person glider—he insisted on its *organic* nature, learned, he said, from a close observation of birds and unlike the "mechanical" contraptions of aeronautical engineers. This might sound a bit strange from a Futurist worshiper of the machine; but one should remember the original meaning of "organic," derived from the Greek *organon,* meaning "tool" or "machine."

Recently, Boris Groys has argued that Stalinist Socialist Realism, far from being a negation of the esthetic dreams of the Russian avant-garde, was their fulfillment; that the dreams were megalomaniacal and totalitarian, whether to create a "new world" and a "new man" or to reveal a world and a man previously quite invisible and unknown. In spite of the radical discrepancy of styles, even in spite of what Stalinism did to the avant-gardists themselves or the systematic way in which it attempted to obliterate all evidence of modernism, there is a certain unhappy plausibility to this argument.[27] And yet all great artistic vision has a touch of the grandiose and the megalomaniacal. Surely what is totalitarian is the means used to realize the vision, not the vision itself. An artistic vision requires artistic means, even when, as Tatlin attempted, it is carried out in the everyday world. Murder and prison are not among them.

A long-term debate within social-democratic Marxism, both in Russia and in Germany, has been summed up in the literature on the subject as one between consciousness (*soznatel'nost'*) and spontaneity (*stikhiinost*, which can also be translated, if awkwardly, as "faith in the elemental"). These terms referred to the desired relationship between the organized social-democratic political parties and the working-class movements they were presumed to represent.[28] All participants in the debate assumed the necessary existence of both elements; what was in question was the relationship between professional revolutionaries (full-time intellectuals) and mass movements. Those who favored consciousness (like Lenin and Karl Kautsky) maintained that revolutionary change could not come about by means of spontaneity alone. The complexity and sheer massiveness of the modern world required study and understanding, which only full-time, professional revolutionaries could provide. The elemental movement had to be *led* by those who represented consciousness. Those who favored spontaneity (like Pavel Akselrod) saw the role of intellectuals and professional revolutionaries as providing clarity to issues that concerned the proletariat—clarification, elucidation, articulation, perhaps consular guidance—but no more than a shaping and articulating of what was primarily a movement of mass desires. One can see that this conceived relationship between consciousness and spontaneity was itself a bit abstract, quite complex, and could easily shift, depending on contingent circumstances and opportunities. In the long run, however, a Marxist revolutionary tended to belong to one side or the other of this debate.

One has to make only a slight transposition into individual-psychological terms (Freudian, if you will) to see the unconscious and the pleasure-principle as spontaneity and the ego and the reality-principle as consciousness, to see the close analogy with what I have called "the Futurist paradox" and the long-term conflict that warred within Punin's psyche. His attraction to the feminine, his need for women's approval, his general association of the feminine and the emotional with inspiration and creativity, his awe before Akhmatova's creativity, his feeling of inferiority confronting it, his longing for "wholeness," and his growing discontent with the mechanical and the abstract tend on the whole to put him on the side of spontaneity. About his diary, he noted: "I am more human here than I am in my daily life, my essays, or my speeches."

Punin's powers as a writer were considerable. His description of the Leningrad flood of 1924 is unforgettable. He captures eloquently both the destructive force of the flood and the exhilaration with which an elemental event could enliven an otherwise flaccid and indifferent human community. Although he does not explicitly state the ironical resonance the flood had in the context of the city's history, he does communicate something of his historical awareness: two previous great floods occurred symmetrically in that "most intentional" city, in 1724 and 1824; in the first, at least according to legend, Peter the Great caught pneumonia and died; in the second, his statue, according to Pushkin's "Bronze Horseman," withstood the elements and crushed the aspirations of the ordinary person. Punin's ironical wit also records what people were saying about the flood: some "blame it on the old regime"; others remark cynically, "Why are you all so happy about the flooding? It won't wash away the bolsheviks." It occurred in the year of Lenin's death, the year the city took his name.

Punin's description of the convent (*monastyr' v Borisovke*) where he spends a vacation with his family is full of sympathy for the archaic lyricism of the nuns' life and their bleak submission to circumstance and persecution. With the years, his antipathy for the bolsheviks and their rule becomes increasingly clear; yet his human sympathies at times include even them. One of his most unexpected insights occurs in the unlikely context of a badly conducted church service: it doesn't matter that the priest stumbles and cannot conduct the service properly; his congregation needs the words, even if they are not well spoken; similarly, he notes, even the incompetent communist agitator serves a certain popular need.

As the years pass, Punin's prevailing mood becomes more somber. During the war, in Samarkand, he thinks of the beauty of Leningrad in the spring. From time to time, a death-wish descends upon him. The storm and intimacy of his relations with Akhmatova are dispersed, yet some love and regard for each other remain to his death, and, for Akhmatova, well beyond.

Sculpture was not traditionally a Russian art; it was banned by the church. There were few Russian sculptors of the first rank before the latter part of the nineteenth century. When Lenin tried to mobilize extant talent to commemorate with fitting monuments historic Russian revolutionaries of all shades, the results proved meager and unsatisfactory. Revolutionaries do have their monuments in some places. But critics? Who has ever heard of a monument to a literary or an art critic?

Punin would not look well in bronze or marble. In words, however, he has his monument: a handful of essays, these diaries, the poems of Anna Akhmatova.

NOTES

Items followed by an asterisk can be found in the Glossary.

1   While many contemporary writers tend to stress modernism and postmodernism as antipodes, few tend to see the latter as a complete rejection of the former; on the contrary, most see it as a softened, more tolerant, less "purist," less "elitist" extension. See, for example, Hal Foster, ed., *The Anti-Aesthetic: Essays on Postmodern Culture* (Port

Townsend, Wash.: Bay Press, 1983); and especially Charles Jencks, *The Language of Post-modern Architecture,* 5th ed. (New York: Rizzoli, 1997). A writer who tends to stress the continuity between the avant-garde modernism and postmodernism is Marjorie Perloff, *The Futurist Moment: Avant-Garde, Avant Guerre, and the Language of Rupture* (Chicago: University of Chicago Press, 1986). Like Renato Poggioli, *Theory of the Avant-Garde* (Cambridge, Mass.: Harvard University Press, 1968), she posits a "Futurist Moment," a historical setting in which avant-garde movements that call themselves by different names and may indeed have had different intentions at their origin tend to take on the characteristics of the most radical (and perhaps "garish") among them. For Perloff that "moment" is 1913, though in her discussions it might well be extended to 1913–1923. Of course, the mixed and perhaps too limited receptions of artists like Cendrars, Magritte, and Ensor were based on the limitations of public taste. Platonov and Tsvetaeva, on the other hand, faced the problem of censorship and political suppression.

2   See Perloff, *The Futurist Moment,* pp. 81–115; 64–65.

3   For Symbolist "New World creation," see Irina Paperno and Joan Delaney Grossman, eds., *Creating Life: the Aesthetic Utopia of Russian Modernism* (Stanford: Stanford University Press, 1994). For Wagner and the *Gesamtkunstwerk,* see Thomas Mann, "The Sufferings and Greatness of Richard Wagner," in *Freud, Goethe, Wagner* (New York: Knopf, 1942), pp. 101–211; Wagner attempted "complete communication to all the senses of all that could be said," p. 120. No one doubts Cézanne's seminal role in the creation of Cubism, but the precise nature of that role has been highly controversial. See, for example, the difference between Albert Gleizes and Jean Metzinger, *Du "Cubisme"* (Paris: E. Figuière et cie, 1912), one of the early attempts to "popularize" Cubism, and Guillaume Apollinaire, *Les peintres cubistes* (Paris: E. Figuière et cie, 1913). No one doubts that Picasso and Georges Braque were outstanding Cubist painters who owed a great debt to Cézanne; but again, the exact nature of their relationship to Russian and Italian Futurism has called forth different opinions. At the turn of the twentieth century and for the next decade, quantum and relativity theory both had a considerable impact on the visual arts. See Linda Dalrymple Henderson, *The Fourth Dimension and Non-Euclidean Geometry in Modern Art* (Princeton: Princeton University Press, 1983). It should be noted, however, that the "new science" and its departures from the Newtonian tradition encouraged a number of mystical interpretations, some by scientists themselves, such as Sir James Jeans, others by mystics with some (sometimes formidable) scientific credentials, like Rudolph Steiner and P. D. Ouspensky, *Tertium Organum: The Third Canon of Thought, a Key to the Enigmas of the World* (New York: Knopf, 1981). Some of the Futurists absorbed the new science by way of its mystical interpreters and also by way of Russian Orthodox mystical traditions in which they were steeped. Among the Futurists, Mikhail Matyushin* was a composer as well as a painter and composed music for the startling 1913 Futurist opera *Victory over the Sun.*

4   Kazimir Malevich, *Essays on Art,* 2 vols. (Copenhagen: Borgen, 1968); Charlotte Douglas, *Swans of Other Worlds* (Ann Arbor: Ardis, 1980); *The Avant-Garde Heritage* (St. Petersburg: State Russian Museum, 1994); *Kazimir Malevich* (New York: H. N. Abrams, 1994); John Milner, *Vladimir Tatlin and the Russian Avant-Garde* (New Haven: Yale University Press, 1983); see also Vahan D. Barooshian, *Russian Cubo-Futurism, 1910–1930: A Study in Avantgardism* (The Hague: Mouton, 1974); Stephanie Barron and Maurice Tuchman, *The Avant-Garde in Russia, 1910–1930* (Cambridge, Mass.: MIT Press, 1980); John Bowlt and Olga Matich, eds., *Laboratory of Dreams: The Russian Avant-Garde and Cultural Experiment* (Stanford: Stanford University Press, 1996); John Bowlt, *The Silver Age: Russian Art of the Early Twentieth Century and the "World of Art" Group* (Newtonville, Mass.: Oriental Research Partners, 1979), on "modern" but not avant-garde painters like Alexandre Benois,* E. Lanceray, etc.; John Bowlt, *Russian Art of the Avant-Garde: Theory and Criticism, 1902–1934* (New York: Viking, 1976), which contains brief excerpts from Punin's criticism; Katerina Clark, *Petersburg: Crucible of Cultural Revolution* (Cambridge, Mass.: Harvard University Press, 1995); Peter Drews, *Die Slawische Avantgarde und der*

Westen (Munich: W. Fink, 1983); George Gibian and T. W. Tjalsma, eds., *Russian Modernism: Culture and the Avant-Garde, 1900–1930* (Ithaca, N.Y.: Cornell University Press, 1976); Camilla Gray, *The Russian Experiment in Art, 1863–1922* (London: Thames and Hudson, 1962); Anne d'Harnoncourt, ed., *Futurism and the International Avant-Garde* (Philadelphia: Philadelphia Museum of Art, 1981); Konstantin Kuzminskii et al., eds., *Zabytii avangard: Rossiia, pervaia tret' XX-ogo stoletiia* (Moscow, 1992); Vladimir Markov, *Russian Futurism: A History* (Berkeley: University of California Press, 1968); Nicoletta Misler and John Bowlt, *Pavel Filonov: A Hero and His Fate* (Austin: Silvergirl Press, 1983); Antony Parton, *Mikhail Larionov and the Russian Avant-Garde* (Princeton: Princeton University Press, 1993); Nikolai Punin, "Obzor novykh techenii v iskusstve v Peterburge," *Russkoe iskusstvo* 1 (1923): 19–24; Karl Schloegel, *Jenseits der grossen Oktober: Das Laboratorium der moderne Petersburg* (Berlin: Im Siedler Verlag, 1988); Richard Stites, *Revolutionary Dreams: Utopian Vision and Experimental Life in the Russian Revolution* (New York: Oxford University Press, 1989); Kirk Varnedoe and Adam Gopnik, *High and Low: Modern Art and Popular Culture* (New York: H. N. Abrams, 1990); William C. Wees, *Vorticism and the English Avant-Garde* (Toronto: University of Toronto Press, 1972) (the Vorticists were clearly Futurists of a kind, though they attacked their Italian cousins as well as Braque and Picasso); see also Peter Selz, *German Expressionist Painting* (Berkeley and Los Angeles: University of California Press, 1974).

For collections of Futurist manifestos: Vladimir Markov, ed *Manifesty i programmy russkikh futuristov* (Munich: Slawische Propyläen, 1967); Giovanni Lista, ed., *Marinetti et le futurisme: Etudes, documents, iconographie réunis et presentés par G. Lista* (Lausanne: L'Age d'Homme, 1977); Umbro Apollonio, ed., *Futurist Manifestos* (New York: Viking, 1973).

5 Edward J. Brown, *Mayakovsky: A Poet in the Revolution* (Princeton: Princeton University Press, 1980); L. Magarotto et al., eds., *Zaumnyi futurizm i dadaizm v russkoi kul'ture* (Bern: Peter Lang, 1991); Velemir Khlebnikov, *Snake-Train: Poetry and Prose,* ed. and trans. Gary Kern (Ann Arbor: Ardis, 1976), *The King of Time,* ed. Charlotte Douglas, trans. Paul Schmidt (Cambridge, Mass.: Harvard University Press, 1995), and *Collected Works,* vol. 1, *Letters and Theoretical Writings,* ed. Charlotte Douglas, trans. Paul Schmidt (Cambridge, Mass.: Harvard University Press, 1987); G. Janacek, *The Look of Russian Literature: Avant-Garde Visual Experiments, 1900–1930* (Princeton: Princeton University Press, 1984); Susan B. Compton, *The World Backwards: Russian Futurist Books, 1912–1916* (London: British Museum Publications, 1978).

6 Leon Trotsky, *Literature and Revolution* (Ann Arbor: University of Michigan Press, 1971), p. 130.

7 Osip Mandelstam, *Selected Essays,* trans. Sidney Monas (Austin: University of Texas Press, 1977), p. 76.

8 "And behold, there was a swarm of bees and honey in the carcass of the lion," Judges 14:8. The biblical reference is to the lion Samson kills on the way to choose his bride. On his return, he finds the honeycomb in the dead lion and shares it with his bride and parents. He then presents a coded version of the incident to his companions as a riddle: "Out of strength, sweetness" was the motif of a prescient essay by R. P. Blackmur, "The Lion and the Honeycomb" (republished later in a book of that title) in which he indicated how the decaying remains of the New Criticism nevertheless could serve as sustenance for a literary revival.

9 See, for example, Bowlt, *The Silver Age.*

10 This is the major theme of Perloff, *The Futurist Moment.*

11 For Gumilev and his "Poets' Workshop," see Sergei Makovskii, *Na Parnase Serebrianogo Veka* (Munich: Press of the Union of Russian Emigrants from the USSR, 1962), pp. 217–222.

12 See the essay in this volume by Jennifer Greene Krupala.

13 Nikolai Punin, *Russkoe i sovetskoe iskusstvo* (Moscow: Akademiia Nauk, 1976); recently some of his writings on Tatlin have been collected by his daughter, in *O Tatline* (Moscow:

Literaturno-Khudozh. Agentsvo "RA," 1994). A proceeding such as that launched against Punin automatically meant a prohibition on publication. The accused's books were confiscated from all public libraries. There was no written legislation on this, but people in "responsible" positions were well aware of the considerable risk of disregarding such prohibitions. Lists of prohibited books and authors were distributed periodically to all public libraries. "Book-extermination" as an aspect of Soviet censorship deserves more scholarly attention than it has received, as Leonid Zykov, the current editor of Punin's works in Russian, has pointed out to me. Picasso, of course, never submitted to the strictures of Socialist Realism. As a foreign communist and a great showpiece for Soviet propaganda, he enjoyed a certain limited license to make the artistic commissars uncomfortable.

14   Punin, *O Tatline.*

15   Suzanne Massie, *The Living Mirror: Five Young Poets from Leningrad* (New York: Doubleday, 1970). Avram Tertz (Andrei Siniavskii), *Fantasticheskie povesti* (New York: Interlanguage Associates, 1967); see also Tertz, *On Socialist Realism* (New York: Knopf, 1960). On p. 83, Tertz mentions Punin on Mayakovsky: "The most daring [critic] of all was N. Punin . . . At that time he was connected with futurism; he is completely forgotten now. As early as 1918 he noted 'the marked classicism of Mayakovsky's verses.' . . . He forecast that 'much as he would like to, Mayakovsky will never again rebel as impetuously as he did in the past.'"

16   Konstantin Kuzminsky, ed., *The Blue Lagoon Anthology of Contemporary Russian Verse, Antologiia noveishei russkoi poezii v Goluboi Lagune,* 9 vols. (Newtonville, Mass.: Oriental Research Partners, n.d.).

17   Punin was an articulate spokesman. It is not quite right to call him an "ideologue." Leonid Zykov is of the opinion that Punin was more caught up by the temperament of the "Futurist Moment" than deeply and genuinely committed in his view of art as a Futurist. There is much in the diaries to confirm this view.

18   Perloff, *The Futurist Moment,* p. 89.

19   Quoted by Perloff, *The Futurist Moment,* p. 12.

20   See Victor Erlich, *Russian Formalism,* 3rd ed. (New Haven: Yale University Press, 1981).

21   P. N. Medvedev, *The Formal Method in Literary Scholarship* (Baltimore: Johns Hopkins University Press, 1978; the Russian edition first appeared in Leningrad in 1928), is widely held to have been written by Mikhail Bakhtin; even those who deny his authorship see clearly the stamp of his influence. It is in this book that the charge is leveled. Relevant here, too, is the collection of Bakhtin's essays *Speech Genres and Other Late Essays,* trans. V. McGee (Austin: University of Texas Press, 1987); see the interesting commentary on these two works by Matthia Freise, *Michail Bachtins philosophische Aesthetik der Literatur* (Bern: Peter Lang, 1993).

22   *The Complete Poems* of Akhmatova are available in a bilingual (Russian-English) edition with useful annotation and supplementary commentary on the poet: Roberta Reeder, ed., *The Complete Poems of Anna Akhmatova,* trans. Judith Hemschemeyer, 2 vols. (Somerville, Mass.: Zephyr Press, 1990). There is a Public Broadcasting System documentary video on the poet narrated by Claire Bloom and Christopher Reeve, presented by WGBH, Boston, on November 18, 1991. See also the essay in this volume by Jennifer Greene Krupala. The most compelling source on Akhmatova's biography is Lydia Chukovskaya, ed., *The Akhmatova Journals* (New York: Farrar, Straus and Giroux, 1994), vol. 1; four volumes have appeared in Russian; *Zapiski ob Anne Akhmatovoi* (Moscow: Kniga, 1989–1994); Amanda Haight, *Anna Akhmatova: A Poetic Pilgrimage* (New York: Oxford University Press, 1976); Roberta Reeder, *Anna Akhmatova: Poet and Prophet* (London: Allison and Busby, 1995). The much puzzled-over "guest from the future," a prominent figure in Akhmatova's *Poem without a Hero,* was almost undoubtedly Punin, as Zykov has pointed out in "Nikolai Punin—Adresat i geroi liriki Akhmatovoi," *Zvezda* 1 (1995): 77–103.

23   British troops were on the Aland Islands under the authority of the Council of the League of Nations. Russia had first occupied the islands in 1709 in the war against Swe-

den. According to the Treaty of Paris that settled the Crimean War in 1856, the islands (which were less than fifty miles from Stockholm) were to remain unfortified. Imperial Russia administered the islands as part of the Grand Duchy of Finland. When Finland became independent in 1917, the international status of the islands was placed in doubt. However, the Alands Convention called by the League of Nations in 1921 excluded Soviet Russia from its participants. War was out of the question at the time—Russia was in no shape to fight one. But the Soviet Foreign Office was understandably very unhappy. Punin makes note of the incident in 1925, because the Soviet Union used it as propaganda, claiming that England really wished to occupy and perhaps arm the islands in preparation for war against the Soviet Union. See the *Pravda* article "Angliia ukrepliaetsia na Baltiiskom more," August 2, 1925, and "Novaia ataka" in the August 9, 1925, edition of *Izvestiia.* The islands were awarded to Finland. In 1939, the Finns armed and refortified them, and Punin's fears were actually realized in the Russo-Finnish War. In the peace treaty that ended that war Finland was allowed to keep the islands, but unfortified and unarmed.

24 | Sheila Fitzpatrick, *The Commissariat of Enlightenment* (Cambridge: Cambridge University Press, 1970), pp. 114, 121, where she calls Punin a "proto-fascist." Lunacharsky was the brother-in-law of Aleksandr Bogdanov, once a rival of Lenin's for preeminence in the bolshevik faction and the main object of Lenin's polemic against the "Godbuilders," in *Materialism and Empirio-Criticism* (New York: International Publishers, 1929).

25 | Robin Milner-Gulland, "Tower and Dome: Two Revolutionary Buildings," *Slavic Review* 47 (1988): 39–50.

26 | Lyubov Popova,* Tatlin, and El Lissitsky were among the artists who designed plates and other china for the porcelain factory.

27 | Boris Groys, *Gesamtkunstwerk Stalin: Die gespaltenen Kultur in der Sowjetunion* (Munich: Carl Hanser Verlag, 1988); translated into English as *The Total Art of Stalinism: Avant-Garde, Aesthetic Dictatorship and Beyond* (Princeton: Princeton University Press, 1992); see also Groys' essay in Bowlt and Matich, *Laboratory of Dreams.*

28 | The course of this argument in prerevolutionary Russia is most eloquently recounted in Leopold Haimson, *The Russian Marxists and the Origins of Bolshevism* (Cambridge, Mass.: Harvard University Press, 1955).

Jennifer
Greene
Krupala

INTRODUCTORY ESSAY
Punin and Akhmatova

In Nikolay Punin's diary entry for July 30, 1936, he writes that "An. has won this fifteen-year war." Fifteen years. Of war. Few would argue that Anna Akhmatova's relationship with Nikolay Punin was simple. From the start it resembled a battle in which the combatants seduced, wounded, comforted, and deeply loved each other. When they fell in love in 1922, both were already married, and there was never a time in their relationship when they were personally devoted only to each other. Even in those moments when they found time to be alone together, their situation weighed heavily on their love. "Our closeness is as fragile as ice," wrote Punin in 1922.

But Punin's relationship with Akhmatova really spanned far more than those "fifteen years — pretending to be / fifteen granite centuries." [1] It had a "prehistory" in their Tsarskoe Selo childhoods and early chance meetings, continued through the fifteen years, resumed on a different level in Tashkent during World War II, and then survived Punin's third arrest in 1949, remaining strong until his death in the Abez labor camp in 1953.

As contemporaries, Punin and Akhmatova both grew up in and remembered the society of prerevolutionary Tsarskoe Selo, and these memories bound them almost from birth. In fact, Akhmatova chided him for having crossed her path twice in her life without her knowing it: as children in Pavlovsk park and later in the 1910's at the Gumilevs. Punin made note of this in his diary entry for December 1, 1924:

> *I cannot forgive you, said An., that you passed me by twice: in the XVIIIth century and at the beginning of the XXth century.*
>
> *How did it happen that we didn't meet in Tsarskoe when we were still at the gymnasium, and how did it happen later that I was at An.'s about three times (at the Gumilevs), and I passed by? I was rarely there because . . .*
>
> *In the fall of 1890 we might also have passed each other by in prams in Pavlovsk Park. We were living there then year-round. An., if she calculated correctly, was brought to Pavlovsk about then, and they lived there until Christmas. She was a few months old.*

Both could remember the town before the revolution, when the streets were full of carriages and "the immortal Annensky" taught at the gymnasium. Tsarskoe Selo was a kind of refuge for the two of them, a place beyond the city and the complications of their lives where they could spend whole days together walking in the park. Akhmatova spent over a month convalescing from tuberculosis in a pension there in 1925. Punin visited her often, and they reminisced about their childhoods in the town and dreamed of a future together, whether at Tsarskoe Selo or some other place. "We spent the whole time talking about life together, about how to rent two little rooms in Kolomna (in order to be further away from people)—and to live. It feels so good to think and talk about it, could it really not be fated to be?"[2] By then Tsarskoe Selo was neglected and abandoned, but, through their shared memories, it provided them a connection that extended far beyond the years when they were physically together.

Punin first mentions Akhmatova in a diary entry from 1914. By then Akhmatova was already famous, having published three volumes of verse, *Rosary, Evening,* and *White Flock.* Punin apparently traveled on the same train with her and simply noted that she was "strange and pretty, thin, pale, immortal and mystical." There are no other references to her until July 18, 1920, when he remarks, "Today I saw Anna Akhmatova with Shileyko* in the park (of the Museum). She carries herself well. I relate to her as to somebody real. I am shy and afraid to see her. I am grateful that she has left the bohemians and Gumilev, and that she is not giving readings or publishing poetry now." Punin would always disdain her associations with "bohemians" and especially frowned on parties she attended at Pavel Shchegolev's.* In 1924, he wrote, "I don't like it when An. goes to Shch.'s—they drink a lot there, and the people are too free and easy . . ."[3] It was a longstanding struggle of wills, but Akhmatova never gave up her former friendships in the face of Punin's disapproval.

In September 1922, Akhmatova and Punin grew closer. Punin married Anna ("Galya") Ahrens in 1917, and in 1921 she gave birth to their only child, Irina. Punin also had close relations with Lilya Brik, wife of Osip Brik and lover of the Futurist poet Mayakovsky. Anna was married to her second husband, the Assyriologist Vladimir Shileyko, but also had a relationship with the musician Arthur Lourie* and theater director Mikhail Zimmerman. Punin wrote of Akhmatova, ". . . I don't know anyone, in whom there has lived such a large and pure angel, in such a dark and sinful body" (diary entry, January 10, 1923). From the beginning, then, their love grew out of a tangle of commitments and betrayals.

Akhmatova would not officially divorce Shileyko until 1926, but by 1922, Akhmatova and Punin were already involved. Punin was often seen escorting Akhmatova to various poetry readings and literary evenings. At this time Akhmatova had moved in with her friends Olga Sudeykina* and Arthur Lourie. Both knew Punin. Lourie and Punin often corresponded and discussed the nature of art and music and the ability to reach the masses through art. Punin hired Sudeykina to make porcelain statues in the State Porcelain Factory,* where he was director of the art department. This work may have saved Sudeykina, who, according to Akhmatova, was not cut out for life in postrevolutionary Russia. Sudeykina, considered a great beauty in her day, had delicate features and light blonde hair that created a striking complement to Akhmatova's dark and austere beauty.

By November 1922, Punin's diaries reveal that he is already deeply in love with Anna Akhmatova, and it is apparent that the feeling is mutual. His entries from this period are interspersed with passages from Akhmatova's poetry, some of which can be found in her 1922 collection of poetry *Anno Domini MCMXXI*. It was reprinted in 1923 with the addition of several poems written in late 1922 and early 1923. Most scholars note that many of the poems refer to Akhmatova's other husbands, Gumilev, who was executed in August of 1921, and Shileyko, with whom she began to break up in that year. Many of the poems do address Gumilev and Shileyko, but several from 1922 are likely to have had their source in her evolving relationship with Punin, including those beginning "Here is the shore of the northern sea," "It is good here: rustling and crackling," and "The fantastic autumn constructed a high cupola."[4] All three poems address a new love; in particular, "Here is the shore of the northern sea" admonishes the love for crying and falling at her feet, closely reflecting Punin's early declarations of love for her, in which he felt "doomed" to her.

> *Here is the shore of the northern sea,*
> *Here is the border of our fame and misfortune—*
> *I don't understand, is it from joy or grief*
> *That you are crying, fallen at my feet.*
> *I've had enough of the doomed—*
> *Prisoners, hostages, slaves*
> *Only with someone dear to me, unyielding and hard*
> *Will I share bed and board.*

AUTUMN 1922[5]

The language in the poem echoes that of Punin's diary entries from this period. He calls Akhmatova his "bitter death" and "dear joy," corresponding to her "from joy or grief" (grief and bitter have the same root, *gor'*, in the original Russian). He too is confused about his love for her, calling it both a "destruction" and "liberation" and "shelter," all feelings related to the state of being a "prisoner," "hostage," or "slave."

The poem "New Year's Ballad" from the *Anno Domini MCMXXI* collection refers to a specific incident in Punin and Akhmatova's relationship. Punin mentions it directly in his diary entry for December 30, 1922:

> *It's finished. I left as easily as usual, not broken and in no way upset. But my heart was weary, as if I had swallowed poison. Life, why are you this way? So you didn't let me dine with you. I am the sixth guest at the banquet of death* (poems of A) *and all five drank to me, the absent one, but I have the feeling that I will never die.*

The poem, which is dated 1923 (after Punin's diary entry), describes the same dinner, the absent one, and the poison:

NEW YEAR'S BALLAD

And the moon, bored in the cloudy gloom,
Threw a dim gaze into the room.
There were six places set at the table
And only one empty chair.

It is my husband and I and my friends
Greeting the New Year.
Why do my fingers look bloody,
Why does the wine, like poison, burn?

The host, raising a full glass,
Was serious and motionless:
"I drink to the earth of our native glades
In which we all lie!"

And a friend, looking into my face
and remembering God knows what,
Exclaimed: "And I to her songs,
In which we all live."

> *But the third, totally unaware*
> *Of when he had abandoned this world,*
> *Muttered, as an answer to my thought:*
> *"We ought to drink to the one*
> *Who is not here with us yet."* [6]

Several images in this poem were to become recurring themes in Akhmatova's poetry, particularly in her poetry dedicated to Punin. The first is the image of the New Year's dinner and toast, which recurs in "The Last Toast" from 1934, in "One More Toast" from 1961–1963, and in the opening scene to Akhmatova's *Poem without a Hero.* In fact, the scene is so similar to the "New Year's Ballad" that it leads Leonid Zykov to argue that Punin is "the guest from the future" in the poem, and not Isaiah Berlin, as is commonly suggested by Akhmatova scholars.[7] "The guest from the future" is also linked to the cycle of poems *Cinque* and the drama *Enuma Elish,* which was written in Tashkent and later burned. Interestingly, the title *Enuma Elish* recalls the New Year's celebration since it refers to an ancient Babylonian creation poem that entered into the New Year's celebratory ritual. It was translated into Russian by Akhmatova's second husband, Shileyko, further strengthening the link to Punin, who was to be Akhmatova's future "husband" after Shileyko.

At this time Punin thought that the relationship was over. He said that their inability to love one another openly (Akhmatova was still married to Shileyko, many still saw her as Gumilev's recent widow, and he was openly shunned by her friends) had caused their love to die before its time. Yet within a week their love had rekindled and burned even stronger.

As the year progressed, Punin's wife, Galya, became aware of the affair, and this caused difficulty in his home life. Punin still loved her and wanted to "preserve his home," to keep his wife and his daughter together with him. Matters were then complicated by Akhmatova's affair with theater director Mikhail Zimmerman. Punin, trapped in his own unwillingness to part with his wife, tried not to judge Akhmatova, but the situation remained tense at the very least. In later years Akhmatova would tell Lydia Chukovskaya among others that her relationship with Galya was a friendly one, but in these early days Galya wanted nothing to do with her husband's new lover.

It has often been said that during Akhmatova's years with Punin she did not write poetry. From the diary entries and from Akhmatova's notes to Punin it is apparent that their relationship did interfere with their work in both cases; yet perhaps most importantly, the climate in

the country was changing. After the publication of Boris Eikhenbaum's*
book on Akhmatova in 1924, in which he coined the phrase "half-nun,
half-whore" in reference to the lyrical heroines of her poems (an expression that would later be used as a weapon against her in Andrey Zhdanov's better-known and much-cited denunciation of 1946), her poetry
was increasingly criticized as being the domestic love poems of a woman
stuck in the tsarist past. After 1925, Akhmatova was not published for a
long time. During these years, she turned her creative energy toward
writing scholarly articles on Pushkin's works and translating books for
Punin's lectures:

> *Today An. stayed on, to spend the night. I put her up in the study
> and all night long I could sense her presence in the house even in
> my sleep. In the morning I went in to see her, she was still asleep.
> I had no idea she was so pretty asleep. We drank tea together,
> then I washed her hair, and she spent almost all day translating
> a French book for me. It is so peaceful to be with her constantly.*[8]

Akhmatova describes the same evening in her own laconic fashion in
the "Conversation Book":

> *9 July*
> **Sheremetev Fountain House**
> *Yesterday I was at K[oty] M[alchik's] for 28 hrs. I read and
> translated "L'art français sous la révolution" and we looked at the
> "Yusupov Gallery" by S. Ernst. It was very quiet and cool. In the
> evening Gessen* came by. Then the evening service—completely
> moving. We parted and said good-bye at my place in Marble
> Palace. My heart was heavy.—Akum.*[9]

From the diary entries and "Conversation Books" it is obvious that
in spite of the threatening times, 1925 and 1926 were happy years for
Punin and Akhmatova's relationship. Punin's life seemed to stabilize at
home; Akhmatova broke with Shileyko and Mikhail Zimmerman and
in 1926 moved in permanently with the Punins. Unfortunately, Punin's
diaries from 1927 to 1933 have been lost, so we have no real written
record of these years.

Akhmatova's poetry always relied heavily on memory and the inter-
section of events past and present, and her life with Punin in the twenties and thirties would later serve as rich source material for her poetry.
According to Nadezhda Mandelshtam,* Akhmatova never wrote about
her lovers until the relationship turned rocky:

Poetry and sex share a mysterious connection so strong that it's almost impossible to describe. Anna was aware of this, and she tried to force me to admit it as well . . . Anna never wrote poems to the men in her life until a crisis occurred.[10]

By the mid-thirties, just such a crisis had entered Akhmatova and Punin's relationship. In 1935, both Punin and Akhmatova's son Lev were arrested. Punin had also begun an affair with the woman who would become his third wife, Martha Golubeva, one of his assistants at the Hermitage Museum. She was quite a bit younger than Akhmatova and Punin. The bitter end to their love was also a new beginning for Akhmatova's poetry, as the crisis opened the floodgates of her creativity. Her friend Emma Gershtein notes the moment that Akhmatova began to write again in her memoirs, recording her conversations with Nina Olshevskaya-Ardova:

Nina Ardova—"It was there that she [Akhmatova] told me 'I've written all I can. The poems no longer come to me.'

"This was probably in 1935," I said, "Soon the poems were coming one right after another, and they never ceased until her death. She made a notation that it started in 1936. I think it all began with the poem, 'I hid my heart from you.' You know the poem."

"Yes, Punin was very cross with her about it."[11]

Many of Akhmatova's poems from this period relate to the disintegration of their life together. Several bitterly describe two people living together in isolation. In "I hid my heart from you," the poet paints a grim picture of her lonely life at the Fountain House:

I hid my heart from you
As if I had hurled it into the Neva . . .
Wingless and domesticated,
I live here in your home.
Only . . . at night I hear creaking.
What's there in the strange gloom?
The Sheremetev lindens . . .
The roll call of the spirits of the house . . .
Approaching cautiously,
Like gurgling water,
Misfortune's black whisper

Nestles warmly to my ear—
And murmurs, as if this were
Its business for the night:
"You wanted comfort,
Do you know where it is—your comfort?"

1936[12]

Not all the poems are bitter, however. In "Beyond the Looking Glass" from the cycle "Midnight Poems," Akhmatova comments directly on Punin's young lover, Martha. The tone of the poem evokes more of a sense of shock and nightmarish inevitability than any bitterness. The poet shares her flowers with the "young beauty," and the lover (Punin) moves an armchair for her. They act as if in a dream and are complicitous in the destruction of their love: "What we are doing— we ourselves don't know, / But every moment is more frightful."[13] The other event from 1935 that generated a stream of poetry was the arrest of Punin and of Akhmatova's son Lev. When Punin was arrested and taken away, Akhmatova was the only one home and recorded the event in "They led you away at dawn," from the cycle "Requiem." Shortly after Punin was released from prison, he awoke to find that Akhmatova had taken her notebook of poems from his wardrobe; it was then that he remarked, "An. has won this fifteen-year war." In that same year, Akhmatova too found another love in Vladimir Garshin,* whom she met while in the hospital.[14]

There is another break in the diaries from 1936 to 1941. Although Akhmatova and Punin were no longer lovers, Akhmatova continued to live in the Sheremetev communal apartment along with Galya Ahrens, Irina Punina, and briefly, once in a while, Martha ("Tika") Golubeva. When Punin began to write in his diary again, Leningrad was in the midst of war. Akhmatova was soon evacuated to Tashkent, and Punin and his family followed in 1943. Akhmatova met them in Samarkand and remarked that Punin was in such a state of starvation that he was unrecognizable. In the Samarkand hospital Punin wrote Akhmatova a long letter begging forgiveness for the injustices done to her and reminiscing about what her love had meant to him:

And it seemed to me then that there was no one whose life could
be so whole and complete as yours; from your first poems of youth
(the glove with the left hand) to your prophetic murmuring along
with the rumble of your poem . . . a lot of what I didn't forgive in

you rose before me as not just forgiven, but even, perhaps, as the most beautiful . . .[15]

Akhmatova cherished this letter and, according to Lydia Chukovskaya, showed it to many people. Both the Punins and Akhmatova spent the rest of the war in Central Asia. They corresponded frequently; and after the tragic death of Galya, Punin traveled to Tashkent to stay with Akhmatova for a few days. He notes that this stay was very comforting and peaceful for him. They may not have been lovers any longer, but they were still kindred spirits. Their relationship reached another, less turbulent level, reflected in some of the poetry Akhmatova wrote in Tashkent.

In Punin's last years, and after his arrest in 1949, he continued to correspond with and to see Akhmatova, but his deepest relationship was with Martha. It was she who supported him most while he was in the prison camp and encouraged him to write letters to stave off the boredom and loneliness, even though he knew he could not send them. After Punin's third arrest Akhmatova wrote the heart-wrenching "Lullaby," which, with its repeating lines of "Bye, bye, bye, bye, . . . aiee, aiee, aiee, aiee, aiee," resounds more as a lament.

Many memoirists and biographers portray Punin as an angry, sometimes cruel and unjust lover and blame Akhmatova's intolerable living conditions on him. Lydia Chukovskaya notes repeatedly in her journals Akhmatova's complaints about missing teapots and dishes and Punin's flaunting of lovers in front of her. The conversations reported by Emma Gershtein and Nina Olshevskaya-Ardova tell a different story. Ardova once asked Akhmatova whom she loved most of all, and she answered, " 'Well, I lived with Punin two years,' meaning that she stayed with him two years longer than she should have, so she must have loved him." [16]

Punin's diary also sheds light on this complicated but very human relationship. It was certainly not one in which Punin was never unjust, but rather one in which Punin and Akhmatova as complex human beings loved, hurt, comforted, and supported each other for over thirty years. Chukovskaya's journals are so filled with references to Punin that it would be folly to think that he did not play a role in Akhmatova's work. Akhmatova herself not only admitted that Punin was the addressee in "I hid my love from you" but also that he had a gift for helping her work out difficult lines: "He understands poetry amazingly well. His ear for poetry is as good as his eye for painting." [17] That is high praise indeed from one of the greatest Russian poets to the most renowned art critic of his time.

Nikolay Punin has received rather short shrift from Akhmatova scholars until recently; as the work of Leonid Zykov indicates, there is much more still to be learned about this interesting and erudite man, who, through his diaries, has left us a lasting account of his life, his generation, art, and the history of twentieth-century Russia.

NOTES

Items followed by an asterisk can be found in the Glossary.

1 Anna Akhmatova, "Northern Elegies," 1942, in *The Complete Poems of Anna Akhmatova,* trans. Judith Hemschemeyer, ed. Roberta Reeder (Somerville, Mass.: Zephyr Press, 1990), 2:345.

2 Diary entry for May 7, 1925.

3 Diary entry for July 25, 1924.

4 Leonid Zykov, husband of Punin's granddaughter, Anna Kaminskaya, is one of the few scholars who have written about Punin's place in Akhmatova's work; his article "Nikolay Punin as Addressee and Hero of Anna Akhmatova's Lyrics" in *Zvezda* 1 (1995) (St. Petersburg): 11–104, argues for Punin's influence on the above-mentioned poems as well as many others.

5 Anna Akhmatova, "Here is the shore of the northern sea," from *Anno Domini MCMXXI* (1923), in *The Complete Poems of Anna Akhmatova,* 1:573.

6 Anna Akhmatova, "New Year's Ballad," from *Anno Domini MCMXXI* (1923), in *The Complete Poems of Anna Akhmatova,* 1:617.

7 Zykov, "Nikolay Punin as Addressee and Hero of Anna Akhmatova's Lyrics," 95–96.

8 Diary entry for July 8, 1925.

9 "K. M." is Akhmatova's nickname for Punin from Hoffmann's character "Kotik Murr," and "Akum" is Akhmatova's nickname, "Akuma" or "evil spirit."

10 Nadezhda Mandelshtam, "Akhmatova," in *Akhmatova and Her Circle,* trans. Patricia Beriozkina, ed. Konstantin Polivanov (Fayetteville: University of Arkansas Press, 1994), p. 120.

11 Emma Gershtein and Nina Olshevskaya-Ardova, "Conversations," in *Akhmatova and Her Circle,* p. 148.

12 Anna Akhmatova, "I hid my heart from you," from *Reed* (1940), in *The Complete Poems of Anna Akhmatova,* 2:85. This poem was originally published in the 1940 collection *From Six Books* under the section heading "Willow." It is interesting to note that in many of the poems referring to Punin the willow is a strong image of their first days of love, as in the poem "Parting." She writes in the first section: "Not weeks, not months—years / We spent parting," clearly referring to the two years when Akhmatova remained living with Punin after the relationship was over; and in the second part she writes: "And, as always happens in the days of final rupture / The ghost of the first days knocked at our door / And in burst the silver willow."

13 Anna Akhmatova, "Through the Looking Glass," from *The Seventh Book* (1936–1964), in *The Complete Poems of Anna Akhmatova,* 2:270.

14 Garshin and Akhmatova corresponded during the war; after the death of his first wife, Akhmatova had agreed to become his wife and even to take his last name. But when she returned in 1945, she found that Garshin had married another woman.

15 Letter from N. N. Punin to A. Akhmatova, April 14, 1942.

16 Gershtein and Olshevskaya-Ardova, "Conversations," p. 151.

17 *The Akhmatova Journals,* vol. 1, *1939–1940,* ed. Lydia Chukovskaya (New York: Farrar, Straus and Giroux, 1994), p. 66.

NOTE ON THE
TRANSLATION

The diaries held at the Harry Ransom Humanities Research Center at the University of Texas at Austin consist of ten slim notebooks, often bound in a handmade cover, each about the size of a school composition book. They span the years 1914–1936 and contain Nikolay Punin's handwritten entries, newspaper clippings, and other enclosures such as a Christmas ornament made by Tatlin, postcards, and even a lock of hair (presumably Anna Akhmatova's). The diaries themselves have had some passages cut out, and others marked out at a later date. The first few notebooks contain comments written by Akhmatova in the margins. All in all, these small and somewhat battered documents are as complex and original as the man who wrote them. Even though the events that shaped his life occurred more than fifty years ago, Nikolay Punin's diaries are living testament to that life, and in reading them one is often transported back in time.

After completing a preliminary translation of the diaries, I traveled to St. Petersburg to meet the Punin family. There I found that the holdings at the HRHRC were actually the middle part of Punin's diaries and that he had kept a diary from 1904 until his death in 1953. Nikolay Punin's daughter, Irina Punina, his granddaughter, Anna Kaminskaya, and Anna's husband, Leonid Zykov, had already organized a great deal of Punin's archives into a collection of diary entries, correspondence, official documents, articles, and Akhmatova's poetry that, like a mosaic, told the story of Punin's life and work. Unfortunately, the scope of the present publication did not allow us to include all of these materials, but the family has kindly granted permission to include part of the collection dating before 1914 and after 1936 in this translation. The first section of this volume, entitled "Early Materials from the Punin Diaries, 1904–1910," and the last section, "Late Materials from the Punin Diaries, 1941–1952," are excerpts from the volume that the family is preparing for publication. We have kept their format in the translation. These sections are highly abridged; we hope that a complete volume will appear soon in Russian and eventually in English as well.

Apart from the aforementioned sections, we have also borrowed the term "Conversation Books" from Leonid Zykov's description (which he in turn borrowed from Johann Wolfgang von Goethe) of the three tiny date books included in holdings at the HRHRC. These little books were Anna Akhmatova's and contain phone numbers and addresses along with short "conversations" between Akhmatova and Punin, in which Akhmatova would make an observation and Punin would answer. They signed each entry, often using nicknames for each other: Akuma or Olen for Akhmatova and K. M. or Koty for Punin.

I am greatly indebted to the Punin family for their cooperation with this project and for their warm hospitality during my stay in St. Petersburg.

Since the diaries are handwritten, there are a few passages that are illegible; these have been noted in brackets. Otherwise, I have kept to the form of the entries and any ellipses, dashes, deletion marks, and other marks are Punin's own. Editor's notes and omissions are bracketed ([. . .]). In a few cases Punin also made footnotes to his entries, which are included in the body of the text. Notes in the margin and those added at a later date are indicated in the footnotes.

Russian proper names and place names have been transliterated using the Library of Congress system, except for using *ya* instead of *ia, yu* instead of *iu, y* instead of *ii* or *i,* and the omission of ' to denote the presence of a soft sign (e.g., "Dostoevsky" rather than "Dostoevskii" and "Vasilevna" rather than "Vasil'evna"). In citations of Russian titles we have strictly adhered to the Library of Congress system. In those cases where a common spelling has more or less established itself, that form is used (e.g., "Tchaikovsky," not "Chaikovskii").

All items followed by an asterisk (*) can be found in the Glossary.

THE
DIARIES OF
NIKOLAY PUNIN
1904–1953

Punin family, ca. 1895: left to right, Aleksandr, Punin's mother, Anna Nikolaevna, Leonid, Zina, Punin's father, Nikolay Mikhailovich, and Nikolay. COURTESY OF THE PUNIN FAMILY.

Nikolay Punin as a young student, ca. 1905.
COURTESY OF THE PUNIN FAMILY.

Anna (Galya) Evgenevna Ahrens, Punin's first wife,
ca. 1917. COURTESY OF THE PUNIN FAMILY.

Nikolay Punin at the Russian Museum, early 1920's. COURTESY OF THE PUNIN FAMILY.

Monument to the Third International, ca. 1920. COURTESY OF THE PUNIN FAMILY.

Nikolay Punin, Kazimir Malevich, and Mikhail Matyushin, 1925.
COURTESY OF THE PUNIN FAMILY.

Anna Akhmatova, photo taken by Nikolay Punin, ca. 1924. COURTESY OF THE PUNIN FAMILY.

Anna Akhmatova, photo taken by Nikolay Punin, ca. 1924. COURTESY OF THE PUNIN FAMILY.

9 Декабря.

"у меня такое чувство, что ты идешь не по моему пути, а лишь пересекаешь мою дорогу; рад к каждому перышку твоих ресниц и боюсь близости твоей, как гибели, оттого и прошу и буду ее от тебя, словно судьбу предупреждаю."
(из письма.)

30 Декабря

Кончилось. Вышел облако — легко, не сломленным и ничем не попрекаешь; как после льда только устало сердце. Что-же ты такое жизнь? так и не пустила меня к себе на урок. Я шестой гость на пире смерти (......) и все пять пили за меня отсутствующего, а у меня такое чувство, как будто я никогда не умру. А умереть вообще хочу, должен, ужасно было-ли не умереть. Сегодня пришел к Ан., холодно, сломана палка (времянка), совсем больна — сердце. Поехал

Pages from the diary. Entries for December 9 and 30, 1922.
COURTESY OF THE HARRY RANSOM HUMANITIES RESEARCH CENTER.

печку, ~~—————~~, потом ~~———~~ гуляли в
Летнем саду. Повеселела, стала улыбаться
своей милой детской улыбкой; зашли в
булочную, накормила меня пироженным, ку-
пили елку, проводила до дому; ~~————— ————
————— ——— · "——— ———— ———— ———"~~;
~~«——— · ———— ———— ————————
————) ——— ——— ——— —— ————.
———. ——————————— ———, ———
———— , ——————, ————————~~

Она разрушена последние дни бесстыдной
и подлой книгой Эйхенбаума, ~~———— ————
——— ——— ——— ————, ————————.
———————— ——————, ——— —— · ————
——— ——— ——— ————————), ————
—— ——————— ——.~~

Ни с кем я не был так терпелив и не-
жен, как с ней. Она удивительно и мило
добра (~~Нет~~ ~~————— —————— ————
— ——— ———, ——————— — ————
———— ———— ———— , ———————.~~

Poem in Anna Akhmatova's hand, with small drawing of a flower, n.d.

Pages from the diary. Entry for May 12, 1924. COURTESY OF THE HARRY RANSOM HUMANITIES RESEARCH CENTER.

Pages from Akhmatova's "Conversation Book." Entries for November 16, 1924, and December 21, 1924.
COURTESY OF THE HARRY RANSOM HUMANITIES RESEARCH CENTER.

19 Января 25 г.
Очень скучал без Ан.
как первый год — я
только еще страш-
нее и безысходнее.

15 Октябрь.

31 Декабря 24 г. ночь
К-М. без Оленя встре-
чал Новый год — было
очень больно, потому
что он не верил
что еще год будем
вместе.
Ан — отплатил
К. М.

Pages from Akhmatova's "Conversation Book."
Entries for December 31, 1924, and January 19,
1925. COURTESY OF THE HARRY RANSOM
HUMANITIES RESEARCH CENTER.

Anna (Galya) Evgenevna Ahrens, 1926.
COURTESY OF THE PUNIN FAMILY.

Anna Akhmatova with her son Lev and mother-in-law, Anna Ivanovna Gumileva, 1927.
COURTESY OF THE PUNIN FAMILY.

СССР

Народный Комиссариат
Внутренних Дел

Управление НКВД
по
Ленинградской Области

ДОМ
ПРЕДВАРИТЕЛЬН. ЗАКЛЮЧ.

3/·XI   1935 г.

№ 860

Ленинград, ул. Воинова, 25.

зак. 797—10000.

Удостоверение

Дано сие гр. *Пунин Николай*
Николаевич в том, что он
содержал*ся* в Доме Предварительного
Заключения с *24 Октября* 193*5* г.
и согласно ордера УНКВД СССР по ЛО
от „*3 Ноября* 193*5* г.
за №*1048-35* из-под ареста освобожден
3/XI 35 сего числа.

Дело № *3764*

Начальник ДПЗ

Секретарь

Photo of Nikolay Punin's document of release from prison, 1935.

Anna Akhmatova with Anna Kaminskaya, 1946.

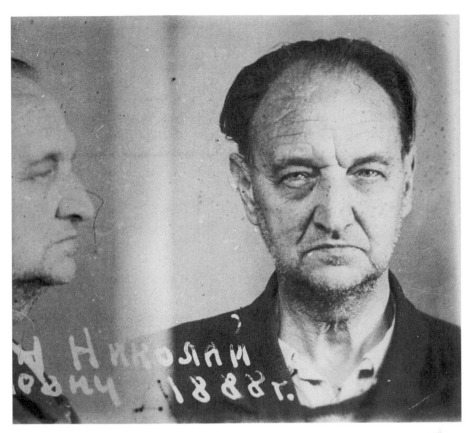

Nikolay Punin after final arrest in 1949. COURTESY OF THE PUNIN FAMILY.

EARLY MATERIALS FROM THE PUNIN DIARIES

1904–1910

<table>
<tr>
<td>Introduction</td>
<td>In 1904, Punin, sixteen, begins to keep a diary. He looks back over the past ten years of his life. Mother's death. 1904–1910: eventful years. Russo-Japanese War and Revolution of 1905. Tsarskoe Selo Lyceum, Annensky, student politics. Punin becomes a left-winger. Reading. St. Petersburg and its upper-class suburbs Tsarskoe Selo and Pavlovsk. First love: "Dama Luni," the concerts at Pavlovsk Railroad Station Hall.* Witte's* reappointment to the tsar's cabinet and constitutional politics. The Dumas.</td>
</tr>
<tr>
<td>June</td>
<td>. . . enough for today. I put down my book and went out into the garden. My brother Sasha* was home and eagerly accepted my invitation to play a game of croquet. Soon all that was needed for the game was done, and the measured, crisp sounds of clicking balls began to echo in the air. However, the sun did its work, and after we had played four games, of which three were mine and one his, I was thirsty. I went to get the fresh milk that was waiting for me and, having drunk my fill of this refreshing drink, decided to take Vera Vasilevna her binoculars, which I had been given yesterday for safekeeping when I was returning from the theater. I donned my coat and stepped outside. The weather was superb. A few white, wispy clouds quietly raced across the azure sky, occasionally darkening the sun; these airy battleships seemed intent on sinking this luminary with their threatening weapons in the boundless ocean in the air . . .</td>
</tr>
<tr>
<td>Tuesday,
5 June</td>
<td>Man proposes, God disposes says the Russian proverb, and it's true, all my plans for today have bitten the dust. I wanted to go to Popovka, but two things hindered me: first, I had to be at a birthday party at the Prokofievs, and second, a terrible rainstorm wouldn't even let me return home. First there was the storm; deafening claps of thunder accompanied each flash of lightning, a black cloud blocked our eternal but seldom-seen friend, the sun, and a slight darkness covered our cor-</td>
</tr>
</table>

ner of the earth with its enchanting coverlet for a while: the cloud delivered a terrible downpour and dispersed, like morning mist. Distant claps of thunder rang out and died in the air. The air was wondrous, it smelled of birch and poplar. Today is the symphony and as I was returning home I thought, "I'll have to go to hear the music," but I confess, it wasn't the symphony at all that drew me, but something else . . .

Be that as it may, I arrived (not alone) in the huge luxurious hall of the Pavlovsk Station. We spent the first part of the concert in the garden. But by the second, we took our places on the right side of the hall. I didn't intend to listen to the music, but somehow involuntarily the magnificent strains of Tchaikovsky's 6th Symphony drew me in. And I really had never listened to anything with such attention, but for that reason it was one of the best things I had ever heard.

Long before the end of all four parts, I was beside myself. This symphony conjured up Tchaikovsky himself so clearly, his life, his soul, and in general the life of each of us and that high reward, which one may still receive in life . . .

They warmly applauded the conductor, Fiedler. Although, as I have already mentioned, I was not alone, I neither heard nor saw that everyone had left, and I alone remained, as if chained to my seat. Even when I remembered that it was time to go home, I was loath to move from the spot, as if it were the spot that had created this enchanting music.

"A performance has been proposed."

The last few days flew by so quickly, I had almost no free time at all. This is explained by the haste with which we took to organizing a domestic theater.* Our young ladies had given us this idea, and I don't know why, because it hadn't yet been developed or worked out, but one of the young ladies and I quarreled. I hastily took to working up this suggestion. Although I was not on speaking terms with the young lady of the disagreement, and my father put forth an explicit and energetic protest, I secured agreement from the former, by way of negotiations through my brother, and permission from the latter, but with a few stipulations: first, that a play of my composition be performed, but only after my father's approval, and second, that rehearsals not be held at home. Without much thought, I agreed to both suggestions. We could very well organize the rehearsals in the park, and writing a play would not be much trouble for me. And so I began diligently and energetically to write a comedy. Three days later it was actually ready and passed the test—it was approved.

Today my brother and I have been drawing the programs and tickets since morning. We must hope that in the near future a peace will be brokered between us; that is, between me and the other young lady. That, of course, would greatly move things forward. In the coming days I want to look at my comedy from the point of view of the audience. I don't know whether it will come off.

Thursday, 15 July

Today I am putting my writings in order; the weather is bad, I don't feel like going out. I expected my grandmother on the one o'clock train. Our plans with respect to the domestic theater have bitten the dust. The opposition to them was put up by the fair sex. But what is to be done? My brother and I can't perform it alone. Strangely, I am not especially disappointed by this, there is so much that's new and cheerful on my horizon. Once a week I go to the amateur theater and write reviews of the performances and plays: I am participating in a choir of balalaika-players (as an alto). On Sunday I am hoping to go to the Bolshoy Theater to see the drama "Olga"; I don't know if there will be tickets.[1]

4 December

The world according to Kant.

In order to understand the world, we must reduce it to its simplest principles, its elements. Sensations do manifest themselves as such elements; that is, the smallest, most indivisible impressions. Yet at any moment, we of course receive a whole series of impressions, and in general in a lifetime we receive an endless number of sensations . . . We can perceive impressions only in time, and distinguish them only in space. Consequently, sensation is the content of cognition, and time and space its form [. . .]

Now that a little over five years has gone by, I want to remember the past—my childhood, the years of my life when my late mother was alive.[2]

I was about six years old then. My father had begun to teach me to read. As I recall, I learned that craft quickly and gladly. I'd go into father's study with a book, sit, and with my heart in my throat (my

---

1   Punin is most likely referring to the drama *Olga* by Yakov Knyazhnin (1742–1791).
2   Punin's mother, Anna Nikolaevna, and father, Nikolay Mikhailovich Punin, had four children: Nikolay, Aleksandr, Leonid, and Zinaida. Punin's mother died when he was six, and his father remarried Elisaveta Antonovna (born Jannine-Perrault). Although Punin makes no mention of having an evil stepmother, Anna Akhmatova would later remark that he always wanted to place her in that role with his own daughter Irina because of his childhood experiences. She said to Lydia Chukovskaya in 1939: "Nikolay Nikolaevich always tried to reproduce the very same sexual set-up as in his childhood: a stepmother oppressing a child. I should have oppressed Ira. But I did not oppress her" (*The Akhmatova Journals*, ed. Lydia Chukovskaya [New York: Farrar, Straus, and Giroux, 1994], 1:28).

father was strict), I'd begin to make out letters, syllables, and words, and, having read two or three pages in this manner, I would usually (if I had read well) model little houses on the floor with my father. I remember that once we modeled a very nice village, and my father began to decorate it with great patience: with glue he made it look like water was pouring out of the well. But it wasn't always so good. Sometimes father wasn't in a good mood, or I read very poorly and he'd really light into me. Sometimes he'd even start shouting, and I'd start crying (father didn't like my tears, just as I don't now) and then he would lose his temper, and I would get more and more confused and read God knows what. This would usually end with him sending me out of the room, and I, crying bitterly, would go off to the drawing room or the nursery, but soon I'd return and, having asked forgiveness, again would begin to read, and by this time would only rarely make mistakes. Yes, it was a good time, and it is both sad and happy to reminisce about it.

Nevertheless I soon learned to read, and on my saint's day, December 6, 1896, I got Ershov's "Konek-Gorbunek." This was my first book, and with what pleasure I read it then: Belinsky* berated Ershov in vain for his "Konek-Gorbunek," I enjoyed it then and enjoy it still, perhaps because I read it during a happy time. What does it matter what I liked, since I'm not yet an "old Belinsky," as my father predicts I will be, calling me (very rarely, unfortunately) "furious Nikolay," although this name does greatly flatter my self-esteem.

Now I will try to resurrect my memory of the time when my mother died. I will start at the beginning. At that time I was still going to Anna Semenovna Syrovyatkina's school. I don't remember precisely when my mother's illness began, but I remember how they sent us away for the summer, how with every day my dear mother got thinner and more sickly . . . I don't know whether my father knew exactly what her illness was immediately, but he, as I recall, was not especially disturbed, while my mother was digging all the time in father's books and looking for clues to her illness and it was not in vain that she searched; she found out that summer that she had cancer. Father carefully tried to hide it from her; once when she was sitting and thinking deeply about something, she suddenly threw herself back in the chair and began to weep, I remember this well, and even now I see and hear her weeping. Father tried to comfort her, but I don't know if there was hope. I think that there was, or else father, who loved her so, could not have been so calm. Summer passed; mother got worse and worse. For whole days she lay in a hammock in the garden and spent most of the time thinking. She knew death faced her. However, father either realized this or at least saw that her illness was serious. And so that's how the religious period of my life began, when I went to church often and prayed there for a long time. My father was also devout, and I used to pray with him constantly and fervently.

We prayed fervently and with faith. But often, I remember, while kneeling before the icon of Nikolay the Miracle Worker, I thought: "Is she really going to die?" and I became very bitter, and sometimes I doubted God, and I thought, is He capable of such a thing? So the days passed. Once we received a letter saying that papa's brother Misha had died, and I thought, what must be going on in mother's soul? But I didn't detect anything in her face. That very day I went to church and prayed for the dead, but found no peace in prayer; and yet that was not the way I regarded prayer at that time . . .

But autumn drew near, and mother got worse and worse. Papa began to go to Petersburg to the Aleksandr-Nevsky monastery and took me along. He wanted somehow to bring the relics of St. Pantaleymon,* I don't remember whether he brought them or not. So far, I have forgotten to mention the arrival of John of Kronstadt.* It was one of those autumn days. It was pouring rain, and we were sitting at home. Evening was coming on. Suddenly John arrived. We children were in the nursery, mother was in the bedroom, and my brother was downstairs, but father wasn't home yet. John came, and we children went out to see him first. He blessed us, tousled our hair. Soon papa arrived, and mother came out to meet him. He began to conduct a service. I am told he said that we were unfortunate children . . .

23 December August came. Mother had only five days of life left, but who could have thought in those terms then? I am told that when mother was very poorly, I began to act up, and that was why they sent me to my grandmother. But that's not true: quite the opposite; toward the end I always read to mother and in general tried to cheer her up.

In any case, I went to my favorite grandmother Varya's in Petersburg on the Vyborg side. There, as always, I was happy. I played "coachman," collected fares from everyone, and so on. And then came the 5th of August. The morning of that day, having gotten up early enough as always, having prayed zealously to God for mother's health, I began to play. Grandmother drank tea. My uncle who lived with her was standing and talking. Then a servant came in and handed him a telegram. I don't know why, but something stabbed me in the heart. Uncle opened it and read loudly: "Anya passed away today at three." Grandmother took sick, I remember. I brought her water and she calmed down. As for me, I remember I felt nothing, and it was only afterward that I sat at the window and thought: "So, it's over. What was the good of my praying this morning? She is dead. Should I jump out the window?" (It was a five-story building.) But I believe these thoughts were not sincere. Grandmother and I quickly packed and went to Pavlovsk. On the way she kept complaining to the old woman sitting next to her that the horse was going too slowly. I recall she explained her impatience by saying that now five of us orphans were left. That word made me feel bitter, uncomfortable, practically insulted. How could that be? Me, an orphan?

But then we arrived. We got on the train and arrived in Pavlovsk at about ten o'clock. There we set out on foot. I overtook my grandmother a bit, and walked a short distance ahead of her. Close to the house a woman met us and murmured something sympathetic like: "Your mother died," while I smiled, maybe even laughed, and answered her: "Yes."

30 December

But I quickened my step and having passed through the garden came out into the courtyard and along the back way into the nursery. As I walked through the garden, I saw that all my sand and clay buildings had been ruined, and I arrived in a state of terrible indignation and decided to have it out with my brothers no matter what. But then, there I was in the nursery. My brothers, just as little affected by mother's death, announced to me: "Kolya, did you know mother died?" Wanting to show them that I knew (and at the same time that their words seemed terribly stupid to me), I answered: "Well, so what?" Later they would often reprimand me for that answer. I was hurt and sad both for my brothers and for mother, and what I really thought was: "I knew it without your telling me," but that is not what I said . . .

When I had taken off my coat, I went into the drawing-room and saw: my father sat by the window with my grandmother (she had come in through the front door), both of them were crying, and I joined them. After we had cried some, we went into the bedroom, where mother's body lay on the bed. I loved her terribly tenderly, and I kneeled before her silent corpse, making the sign of the cross and kissing her, yet I did all this only because it was what had to be done . . .

*5 February
1905*

So, we have been drawn into the whirlpool of the revolution. We are spinning around in it, but we await bright new days. A little longer and a clear dawn will shine on the gloomy horizon, and then, then a bright sun will rise and warm us with its warm rays. We will wait and hope.

17 February	Today on the 40th day since the bloody slaughter in Petersburg, we gymnasium students sent a deputation to the director of the gymnasium with a request to perform a requiem for those killed on the 9th of January.[3] The deputation consisted of the following: Vengerov, Starikevich, Vasilev, Stepanov, Kosych (8th class), Shpakenburg (7th), Volkenau, Antonovsky, and Punin (6th). But the director, using an extremely complicated and unfair argument, refused our request, so during the fourth break we decided to sing "Eternal Memory" in the corridor. The authorities took measures, doubling the supervision. We began to whistle.
18 February	Difficulties have arisen with our deputation. The director was very displeased with the conduct of the students after his refusal, and today all the deputies really got it.[4]
11 March	. . . Bored again! Again my soul is torn apart! What do I want, what do I need! Love? Don't mention it. Spring? Well, it's spring. What do I want? Something exotic, unearthly. Suppose I were stopped on the street and asked to sing "God save the tsar," under pain of death. What should I do? Sing or not? I put this question to Borodin.* "Sing," he answered. Yet it seemed to me that out of a moral sense and on principle I should not sing. But after a long debate he (B.) said that these were not real questions, there was nothing to argue about. "Suppose," I said, "you had to be a liberal if you wanted to stay on at the university?" The same answer: an artificial question. When I said that I didn't care what kind of question it was but I needed to know his moral point of view and that I was sure he would stay at the university and become a liberal, he became angry, and after telling me that I needed to think before I spoke, and that one can't insult people, he left. Could Borodin, to whom I had trusted all my unripe thoughts, really be offended by my thoughtless words . . . ?
17 March	I don't have any strong convictions yet. I am not aligned with one political side or the other; nor do I have anything of my own to sug-

---

3 See the Glossary entry for "Bloody Sunday" for an account of the events that loomed large in the life of Punin and in the life of Russia in these years.

4 In several passages omitted here, Punin remarks on the shocking effect the war with Japan had on him as well as on his growing love for the theater and early attempts at criticism.

gest. I only know one thing, and it is my primary and main conviction: to live so that every word, thought, and action is sincere. That has been my ideal since childhood. Maybe it was unconscious, but it manifested itself long ago.

[no date]

In a year of political passions, I forgot about my diary.

1906

18 May

[. . .] My plans have fallen apart, terrible swinishness. My "Grushnitsky" is leaving a day after me, for a whole month it would seem. With him away, I'll have a long time to frolic reluctantly with "Mary." [5] Without him around, there is no one to provoke, so what would be so amazing if I made up with her in his absence.

22 May

[. . .] Life is both physical and spiritual, the opposite of death. Life is struggle. Struggle means suffering, since we struggle when we lack something, when we don't have something we want, which means we struggle when we are unhappy, when we suffer. Therefore, struggle is suffering. So life means suffering. Happy or unhappy. Life is suffering. To live means to suffer. Happiness is a chimera. Enjoyment is suffering.

25 May

How I would like to pray. To pray fervently and with faith. But there is no one to pray to. I wanted to try to seek out God, but no sooner did I lift up my head than I laughed. To this fantastic idol? To pray? There is no one to pray to anymore. But how I want to! If only to believe, to hope! To pray? The world is so cold and empty. There isn't a single spark in it. Everything is ruined, everything is trampled underfoot. If only some holy splinter remained. Nothing!

AFTERWORD TO THE DIARIES OF 1904–1906

*5 September
1908*

I have paused at that moment in my life when the first-period inner crisis that most people go through came to an end and the second stage of my metamorphosis began. I became acquainted with Ivanov and met with him, and we had long philosophical disputes. I cannot say that his influence on me was strong. It seems to me that he had already done

---

5   "My Grushnitsky" is a reference to a character in Mikhail Lermontov's novel *Hero of Our Time* (1840). Grushnitsky is the hero's rival in a love triangle; when his rival leaves, the hero finds that he is no longer interested in his love. Punin places himself in the hero's shoes here, most likely referring to his love for Lida Leonteva (later referred to as "Dama Luni" in the diaries).

his part when he drew me away from the class crowd. Later on I stood apart from him and perhaps served him more as a support than he did me. After that, Borodin began to play a major role in my life. Little by little this strange person became the only one to whom I would entrust my experiences. I have called him strange, and that's the only thing I could say about him now. Having been born into a quite well-to-do family, he received a brilliant education, pedagogically speaking. He was also by nature a completely balanced person, but his mother developed his will to such an extent that he could dominate many of his desires. This situation along with his strong, yet by no means profound (he had more of a cold practical mind rather than one which reflects all the inner life of mankind), mind would make him a cold, just, honest pedagogue in the old sense, which he became in his future field. He was always capable of hearing out the confessions of ailing souls, yet he wasn't able to talk to them, nor could he give them that calm, deep, and fully spiritual give-and-take that my mind, terribly tormented as it was by its inner discord, so insanely, so persistently demanded. I almost always left him dissatisfied. I am inclined to think that he never really understood me; whether this was due to those insane, unbearable impulses of my soul, which were absent in him, or simply that it was a consequence of his characteristically deep egoism I don't know; but he lacked the ability to answer my most secret thoughts, or he answered them in a way that made me later regret my inappropriate sincerity so greatly that I now remember him partly with hatred and contempt.

After these horrible storms of the fourth class, after I saw school in its true light and especially after the "domestic unpleasantnesses" (I call them this, because I am ashamed to call them by their real name), Borodin became for me the only person whom I sought out for meetings and conversation, and who gave meaning to many days of my life. Along with these outer events, my inner life developed strikingly quickly. My studies in astronomy did not last long. I was mainly interested in the biographies of great astronomers and the philosophical implications of this science, so that no sooner had I exhausted all the popular and general-philosophical books on astronomy than it was necessary to begin to study pure mathematics, and my interest in astronomy dissolved like a fog. In vain I listened to the reproaches of Ivanov and of the math teacher Travchetov, a very original man and a talented mathematician. Astronomy had left me forever. I devoted myself to literature, and my idols—forgive me, oh gods—became Belinsky and Rousseau. I remember very well how hard I tried in Russian class, with what impatience I waited for the return of my written essays, for which I always received an F or D, because I had not mastered any style and didn't know orthography. How earnestly I studied literature and what a great celebration it was for me when I made the teacher of Russian (Mukhin)—he didn't want to do it—give me a B for the term. I wrote essays, both those that were assigned and those that weren't, and in this way I was able, in the course of a year, to correct my style to such an extent, and learned how to think, that for my essay on the theme of "Autumn in the Tsarskoselsky Park," I received an A- (orthography). And I have yet to master orthography.

That same winter I very quickly moved from Belinsky to philosophy, history, religion. . . . I passionately loved those little books of the biographies of great people published by Pavlenkov.[6] With boundless joy I plunged into the souls of great people, with a strange pride I found in them features resembling my own, with a mad suffering I acknowledged their preeminence. I wore myself out over those little books more than I had in all my life up to that time; I examined myself to the point of idiocy and attributed significance to every small point: a pose, a manner of dressing, the type of life of each of the great people. I compared them with my own and was delighted when they had something in common, and I was endlessly tormented when they were different. Schopenhauer's notion that a genius must have a short neck tormented me terribly, because I have a long neck. I remember that I escaped into the park to devour these biographies with all the passion of youth. I bought them myself and, having spent all my money on them, checked them out of libraries. How many of them I read and reread and bought, I don't know. I have only a few left now; obviously these books had other fans. It is also true that these books had another significance as well: they provided me with a mass of historical material and fed the embryo of my future love for history. And thanks to one of these biographies, I became acquainted with the philosophy of Schopenhauer, and it immediately caught my attention. I received Schopenhauer's essays as a gift for Easter, and all spring I intoxicated myself with him, only dimly perceiving his pessimism, but grasping quite well those many thoughts already familiar to me.

All of this was during the winter of my sixth class. But then the summer of 1905 came. Late that summer I met Lida Leonteva.

---

6   This popular series by Pavlenkov was later revised and republished after the revolution by Maksim Gorky in the series "The Lives of Extraordinary People." It was part of Gorky's campaign to bring literature to the people, along with the publication of popular editions of the classics of world literature.

The new academic year began. Even earlier the Tsushima battle had been fought, and I always remember that dark, sad day when we learned of this horrible event.[7] I was choked with tears; sorrow filled my soul. Russia was sad and the whole country silently mourned the impossible defeat.

Time passed, October came, there was agitation everywhere, everything overflowed its banks. I was morally exhausted myself, thanks to the biographies and Schopenhauer. Borodin didn't answer my questions, and everywhere everyone was awaiting something, hoping for something. An important change that concerned me occurred on the pedagogical staff: we had a new teacher of Russian language, V. Orlov. He was a well-educated person, but one of extremely doubtful morals: he was simply nasty, as Ivanov said of him. The point was that he was of quite a liberal frame of mind and subtly and slyly liberalized the gymnasium, almost always having the class on his side. He very deftly closed the eyes of the administration and said in class what seemed then to be the most terrible things, such as: "The censor of Pushkin was the Chief of Gendarmes, Count Ben-ken-dorf," and moreover he pronounced "Chief of Gendarmes" in such a way that a naive person might think it was a great honor to Pushkin, while we students, of course, clearly saw sharp irony in this enunciation. He was always like that. In any case, the Tsarskoe Selo gymnasium owes its participation in Russia's political movement to him. I, thanks to my knowledge in the area of literature, and especially of Belinsky, immediately was moved to the head of the class; from that time on I never received less than a B for an essay.

The days passed, the October strike began, the Petersburg gymnasiums were vaguely troubled, something also occurred among us, but at that time I couldn't understand exactly what. Shut in my own inner world, noticing little that went on around me, I saw with amazement that life had touched our gymnasium and when suddenly, so unexpectedly, so strangely, a threesome or foursome of my "comrades" arose, and in place of Russian lessons debates on social themes began, then Orlov's practical advice, expressed for example, as follows: "The Workers' Soviet sends a deputation in such cases," oh, how well my comrades understood this phrase![8] I sat there amazed. But then our deputation

7   See the Glossary entry for "Bloody Sunday" on the impact of the Battle of Tsushima.
8   See the Glossary entry for "Bloody Sunday" on the importance of the soviets or revolutionary councils in the 1905 revolution.

was also sent; we demanded (I don't remember what), we threatened to strike, and I and two others, agitated by ambition, protested, didn't agree, and refused to strike. Later they wanted to hand us over to the comrades' court for this, but the situation and the influence of my speech alone saved us from these excesses.[9]

It was, I recall, the 14th of October. The whole 7th class, beside us three, asked Orlov (he was then the form-master) to present our demands to the director. In case of noncompliance we threatened a strike, and not just us, the whole gymnasium; because this new, extremely engaging idea, such a beneficial one at that, succeeded in catching on in all the classes through the work of the deputies. The next morning the gymnasium was closed. I was still asleep. True, I had already read Bebel,* Lassalle,* and Marx,* but since I was more interested in their philosophy and inner experiences, and since I still couldn't break out of my inwardness, I didn't understand what kind of connection these deep meditations on suffering humanity could have with our strike.

But the atmosphere became more intense hourly. Every morning and every evening we learned of new demands and new strikes, and then that famous general strike was called which caused the events on the 17th of October, and everything that followed to this very day. On the evening of the 16th of October, Borodin and I were sitting together arguing about "politics." My heart felt somehow strangely constricted and there was that exceptional mood of expectation which occurs before sunrise services or before the observation of a lunar eclipse. [. . .] The next day the manifesto was announced and after 12 o'clock flags appeared. And then there was something ominous in the northeast, blood and demonstrations, Trepov* and cartridges.

I didn't know for sure what my comrades were doing at this time: they told me that they went to Petersburg, gathered in groups, organized societies. Not having been closely associated with them in the past, with my protest I now acquired in them my true enemies.

Finally the gymnasium opened. The director—the immortal Annensky—made a speech, it was answered. We dispersed to our classes, but once released to freedom, like waves, we could not so quickly be calmed. Especially since all around us everything still raged, everything was alive and full of life. By force of the new resolutions we

---

9   The "comrades' court" was a system of justice instituted by the soviets by which a person charged with an offense would be judged by his or her peers.

had the right to organize assemblies, and these assemblies became the meaning of our gymnasium life. After classes we usually met in the assembly hall, set up rows of benches, a table, and a tribunal, and opened our meetings.

In the beginning the discussions concerned the recent days of our life, our further relations to the political life of Russia, our organizations. Permanent assemblies were established, a battle organization and comrades' court were worked out. All these special terms are all too well known to those of us who have had the joy and grief of having lived through this most interesting period. As before, I was in disfavor, and only a small group, the majority of which consisted of sons of the wealthy, concentrated around me, and two or three of my comrades. But irrepressible ambition, that strange desire to be involved in this spontaneous movement, forced me to approach the "left" more closely. Once I demanded to speak, not knowing ahead of time whether I would speak in favor of the right or the left. I spoke heatedly and passionately, I didn't know I could speak like that. I was carried away by my own talent, I saw transfixed faces before me, how the president and his comrades behind the table to the right turned toward me. I saw their amazement, their satisfaction, and a boundless pride filled me and motivated each of my phrases. This was my only well-delivered speech the whole time (I tend to stammer, if only rarely). It was on a topic so very fashionable at that time, on how our constitution existed on paper alone. As I finished, the thunder of applause drowned out my words— my first applause. Since that day every one of my speeches has been accompanied by applause. But I had spoken for the "left," I had escaped the court, I stood at the head of the crowd. But I had lost my independence, my world, I had poisoned my soul with that mercenary speech.

And then everyone blamed me, and with good reason, beginning with the director, ending with my comrades, for "sucking up," for betrayal to the leftists. True, my passion, my decisiveness, the absoluteness with which I then joined the left, made it easy for them to lay many risky and difficult tasks on me, like the deputations for instance, or mediation between the assemblies and the director, and so forth. But the hatred of my comrades always weighed heavily on me. When, after the Christmas holidays, the gymnasium was left without its ringleaders, who had not arrived yet, I reigned in it almost alone. Those were wondrous and bright days in my life.

I arrived at the assemblies fired up, agitated to the point of nervous tension, somehow or other ate, and, of course, didn't study (one could get away with that then). I spent the evenings at organizing circles and committees. Soon I established contact with the Petersburg circles and through my brother was prepared to take the 2nd Cadet School under my leadership. But winter passed, Russia became calm, the workers' organizations split one by one, a series of announced strikes fell apart without ever having managed to start. Witte's politics were irreproachable. Reaction began. Our gymnasium, like almost all gymnasiums, stood under the socialist banner. We prepared a strike, awaiting only our call from the Soviet of Workers' Deputies. True, we already had lost hope for the solidarity of all classes and were resorting to obstructions. I had been ordered along with Vasilev, who, by the way, is now in prison, to set fire to the gymnasium with our speeches. This was not successful. We resorted to violence and let loose a stink in the classes. The gymnasium was closed again, but by that evening the pedagogical union had quickly expelled seven members of our class from the gymnasium, including me, citing our excitable and nervous temperaments.

At almost the same time the head of the 2nd corps, having learned of the ferment of the cadets, threatened to expel my brother. Then the domestic dramas began. My father, with tears in his eyes, begged me to give up my intentions, promised to do anything I wanted, if only I would break with Antonovsky, who was the center of the organization. A cold man, but tough and practical, and he carried invisibly on his shoulders the whole external side of the gymnasium perturbations. For me, insanely tortuous days began, when my whole soul moaned from the battle between ambition, power, popularity, a vigorous life, and the tears of my father. I escaped to Borodin, but didn't say a word to him about all this, all the more since not long before I had precipitated a quarrel over convictions. That was also very much in fashion then.

Then I vainly hid myself in the Tsarskoe Selo park. In vain I wanted even just a minute to forget everything that had happened at home. And at home it was terribly difficult: beginning with my grandmother, ending with my little brothers, everyone fussed around me. No sooner did I come through the door than I had to deal with my father. Everyone hated me, wouldn't talk with me, and all the while they'd be conversing with each other, using expressions of amazement, anger, or hatred toward sons like me who did such things to their father. I was extremely exhausted. My father, that dry, pedantic, iron-willed man, cried and implored me—what was yet to come! So I made up my mind. All my decision cost me was my ambition and my glory, but God, how difficult it was for me. And when the gymnasium opened again, I was no longer the same. It's true that for a long time I still mingled diplomatically with the lefties, but I never played the same role again and I really couldn't anymore. I began to lose all my bearings, and that is how the third period of my crisis began.

Spring came, and as always overflowed noisily and majestically in the Tsarskoe Selo park. The colors became brighter and more alive, the sky was a marvelous blue. But deep down I felt dark and heavy. This past year of such terrible storms and crises weighed on me, and more and more my desire for life weakened. I still believed in the socialists, but I no longer lived by them. We moved, as always, to the Pavlovsk dacha. And I was amazed, when I saw the familiar places, at how much I had changed over the winter. But then I met Lida Leonteva. Since the previous year her image had remained with me, her mood, her speeches still rang in my ears—I had never forgotten about her.[10] We went to the park. She started right off talking about my deeds of the past winter. She knew about them. Echoes of my gymnasium fame had reached the vicinity of Tsarskoe Selo. She was the first to show me the true reason for my attraction to socialism; she penetrated to the very depth of my soul, and there she dug out my ambition and laid it before me, washed clean of any so-called ideals. In half an hour she had convinced me of the lie of socialism by the most simple means: she asked me about the sufferings of mankind—could they really be simply material? When I returned home I was no longer a socialist, not in body or soul, and I no longer bore within myself those stupid ideas. Instead I had her sad, her wondrous image.

A marvelously hot summer unfolded, with dark blue skies. And every day I walked deep into the Pavlovsk park and waited there for meetings with Lida. She came often, but not always. These were not prearranged meetings, but I knew that she walked along a certain path, and she understood that I always awaited her there. She came and told me about her sufferings, about the sufferings of the world, about the difficulty of life. Maybe she embellished a lot, maybe she lied, but for those moments of sincerity, for those moments when she responded to my torn and imploring soul, she responded not like Borodin, but full of feminine concern and full of a deep understanding such as I have never encountered since. For those moments, I forgive her every lie and all those wounds which she purposely inflicted on me later.

Schopenhauer again appeared on the scene, and by this time in full force. With each day I understood better and better that to live is horrible.

10   See note 5 above.

There were white nights. And almost every day, when everything was quiet in the house, around 1 A.M., I climbed out the window and went to get her to walk in the park (she allowed this). We walked until three or four and talked the whole time. Strange, such a setting, night and spring, yet I desired nothing but conversations. I heeded her every word, every thought. By that time there was nothing in the world I valued except her. Usually, I am stubborn and willful with women, but I obeyed her slavishly. I knew that I had to go and I went. I knew that this was weakness and humiliation, but I did it.

There was only one strange thing about all that. When I saw her, when she touched upon our relationship, I obstinately resisted, I never allowed her to get closer to me, and, sooner the other way around, rejected her.

Summer passed, I left for a week, but returned because I couldn't be without her. The days became shorter, the nights were dark, and our walks came to an end. But I was with her daily. Often she met me coldly and with hostility, but I couldn't not go to her.

Across from the Leontevs lived a student, Evgeny Fedorov. I don't know, don't understand, what kind of relationship there was between him and Lida, but he was at their place every day. He was a very interesting type. Lida said that he was terribly like what I would be in the future. Very probably, he suffered a lot because of himself. Then he was, like Lida, like me, disenchanted with everything to the extreme. He spent his nights at billiards and wine and slept during the day. I know he was sick. In his student's outfit, not at all new, he dressed half-mussed, Byron-style. He had a weak gait, a result of illness, a pale, even yellowish face and attractive deep dark eyes. He was basically nice. He treated me well, thanks to Lida. With time, I got the feel of his soul, and then how familiar it seemed to me! I know almost nothing about his life, just as I know nothing about Lida's. He had been in the Japanese War in the East while still a student. Whether he loved Lida I don't know, but she . . . she, it seems, loved him. Most of all, she was afraid. Once she told me something about him, and I carelessly let him know that I knew. He left immediately after that, and I could hear him on the stairs, my God, calling her a swine. She turned back to me, there were tears in her eyes, and she asked me never to speak to him about anything that was said between us.

Fedorov had only to enter the room for her to become cold with me and to make eyes at him. That was the situation with which I had to live. Endlessly loving Lida, I saw that she loved Fedorov, but what he felt for her . . . Perhaps he was tormenting her, perhaps it was his sufferings, about which Lida's eyes and lips spoke to me.

Then everything was destroyed in me, over everything stood the cross of rejection, and I was exhausted and lost.

Fall arrived. The woods breathed more and more quietly, the sky paled, clouds, white and soft like sadness, spread across the sky in shreds. Everything bright and alive was dying, and the happiness I had experienced also died. I was broken, spent the evening in the restaurant where Fedorov played billiards, drank, and returned home drunk at night. Sometimes I bought vodka and in the evening, when everyone was going to sleep, I got drunk alone in my room.

Once Lida, and this was the only time, arranged for us to meet at a concert. It rained, but I went, and she was there. I will never forget those hours when we sat in one of the corners of the hall and she bared her soul to me. She spoke of the world, of people, of Fedorov . . . We strangely understood one another. It was as if she had forgotten about me, forgotten that this conversation could torture me, because I saw how her soul ached, for the sake of which I was prepared to do anything.

Meanwhile all around me it was already really autumn. The leaves flew off, day and night a northern wind wrangled, to the like of which to this day I cannot calmly listen, which awakens the past in me, which sings the song of sadness and longing and the suffering of the departed, [. . .] of Lida.

It was the end of August. I was walking Lida home at night after the theater. We walked through the park; above us the green of the trees melded with the darkness of the heavens and it seemed as if the sky swayed together with the branches and rustled in troubled longing; the street lamps dimly threw light through the trees and patches of light lay on the sand of the path. She said this was her last time in Pavlovsk. She spoke of my love for her and comforted me, explaining to me how I had no need for her, nor her broken life, nor her ailing soul; that I was so intelligent, so competent . . . and then she began to sing and her voice blended with the sound of the wind. Her notes rose above it at times, at times faded away, and this sound and the wind and leaves all whirled and blended together.

I didn't see her in Pavlovsk any more that summer. I remained alone. I spent all my days at the edges of the park, where we had walked. I wrote Lida a letter, but there was no reply; wrote another, the same; finally I succeeded in going to see her myself. It was dark at their place, but she and Fedorov were home. Some young man arrived at the same time as me; we went into Lida's room, no one was there, but then Fedorov entered from the adjoining room. He greeted me very cordially and, when Lida's voice asked who was there, he told her. Lida invited me to come to her, but my fellow visitor was not received. When I entered I saw Lida, thin, pale, with disheveled hair, in an unbuttoned blouse.

I learned that evening that she was marrying Fedorov.

That night was disturbed, but although the next, and the next, and the next day after day passed slowly and grayly, I was calm, strangely calm. But when my sufferings became too strong and rose in my throat, I whispered the prayer of Lermontov:

I don't pray for my own deserted soul,
For the soul of the homeless wanderer of the steppe,
But I want to entrust an innocent girl
To the warm intercessor of this cold world.

For three more weeks my calmness continued. In mid-November it overflowed into the diary, and even earlier it gradually subsided thanks to the essay "The truth of life and the truth of creation," which was indebted to Lida for its existence and which brought me praise. Then I became acquainted with Nietzsche. My return to health and success at the gymnasium began.

When I related this purely outer material of my past life, I completely ignored what happened in the depths of my consciousness, even, moreover, my soul, since consciousness, which has only now been born, was then just blind instinct. But to talk of the life of the soul is to judge it. I couldn't and cannot do this, since I am not able to judge my own soul; since for one thing, it is mine. In this afterword I only want to say that I wrote my reminiscences as much to reveal the grossest and most criminal mistakes as for the satisfaction I get when images of my own experience appear before me again with greater consistency and more detail and connection. Yet I wouldn't want them to give the impression they were shaded by my mood at the moment of writing.

I judged myself unflinchingly, but I have not so much as hinted at the fact that had a huge meaning in my life: my struggle with myself, with my own nature, in the name of morality. I received an impeccable *theoretical* moral upbringing. Very few were instilled with such theoretical virtue as I was from my very first years, and few assimilated these inculcations as deeply as I did. Perhaps my family's relatively moral life greatly aided this. My father never betrayed my mother, never stole, never undermined others. His diligent attendance at church gave him a Christian reputation, his conscientious attitude toward his responsibilities inspired respect, and, finally, his dependability, honesty, along with his humble pride, created a distinct aureole around him and around us, which for us had the value of providing a living example of the virtuous life, and yet . . . These theoretical positions of morality which we accepted differed from real life and even from the life of our father, if only because these positions were unrealistic. Therefore, as soon as I began to understand and analyze my surroundings, this distance between the morality and life of my father, and even more of other people, struck me. By measure of my knowledge of the practice of life I could see that there was such a thing as ideal virtue, but there was also something different called real life. And third, there was also deception, which occurred when people realized the impossibility of applying an ideal morality to real life and created a soothing in-between, a life-morality. I had to choose between these three paths. Deception was not for me, thanks to my upbringing and youthful idealism. I dedicated myself to an ideal morality for two years of my life (8–9 years old), when I gave myself to Christ with all the force of my soul, in order to conquer the world, its evil, and myself, my evil. But I endured the most calamitous defeat, because I wanted to live.

I went from being an excessively virtuous follower of Christ to being virtuous in general, attracted to good people, to the philosophy of morals, to the morality of the so-called ideal, and each step in this direction threw me into battle, because I, as an animal organism, could not accept morality, every morality was a frame by which I was supposed to limit myself. It was impossible, and my whole life, all of it, to this very day, has been a battle of my whole being with the limits of every system of morals.

It was the month of November before I began to understand what had happened. And if up to this point I had hidden my love from myself because that was the common way, I could no longer do that. I began to understand that this was a love possible only once in a lifetime. Many people experience this period just at this time in their lives, when their childish idealizations are destroyed, after which, finding themselves prisoners inwardly, such people are confronted with real life.

DIARY — 1907

12 July

There is no good and no evil. This is the truth, which, if not just yet, then in the next generation will become the "Lord's Prayer." We will not find two people for whom identical events would be desirable or undesirable for one and the same reason. (The philosophy of Nietzsche, which I openly profess.)

19 December

For two months I have been taking painting classes. Now feverishly. My teacher wants to save me for the sake of art—but has he thought about whether it's worth it? Perhaps I was not called to serve before the altar of painting, that radiant, most holy of altars, just as I was not called to serve before all the other altars I have approached. With what scorn I was pushed aside by poetry, astronomy, and science when I attempted to lay my incense at their fires. How angry the muse's answer was: "This incense is too dirty—made from rotten pines. Go burn it before the masses." But I could not go to the masses, because I was among them searching, disdaining them. I could not go to them, because I desired goddesses and their fire. God knows, I loved the goddesses with too strong a love. Is it really my fault I was given poor incense and a great love? Am I really to blame that I cannot breathe without sacrifice?

He [my teacher] wants to save me—but is he allowed to? Let him tell me I'll find out myself sooner or later. Let him speak now, let him not torment me. That could be the final blow, and I disdain it in advance . . .

DIARY—1908

21 March

So what am I in the end, a poet or a philosopher? I am a thousand times closer to poets than philosophers. Even in Nietzsche, it was always form that interested me much sooner and more deeply. When I read Zarathustra for the first time, I got as much enjoyment as I have ever had out of it even though I didn't understand a single line.[11]

LETTER FROM E. A. PUNINA* TO N. N. PUNIN

Pavlovsk 19.VI.1909

Dear Kolinka

Not having received any word from you, I decided that you must be doing fine. Your letter confirmed my thoughts. Papa and I often think about you and it seems to us that one fine day you will suddenly clearly see that you are among strangers. Everything so pleasant to you, everything you are using, all this is the goodwill of strangers, and even if these strangers are very kind, attentive, endearing, all the same your inner voice will ask: "What do you give in return, how can you thank them?" Wouldn't it be better not to abuse their hospitality and to return to your home? And if you would just bring your gaze to rest

---

11   Punin's entry from August 1 is omitted. In this entry he compares his feelings toward two female friends, Dmitreva, who is beautiful and well-bred but shallow, and Ritova, who is not of his class, but who has a wonderful depth of soul. He treats Ritova rather shabbily and later regrets it.

here, your soul would catch fire from the closeness of your own people, who love you.

Everything is the same as usual here, everyone is healthy and satisfied with their fate. The children loved your mademoiselle and Lev* [Punin] is succeeding bit by bit. Zina is earnestly studying French with Lev, although it costs her some hard work. We received a short note from Lenya*—a postcard from Constantinople. He is in ecstasy over the Black Sea. Last Saturday grandmother Dunya came to visit with Valya . . . today they are getting ready to leave. Valya came to see us with joy, but Zinochka quickly dampened her spirits with her harsh and inhospitable character. At first, Valya wanted to go home, but then grandmother and I succeeded in brokering peace between them. Lev relates to girls as he does to cadets. They play in the neighboring yard all day. Thankfully, the dacha isn't rented.

Give Madame Shatko our sincere, heartfelt thanks for her kindness to you and for her hospitality . . . To Volodya my regards and my request that he look after how you are eating to make sure that you're completely O.K. At first, shy of large company and unfamiliar people, you probably looked after your appearance, but having made yourself at home and interested yourself in everything around, you probably put it on the back burner.

For me, my summer joy is arriving soon; the theater season opens on the 21st. The theater is rented not by the Petrovs but by someone else, I have forgotten the name; Maria Sergeevna is still in the box office, which makes me very happy . . .

I sincerely wish you all the best, and kiss you warmly, your mother.

DIARY, 1909

26 June

This whole time I've been thinking about those days, and more and more it seems to me that something great happened; that perhaps defined the character of my future life; that perhaps my fate depends on those days. All this is "perhaps"; but one thing is clear: I carry within myself a defined, complete, beautiful, original world view.

Now I will bring forth my three main positions, from which I can take everything, and which resolve all questions.

1) I have faith in man's instinct

2) I will not permit myself to construct any ideals

3) Creative work is a manifestation of human instinct (the more creative, the higher the human being)

LETTER FROM N. N. PUNIN TO N. M. PUNIN*

3 August 1909

Dear papa!

I was ill and got out of bed only yesterday. I didn't write you earlier, because the doctor shook his head and said it was almost probably typhus. Now everything is O.K., I am just a bit thinner.

And now, Greek. Of course, my hopes of passing are even more diminished, and I think there is no reason to delude myself on this account. It is better to think about it and come to a resolute decision about what to do. To tell you the truth, what is of most interest to me is whether you will let me make this decision myself or whether you want me to do what you think is best. I myself think there is no special basis for remaining in the historical-philological faculty. In principle, I am completely indifferent to where I finish, since no matter where, I will not become a professor. I need nothing from the university but the "piece of paper," and the law faculty gives me more free time, and by the third year I can already get private work, as the majority of lawyers do. As far as all the talk and gossip, I am completely uninterested. Well, no matter what, I would like to know what you want and think. The exam in Greek should be taken between the 20th of August and the 1st of September, and for the exam I need to know Plato and the Iliad, and I can't even make out Xenophon completely. Judge for yourself how it is possible to think of this. As for my further residence in Ladoga, I would like to stay here as long as it's possible, because I haven't seen anything yet. I arrived on the 15th and by the 20th I couldn't walk because my head hurt so. I have been only in Old Ladoga. So I leave this question, too, for your review. I await your letter. Aleksandr Mikhailovich and Olga Lavrentevna send their regards and thank you for the letters.

My regards to all. Love, K. Punin.

LETTER FROM N. M. PUNIN TO N. N. PUNIN

Dear Kolya! Your letter saddened me greatly. First, of course, your illness. You shouldn't go anywhere away from your own home. While you're at home, you are healthy. Poor Olga Lavrentevna and Aleksandr Mikhailovich!

The second problem is no less saddening: your desire to change faculties. You know very well my view on this question. I cannot stand people who run away, and I know that there will be little benefit from it. It is no small thing to lose two years. Later the student himself will regret this. As far as your suggestion of some kind of work for lawyers, there is nothing to hope for under any circumstances: the supply exceeds the demand a few hundredfold, and one must have extensive connections in the legal world to find any kind of work. Anyway, you could also find work in the historical-philological department; the lecture schedule won't bother you much. So my advice is to study Greek no matter what and to take the exams. I am sure this exam is not as terrible as you imagine it. As far as your stay in Ladoga is concerned, I give you full freedom, but only if you don't embarrass your dear hosts. Give them heartfelt regards from me and your mother and deep gratitude for their care and troubling about you.

Love, N. Punin

DIARY — 1909

19 August

Today I depart. I really don't want to leave this place. I don't think that there will ever be more joyful, brighter days in my life. I really don't want to see people. I've been almost completely alone here, accustomed to sit for whole hours with my fantasies. I dreamed and wrote by the window, looking at the Volkhov. Only one notebook left from this, which, God knows, can express only a droplet of my soul . . .

19 October

I have fallen in with our literary bohemians and was warmly received by Auslender.* Now that the first waves of contemporary Russian literature have reached me with its aches and pains and all its searching, the first thing that strikes me, the first foamy wave that strikes my soul with a fearsome cold, is the question of Russia. It is not the abyss that exists between me and those "realistic symbolists" that frightens me, but precisely the difference between their and my relationship to Russia. . . . what is there in Russia, what is its content and what is its form?

The content: the pursuit of what is Russian — the desire to be Russian at all costs; that is, to blurt out the idioms of the Russian muzhik, to sing the praises of Russian house-spirits, although before their time these were not the poet's business. On top of that, there is their eternal "communality," their tendentious, long, servile, idea-less intriguing, their stupidly deep questions: "Vanya, oh Vanya, why live, is life worth it?" and so forth. This is their content . . .

How lonely it is to think that I am far from my homeland, that there is no place for me to cling when things are hard; that perhaps, uprooted, I am in no state to create anything, because cosmopolitanism is still a volatile word. In any case, art is still almost everywhere deeply national and perhaps the idea of a non-national art has not yet been fully born, although there is a lot of talk about it. How to live without a Homeland, how to make one's way in the world, taking everything into one's heart, everything that is beautiful, yet remaining a foreigner to it all.

16 November
1909

Today I turned 21.

26 November

Auslender said that my composition "Mood" was pretty awful. "Literature," written as they all write it. It is a cliché. The fact that I could write such a "big" thing, of course, shows my obvious attitude to literature—there, that's what he said.

The first hours were very hard for me, yet the suffering uplifted me. Now I feel such a lack of light, such full despairing darkness. In a word, everything has been taken from me—everything—and I have been left to live. I am leprous, exiled from the world. A leper, who lives only to die.

He didn't read all my things (he couldn't have), he only looked at the first pages.

18 December

Divine Plato! As the corybants hear the sounds of the flute, so I hear in my breast the singing words!

I sat with the Greeks for ten hours today and I didn't want to leave, Socrates (or Plato) are [*sic*] great, like gods of a sort.

DIARY—1910

28 January
1910

I just read Maeterlinck's *The Intelligence of Flowers*. I know what he needed to express; that this is empty fiction. Yet with my whole organism, with all my soul and mind, I don't want such insane and terrible resolutions. It is terrible to see a world deprived of God, to view the world as an eternal evolution of reason or instinct while at the same time excluding the soul, excluding innate and predetermined beauty and reducing man to the level of a worker-bee. Or this mad fabrication of the Flamand or Parisian enslaved by culture! All culture, all the centuries, the millennia that have passed since the day of creation, can be thought of from his point of view. The soul is dead, the soul died on the threshold of everyday life, having only just been summoned, killed by the hand of him who had torn it from the eternal mystery of the Unknown. And what, damn it, is to be done? Be calm and think, having closed these harmful, immoral books, never to open them again.

NOTEBOOK ONE

1915—1917

APARTMENT NO. 5 — A FRAGMENT
FROM THE BOOK *Art and Revolution*[1]

"Apartment No. 5" was a special chapter of our lives, and it should be
written about. When I began this book, I thought I saw it absolutely
clearly; as if it had already been written. But now . . . I am so aware of
the rumble of that time and our individual voices that were lost in it
that "Apartment No. 5" seems to me to be a private episode, perhaps
even autobiographical. Strictly speaking, this is not the place for auto-
biographies. When you live in an epoch like ours, when the events of
half the world become your own business to such an obvious degree,
you have to yield to its scale.

In 1915, it seemed to me, as it probably did to many of us, that life
in apartment No. 5 was lived more intensely and more fully than anywhere else. We gathered there, shared our work, and, in the interests
of our work, followed literature: we read articles and listened to poetry.

[1] This passage was actually written sometime in the thirties and was part of Chapter 5 of
Punin's unfinished work "Art and Revolution," which was envisioned as a history of art
and life in St. Petersburg in the 1910's and 1920's. It was never published during Punin's
lifetime, but Chapter 5 was published in 1989 in Moscow as part of the collection
Panorama of Art 12.

We drove out the lazy ones and we put the willful ones in their place. We looked after each other and we studied art . . .

A lot of people gathered in apartment No. 5. Not everyone knew each other; we got acquainted, and we listened with interest to what the Muscovites had to say. Besides us, the people who were consistently there included: Arthur Lourie, Altman,* Tyrsa,* Mandelshtam, Nikolay Bruni,* Mitrokhin,* Kluev,* Rostislav Voinov,* Nik. Balmont,* and that evening [when K. Malevich came—ed. note] Puni,* Boguslavskaya,* Rozanova,* Tatlin, Klun,* Udaltsova,* Popova,* and Pestel* came. And there were others, who were neither artists nor writers but of some importance to art.

We gathered in Bruni's studio, in a large room with a window looking out onto the corner of the Fourth Line of Vasilevsky Island and the bank of the Neva . . .

Apartment No. 5 was in a De La Mothe building of the Academy of Arts and belonged to K. S. Isakov, the assistant to the curator of the Academy Museum. L. A. Bruni* was his stepson.

. . . in apartment No. 5, "isms" were immediately and forever banished, no one shrouded his works with such labels, and we only used those that were meaningful and indispensable: Impressionism, Futurism, Cubism.

When Malevich introduced Suprematism with his exhibit "0,10," no one was seduced into thinking that this new "ism" was new. The time of Futurism had already passed, and no one wanted to rack their brains over it . . . Most often we discussed method in Bruni's studio. We weren't searching for a new method; we were looking for a means to seize reality, devices, by means of which it would be possible to grasp reality with an iron grip, without tearing it up or being torn up by it, by its convulsions and moans, its agony, and put it on canvas. Artists had to have a keen eye, a trained hand, a nose for the hunt, the knack for hunting. The beast was fearsome: no one expected or wanted mercy for wounds and mistakes. There was rigor in all our work and research, in everything we did then. People were serious and sincere. We were all abnormally exhausted by the approximate nature of estheticism, and (in no less measure) by the feeble trotting of the Futurist derbies. We were searching for an art that was strong and simple, so simple, that it *could* remain simple even in those incredible years of transition.

For a long time a turning point had been developing among us, a point toward which we were all headed, either consciously or blindly, eagerly or reluctantly, impatiently or taking into account success, money, and the past. We were all heading toward it, leafing through those pages of days and months, just as constantly as the life that passed by our window: the life of the city, the fate of war, everything that we considered our own and that seemed to us to be contemporary.

We valued contemporaneity, or in any case, none of us wanted to outdistance time, no one wanted to be above everything, we weren't seduced by pretense. Art should be comprehensible and beloved. If it is good art, it should be immediately comprehensible. You could love only that which was needed, and so the art we worked on in Bruni's studio had to be needed. And we believed that our art was simple, comprehensible, and necessary. We believed that earlier, in 1915, and we believed it later, toward the end of 1916, as we entered our "Cubist phase" and even as we left "Cubism" for Tatlin's "Constructivism," because neither one nor the other signified a direction for us, not really "isms," but a method. The war took its course, and lay between our life in apartment No. 5 and "the first Futurist struggles," tearing from us pieces of the past that should have belonged to us. It shortened some things and drew others out, as a candle shortens and lengthens the shadows on the wall, and having brought the world up to a new speed, the war placed an evil backdrop on all our lives, against which every-thing seemed at once tragic and meaningless. We realized early on that the device of skewering the bourgeois, which the first participants in the Futurist movement had used so widely and with such stunning suc-cess, was harmful and inappropriate under the conditions of 1915–1916. It was harmful because it conditioned us to treat art as a scandal, it took away the quality and actual meaning of the artistic struggle. It was inappropriate, because the "bourgeois" was already so skewered by the war—by this Futurist who roamed the globe in a bloody coat of end-less sunsets, that any additional skewering was simply stupid. And so we developed, little by little, an ironic attitude toward everything that was connected with the Futurist campaign. I've already spoken about Burlyuk*—it was quickly ended for him, but even more significant were Larionov,* Goncharova,* Lentulov,* Malevich, Kamensky,* and Mayakovsky . . . it seemed we looked at them askance, with alien eyes.

Only Tatlin and Khlebnikov remained indestructible: we saw in them the shortest path to the mastery of quality, especially the mastery of the quality of material in Tatlin. We were living in Petersburg and were caught up in that Petersburg, "World of Art,"* graphic relation-ship to material; that is, we simply didn't feel it well. We needed Tatlin as we needed bread . . .

Besides, events soon occurred that made us more aggressive in general.

At the beginning of 1916 Bruni and Altman, as always, presented their new works for the next exhibition of "World of Art." The judges rejected some of them, and so they refused to participate at all in the exhibit. The break with "World of Art" that had been long in coming finally came to pass. We immediately composed an open letter to Alexandre Benois* and published it in *Rech'* with his reply. This letter and Benois' reply was part of the polemic I mentioned above. The forces opposing "World of Art" gradually consolidated. Our activity gained a notable foothold.

In his reply, Benois, among other things, wrote: "I am personally interested in both artists (that is, Altman and Bruni), and for that matter 'World of Art,' too, by no means rejects them. Quite the contrary, up to now, the most significant works by both artists appeared precisely in our exhibits. But my God, how could we cite them as some kind of new prophets, as a 'new way,' of painting. The 'Cubistic academism' of Altman and 'academic Futurism' of Lev Bruni are really ours through and through. It is very talented and clever art, but there is no world view and none of that discovery at which Punin hints (the open letter was written and signed by me). Now take Lentulov, Tatlin, or Malevich. Those are innovators. There's the 'new way' and so forth." Benois was right; he gave us a good lesson in revolutionary tactics. The situation was already such that for those who wanted to sit on the fence, there was no fence, just a hole. You had to decide: either for us or against us. All of 1916 passed under the sign of a sharp and uncontrolled movement to the left.

If only it were possible to resurrect Bruni's studio as it was at the end of 1916! Canvasses, stretchers, and easels had been pushed into the corners; everywhere there lay "materials": iron, tin, glass, cable, cardboard, leather, some putty, lacquers and varnishes; a lathe, saws, files, various pincers, drills, sandpaper, and emery paper of different sorts and grades had appeared from who knows where. On the tables and workbenches stood finished and unfinished reliefs, collections of materials and constructions. All this was presented with fervor, not without snobbism, but with a real taste that reflected the new passion that moved people. Tatlin's "Corner Counter-relief" hung by ropes in the corner, left with Bruni after the exhibition "Streetcar V."[2] Tatlin himself came from Moscow, summoned (I don't remember how), perhaps by letter or telegram. We awaited him, as one awaits an event which could warrant expectations and bring new discoveries, as one awaits a leader.

---

2   "Streetcar V" was the first Russian Futurist art exhibition. It opened in Petrograd on March 3, 1915. Klun, Malevich, Morgunov, Popova, Puni, Rozanova, Udaltsova, and Exter also took part in it.

When he arrived, many who only rarely visited apartment No. 5 now came "to take a look at Tatlin." He really did bring with him new tastes, a new understanding of art, an elemental will to create, an indomitable faith in the future of "Constructivism." He was a person of revolutionary will, incapable of compromise, a participant in the "first Moscow battles." From Paris, to which he had traveled, as they were saying then, with his bandura, earning his train fare by singing with a group of blind bandura players, he brought "the last stage of Cubism"—the spatial painting. Tatlin was one of those few Russian artists who had deeply plumbed Cubism. His gifts, obviously, surpassed the gifts of all of his contemporaries. He had a completely unique, pure, and defined taste. I am sure that even now no one can compete with his sense of the quality of material. At that time, his every judgment, every expression of thought on art, was for us a breakthrough into the new culture, into the future. We had only to listen to him, adapting our personalities to this huge machine which breathed energy and tore up the age-old layers of artistic culture, in order to lay them back down in a new way. "Let the Milky Way split into the Milky Way of inventors and the Milky Way of acquirers." [3] Khlebnikov's words describe our meeting with Tatlin in 1916 well. He was on one side, and all of us were on the other. We took everything he had. All of our new thoughts, which seemed independent to us, were in the end either a fragment of or a small reflection of one of his thoughts. We were impressed not only by his work, but, as always when meeting a truly great person, by his manner of speaking, by his way of moving. We walked like him, put our hands down like him. Moreover, it would have been difficult to act otherwise. Tatlin not only had a creative power, from the pressure of which it was almost impossible to escape, but also in everything that served to transmit that power, in his "appearance," there was a certain combination of qualities, usually called "charm." Each age has its own "arbiter elegantarum," and in the age of industrial Cubism this term applied to Tatlin. He was a man who set the style, a man of beautifully organized form, beautifully made of one piece.

Tatlin's influence on us in 1916 was, as I say, boundless; it continued into the following years as well, and much of what in the period of War Communism became the artistic-political program of the Department of Fine Arts of the People's Commissariat of Education was based on Tatlin's principles.

Throughout 1916, energetic work on explication of the principles of

---

3 | Khlebnikov, "The Martian's Trumpet" (1916).

"Cubism" progressed in apartment No. 5. Both under Tatlin's direction and without him, but in resolving tasks set by him, we sweated over the construction of spatial models, over various types of collections of materials of different properties, qualities, and forms. We sawed, planed, cut, ground, stretched, and glued. We almost forgot about easel-painting. We spoke only of contrasts, of links, of tension, of the angle of a cut, of "textures." From outside all this might have seemed to be just crazy, but in reality it was the creative tension of people who thought that through their efforts the world could eventually be moved away from its ageless canons and "enter a New Renaissance."

Bruni made one "assortment": stretched hide, cable, glass, mica, and tin, with a steel rod controlling the whole composition, and began a second, with a wooden butcher's board. The board, soaked with meat drippings and scarred by knives, "had" its own texture. This second "assortment" lies disassembled in my closet. The first probably hasn't survived at all. Miturich built a composition of glass, veneer and paper, lilac paper, and glass splattered with wax, joined by a piece of the "silver" in which chocolate comes wrapped. It was a simple construction, created by the sharp eye of a good graphic artist. And there were other works I don't remember. There were drawings, one of which I remember because Bruni and Miturich tried in vain to draw the square root sign into it.

Then many intelligent words were spoken in artistic jargon about the constructions, assemblies, and drawings. Arthur Lourie, the only musician among us and perhaps the only one capable of abstract speculative thought, translated this *zaum* into the theoretical language of art. I found it easy to discuss the bases of the new art and Cubism with him; he was calm and calmly brought forth issues concerning theoretical problems. Later we often appeared publicly together.

The passion for "Tatlinian Constructivism," "living materials," and "living space" continued in Bruni's studio throughout 1916 and all of 1917. Then two-dimensional canvas and oils reappeared; no one became a Constructivist "forever."

Yet the work of these years did bear fruit. A sense of spatial relations remained, an ability to create complex compositions was developed, and a receptiveness toward the various qualities of material was heightened. People were steeped in the cauldron of the Tatlinian method and emerged from those years more stable, having grown into painting, and attached by this sensibility and movement to quality as the basis for all painterly elements and the actual basis for any reality that might confront the artist. Of course, a lot was lacking and a lot might still have been achieved, but 1916 passed, the last year in which our generation had the chance to learn something and to work somehow. "Somehow," because many had already put on military protective gear and leggings and were leaving for war. We still lived at home, and not in barracks, but this all soon came to an end. The Petersburg garrison had to be brought to order . . . The war slowly turned to revolution. When the revolution began we don't know: the war had no end.

DIARY—1914

"Love"   ~~by Punin~~

"She did not dominate them entirely. She was jealous of Massival's music, Lamarthe's literature, always something; she was dissatisfied with her achieved half-triumphs, yet was powerless to banish everything that wasn't her from the souls of these ambitious men, men with a name, or artists, for whom their profession was their first lover, and nothing and no one had the strength to tear them away from it."[4] Maupassant's words are not an excuse for me since I belong to you and don't want to make excuses. But they testify to the fact that I am sincere when I speak about art and about you and that we artists have long known about the peculiarities of our organism. I replaced you with a more powerful lover, to whom I have dedicated my life. Perhaps it would be more precise to say that I returned to my former lover after I lost you, not knowing whether it was for months or for years; lost, because I wanted it, and because someone demanded it with terrible persistence. Sufferings—and I suffered, this you understand. Creative work heals an artist's suffering, and does this so powerfully that the mere thought of creative work can disperse whatever sorrow there was down to the last hint. When this notebook first occurred to me, when it occurred to me that I could always write everything down in it, the longing which filled my breast, and because of which I felt horribly broken, passed in almost a moment. It's true that I ironized about myself in this regard, and felt some stir of conscience, but that is human . . . I cannot be just a puppet of art, and I, even I, have committed myself to suffer together with you, if only a little. But is this even worth talking about? I opened it, this notebook, and I wrote, so I stopped suffering and I can't do otherwise. May God, in whom I absolutely believe, judge me and may mankind, which I presume won't forget about me, judge me . . . but no one else, since you, no matter how you controlled your mind, could not judge me, because you love me. If I beseech you and seem to

4 Guy de Maupassant, "Notre Coeur," in *The Works of Guy de Maupassant* (New York: National Library Company, 1963), 10:43.

address you, it is not because I think that sooner or later I will give you this notebook, but because of a romantic desire not devoid of sentimental tenderness to talk to you, just as if you were here, to speak as I would in a letter or a conversation, as if . . . I only *write* because I love you . . .[5]

24 September
1914

Wednesday

I woke late today and with a heavy heart. My first thought was of you. I had to hurry to catch the train and I didn't think or listen, but felt this immense weighty sadness under my heart. I was gloomy and preoccupied, but essentially content, because yesterday, since that hour when we parted, my life had acquired a new interest, new strength, something alive and genuine, which the day before yesterday Dama Luni had called "real life." Yes, my life became real, full of movement.

I couldn't figure it out at first. I thought it was love. No, it wasn't love. It was interest in what I would do, what you would do, how I would establish my relationship with Lev, Sasha, Zoya* [Ahrens] (with everyone) from the time I decided not to go anywhere that I might meet you. In addition, it occurred to me that my lengthy absence from your home might be interpreted as evidence of an affair, my absence from Sasha's as a sign of our disagreement.[6] Both notions pleased me, flattered my self-esteem, made me look like an insulted youth, who at the same time romantically disappeared. Leva upset me more, since I feared his obtrusiveness and his inadvertent perspicacity. I also thought about my friendship with Poletaev, whom I, in any case, will try not to see or not to see before I see you. On the train I read that same book by Maupassant from which I quoted at the beginning of the notebook. As I bought it, I thought of you. I thought about how I would send you all the books I read. But I won't send them since I don't want to hurt you more and I don't want you to think I'm weak.

As I walked down the stairs of the station, I suddenly felt really bad because a painful thought came to me: you aren't here, you won't meet me; maybe you never will again . . . but since the streetcar came quickly, and precisely the #15, I ran, immediately banishing all these thoughts. It is difficult to say now, what I thought about on the way. I felt weak, sickly, broken. From time to time my head throbbed, the pain came and went, then turned into a sort of dull ache that never left me even when I thought of other things. What exactly is suffering? A bursting

5 In this passage Punin is addressing his wife to be, Anna ("Galya") Ahrens.
6 Leva, Sasha, and Zoya are Galya's siblings.

heart, exhaustion, a feeling of tiredness and sorrow, the wish to die; yet at the same time a kind of satisfaction, happiness, as a result of new strength . . . Do you know what suffering is, my beloved? I arrived at the Museum, constantly returning to you in my thoughts. I reminisced, analyzed, missed you. I went into my office, where I noted down the crosses (*nomerki,* as you used to say). I threw down my pen from time to time and thought of you. When Okolovich asked me why I looked so "autumnal," I answered wryly, "Not every day is July." [7]

Since yesterday I have been madly joyful. Then I thought of you again. Then I sat for four hours and wrote and thought. I asked myself: are you suffering? Yes. But don't you want to suffer? No. Why? Don't know. Do you love her? Don't know.

I decided that I don't love you. In any case, seeing you would be unbearable. It would be interesting to live at a distance, suffering, longing for you, hiding from everyone like a thief or a very busy person, knowing that no one would come, that you'd be home all evening, that you're free, that a book, art, creative work, awaits you there, perhaps inspiration, happiness, an unexpected moment, a metaphor, perhaps even poetry, in any case emotion—and solitude. Oh, that would be happiness, mad happiness!

I realized this, but the pain that swelled in me grew stronger, from the loss and from feeling insulted. As a man I was insulted by you yesterday. I cannot possess you, so I am sick, physically and morally. All this is due to the sickness. Acknowledgment that I could not do a single, decent thing, that I was a weak sexless being, egotistical and worthless, bringing you torment, makes me suffer.

I wallowed in these feelings to the point of stupefaction, of unbearable torment, of despair, until I wound up filling the room with groans, calling your name. Why, and for what? When I left the Museum, pitiable and haggard, I grimaced, afraid that you might see me. I walked by the Passage,* and strangely, I had this disturbing desire to meet you, yet I didn't want to, didn't want to. I only wanted you to see me, precisely as such a grimacing, suffering—poseur!

And you saw me.

When I got off the trolley at the station and slowly moved along the pavement, you came toward me. You saw me and you shied away, crossed the street. I hunched lower in order not to see you and to seem even more unhappy. I walked past in terrible agitation, wanting to turn

---

[7] Punin worked in the Russian Museum from 1913 on and was one of the organizers of its icon section, as well as organizer of its collection of new art in the 1920's.

back, walk up to you, call you. You seemed to be following me. I slowly climbed the steps and went into the hall. Were you behind me or not? I was scared to turn and look. One minute I wanted to rush after you, then the thought that all my interest in life would be lost held me back. But I suffered terribly from yearning and horror. When I sat in the car, I looked out the window. Maybe you would still come, catch up, walk past. My throat constricted with sobs. Tears were in my throat, but my eyes remained dry. Sufferings—they are already familiar and beloved! Accursed organism, I want to die. I am tired of all this. Will you return, dear, beloved . . . ? I am tired of my own egoism, of my pride, of my baseness, of the fact that I am not able to be happy, of the fact that I should make you suffer. And I am ready to give up my art, if you inspire in me everlasting, unceasing love for you, to give up everything I have, if you teach me love.

This writing has convinced me that these pages don't succeed, that they are not, in any case, art, and my yearning springs up, returns. The nights are so cold, life is so lonely. I cannot, cannot write you. I don't know why. If I can't write differently, I'll quit, but love you differently, that I cannot do. Sincerity and art, it seems, are truly enemies; nevertheless, I am glad the longing returns. Maybe I'll soon turn paralytic or feeble-minded. No matter. Life doesn't comfort me; the thought of not loving you depresses me. Yet again.

25 September　　There's no peace for my sinful, sick, weakened soul, and from time to time I can't bear all this. Twice I have been prepared to send you a telegram or go myself, but the thought of seeing you held me back. To what extent this is abnormal I don't know, but I can't think about the fact that you have a physical presence, and that it is possible to see you. Sometimes it has seemed to me that I didn't suffer from the fact that I loved you, but only from fear or self-pity, for the sentiment of love I had within me. I would gladly show you myself and my feelings, yet I cannot see you or know about your feelings. I yearn ceaselessly nevertheless, hour by hour, hysterically, until my hands tremble. I yearn as I had never yearned for "Dama Luni," with all the shuddering of my heart and the coursing of all the blood in my body. And I want to talk about you, to yell, to throw out in words, with my voice, the thought that struggles with some sort of secret yet I can't grasp it, the whole time diving into the depths of consciousness, dragging out a whole heap of emotions and ideas, powerless to grasp only one, the single, the most secret in me, the most needed, which would immediately lay me to rest or give me life. Sometimes it seems to me that all this torment simply amounts to a release from a habit that has sent out terrible roots these two years. Yet at other times I think it a volcanic explosion of creativity, of the creative force of literature and life, of that which you were involuntarily crushing, killing in me through the whole course of our acquaintance. Why did I constantly want to buy a mirror, powders, cosmetic pencils today? Why did I want to look elegant again, to be beautifully dressed, to be unsullied by life as they understand it in the Ahrens circle? I dreamt that I would send you a ticket in two or three months for the theater, where I could see you for a moment in the splendid beauty of society. To strew you with flowers, lacquer boxes, candy, to give you all the ephemera of life without ever discussing literature or genius or mentally sharing with you all the shades of expression, all the novels, all the feelings about which I write or which I read. There. That is what I have fruitlessly and tormentedly dreamt of for a long time. I eagerly agree that all this is sick, abnormal perversion, the fruit of sexual exhaustion; in short, the filth of a literary man who deliberately deadens his feelings and is not naturally aroused. But if I were guilty of this, if just for one day! The preoccupation which has made me too fickle and nervous is life that no longer remains in normal strength in my body. My will has corrupted my soul, mind, and heart. I did not sow these seeds in my body, and I wasn't conscious of it. Besides, I am not pitiable. My sufferings, if they really exist (in the end, this, too, is not so easy to discern), transport me into a world where life is majestic, royal, and full. I don't have the right to grieve or grumble and I do not, at least insofar as it has to do with myself alone, only me, in my loneliness and my egoism. But as soon as I think of her, of women, of friends, of you, pain pierces me from head to toe like trembling or fear. I would gladly lock myself up among my books and work, lock myself up like a parasite, like some absolutely harmful being. If I break it off with you forever, I will perish, I will force still more, more women and people to suffer. Allowed freedom, I will always be horrible. But I cannot remain without freedom. Certainly, if I don't lose my mind now. Oh, you don't know what it means, what it means to feel like a parasite! . . . To feel like there is a mark on you, horror and longing. To feel that there it is—your filthy organism—and that it is not really possible to be any other way. I don't know how much all these thoughts increase my pain; perhaps you inspired this contempt in me for myself when you spoke of how there was little difference between Georgek, Sasha, and me; or perhaps I engendered it myself. But isn't all my longing, this pain of a truly contemptible person, perhaps only my outraged vanity, pride, and my belief in my own purity? Oh, I don't know. Don't ask me, don't touch this heart, which is all atremble and pounds at the thought of you, because of my love for you. At times it seems to me that this suffering is almost physical. And it is just like scratching at an elusive but persistent wound that is oozing a little and terribly soft and bloody. Perhaps I never did love you, I was only intrigued, and, as a true artist, got myself involved. But maybe I have loved you with all my strength. I looked for you twice today in the halls of the museum. Once a display's glass case seemed to catch a flash of you in a blue dress. My heart shuddered and beat fast, fast, and I shrank back. It wasn't you. Of course that pleased me, since I was in no state to see you. But later when I thought about my scare, I told myself, "See, you do love her," and I rejoiced, rejoiced like a child.

26 September, Morning.

My morning sleep was heavy. Maybe all this only happened thanks to my strange longing for a dream. Why can't I see you? Yet almost every hour I think of you, speak to you, search for you on the street, and all the while it seems that you are there in the crowd somewhere. I lay there and thought of all this, and again the idea that I would soon lose my mind gripped me. Oh, how I love life, the very force of life, the ability of the organism to live. Should I die, right now, so soon? If that were the case I would beg for a child. A child to whom I could give my life, blood, thought, and meditations; even if he were sickly or an idiot. If only he would live to be old enough to then pour his life into another. Let it even be a long and useless struggle. Even if this child were to be born of a prostitute, if only my life, soul, and blood would go on! I don't understand this longing, why this desire—to live at all costs?

Afternoon.

It pleased fate to make our paths cross. I saw you and spoke with you. Now I know that I will probably not leave you, not for a month, not for a week, that I love you, I love you with endless strength, to the very end, without anything left in my heart. Before our meeting I still resisted, but now I am agreed to everything, to roaming the streets exhaustingly, to your house, to Serpukhovskaya, to the streetcar—to everything, if only to hear, or not to hear at all, but to feel with my whole organism, not only with my ears and eyes, but with my whole organism, to feel your presence. I just spoke to you on the phone. I will go now and I will take the notebook. I will do it all again, all that even this morning I hated so much, so much . . . it seems like it's not important that it's been not just three days but a whole year since Tuesday.

17 October	Oh, you are so endlessly beloved. I listen to you and do not tire, look at you and cannot get enough. Because you are in my life, death frightens me so, and I love the bustle of life because you, my love, are with me.

1914

——— ———

1915

15 March *1915*	I never thought that life would give me such strong wine to drink. Beneath the beneficent, gentle, spring sky my heavy sadness blossoms; my heart is like a stone, and there is no comfort for my life that's gone astray. Only save and forgive it, Lord.

25 March
1915
	In a word, all thoughts have gathered around you, and you pour your blessed light on them, oh, my love.
	    My thoughts are with you, day and night, guiding me along all paths, but, like lightning, the thought of the possibility of you dying strikes, cuts through, and burns my heart.
	    I love you, but in love, life dims and dies. Are you dying of my love?
	    I forgot everything and devoted everything to you, you are like a pyramid in the desert, but your bones are fragile and your body ephemeral. Truly, God commanded us not to love this ephemeral world.

6 April	She returned from the hospital.
25 May	Pavlovsk The whole tragedy of a great person (genius) consists, perhaps, in the fact that having been born he awaits his audience, suffering until the hour of its creation and awaiting its arrival in deep loneliness. Tolstoy didn't wait for his audience. There are geniuses who don't wait.
26 May	I have seen women, deceived and frightening, depraved ones, exhausted by their filth. I have seen people who have lost other people's money. I have seen a mother, bargaining for the price of her 13-year-old daughter and I have also seen the buyer of this daughter on the eve of the trial against him. I have seen a father who had never been servile begging a colleague, who had at one time seduced his sister, for the sake of his son. I have seen a drunkard who had drunk away the cross left him by his sister. I have seen a student raped. I have seen a poor boy whose legs were scalded by his aunt because he didn't bring her 3 kopecks. I have

seen a working mechanic shove a soldering iron into his lover's vagina because she hadn't given him money. I have seen a young girl who set fire to her governess' bed one night because she had beaten her. I have seen a man who every day took a ruble from his father the general's writing desk. I have seen an accountant who kissed his department head's hand to get the rank that was due to him. I have seen a scholar send a lackey-minister his card. I have seen two sisters fight over a husband. And I have seen dozens more small and great sufferings, all sorts of sufferings, which it might seem possible only to invent, all horribly tearing and pitiful. But I have not judged your world, Lord; I bless it and I accept it with my heart and with my unyielding reason, for there is no truth and no judge, but love and happiness save the world.

27 May

My love, I am just as devoted to you as the first day.

6 June

Oh, I long for you my love; my happiness is unspoken, I haven't the words.

5 September

Fear, longing, bitterness, expectation, sorrow, agitation, indignation, tears, secret tears in a corner of the train compartment over a magazine already read. You know this, have experienced it, have seen it, and now I ask of humanity, who feels life more strongly than we do?

Social calamities, terribly irreconcilable, a constant passive pressure on the will. A lofty arrogance lightens and almost destroys the individual gravity of the cosmic feeling, but this gravity becomes excessive when whole crowds of people carry it, constantly and tirelessly recalling the huge expanses of the world and the terrible pathos of death. You lose your bearings at the sight of a bourgeois or a lady, bearing the image of pettiness, at the sight of mediocre minds and petty hearts, which now always and constantly think and feel that the eternal world and terrible death are the most genuine and active reality. The fact that these heads and hearts feel the universe and suffer for human lives— this is indeed a great spectacle, from which the soul spins and dims.

Oh terrible, terrible months of this unequal and shameful battle.

10 September

We are not worthy of the great significance that has befallen our lot. In realizing this, the last strengths of our will perish. Our fatherland is out of danger for the time being—such are our feelings, and they lack love and passion.

We are uncoordinated, we are impotent, we are melancholic, yet in the depths of our hearts we are indifferent, like little bronze idols. And a deep, fathomless horror controls our lives at its roots. Not we, but you, the future, will bring our native fields back to life; don't judge us, you don't understand us; forgive us, you didn't know our childhood. The efforts that we made were great; count our fraternal graves and listen with us to the hysterical cries. But we lacked strength; we were beggarly, poor, and corrupt in the depths of our hearts.

9 October

Romain Rolland* has renounced politics, England has acknowledged the victory of the German principle of organization; we, as always, stumbled in chaos, not knowing with which of our two enemies, internal or external, to come to grips. As always, we were without conviction, without a mission, without law.

12 Oct.

Lord, calm thy unfaithful and rebellious servant, like the surface of a wave.

3 November

The world—as I see it now—is shameless, pitiful, and horrible, but I love the wonder of its laughing eyes and the depth of its heart. Forest, sky, and stars awaken in me a childlike and wild joy and tears. Blessed land!

18 November

Calm my tormented spirit, God of righteousness. Remove pride, vanity, and falseness from me, You, who are the Enlightened One, shining in me, have mercy, dispel the chaos and darkness. Dissolve me in your great light, Almighty God. My soul burns in the name of truth, reveal Thy Path. I am weak; heal my suffering soul.

25 November

Russia, beloved, what have they done to your blessed body, these barbarians, these swine!

1916

5 February
1916

I have lost the sense of truth, of any cognition. The world is not so much an evil and repugnant vision as it is an empty spectacle, harsh, mottled, irrational, and somewhat boring. I wouldn't want to change this dear puppet-show because I don't understand it. If life seems irrational to me today, on another day it may act predictably. Not only is the cause for any phenomenon unknown to me, I don't even know its first element. I allow myself to be ironic or to be indignant only because I am alive. Life itself, probably, or so it seems, does not deserve irony or anger. I don't believe God or in God at all, and I only have a superstitious fear of disbelief. I think that it is an atavism. And I am happy to the end, moreover, deeply and childishly happy and at peace. Joy informs only love and the little cares of life: a book, a meeting, an observation, a conversation. Love is the life of my soul and body, an ordinary love, strong, bitter, at times tortuous, persistent, great in its intensity and concentration. Love for the woman about whom I have been writing; it will soon be three years. In this love there is neither romanticism, nor creativity, nor springtime. It is the simplest and strongest love. It is beautiful thanks to the fact that it is not exactly in the accepted form.

I no longer seek praise, and I don't seek brilliance. I want to live in peace and quiet for now. I am not tired, I love living, I very much want to live, because only by living can I experience love, see, kiss, and desire her.

*8 February
1916*

Today I thought about creativity, of which, it seems, I have little. I reread my articles; they are short-sighted and pale. I suffer. A passion for the monuments of old art is a pitiful passion. It is necessary to burn and destroy all pictures and likenesses of the world. It is necessary for the living, for the salvation of the future. We should leave only a few examples for memory. I would leave Morales and Greco, some icons, old English paintings, one or two Danish, Cézanne, Picasso, a few early Italians and Germans. Walter Pater moved me yesterday with his "Denis." A symbol has only one meaning—laconic brevity of expression. All else is conjecture. I want to create and I suffer.

*16 February
1916*

I am lying in bed to write down some kind of weak, sickly thought? Suffering and hysterics. Oh, I'm tired, tired; be ye cursed, mankind.

*16 April
1916*

With that, I hurl my anger and my crown of fame at it, at the world. I want no part of its iron or the vise of its chains. I have never given it my heart, nor even my creative work: the intensity of my torment, or my weeping in the depth of nights that were like centuries, or my piece of the eternal ring, or what resembles love or death—oh, earth, earth, to sink into your darkness as my final resting place. Mutinous stairway of luck, outcry and purity of fire, and nights fragrant and indifferent— you are the heart in me and you are my intellect. A blessed pearl . . .

25 May

Today none of my desires are here. They are all there, on the battle-fields. The crown of martyrs and of those who have sacrificed their lives is not to be found among those of blue blood. I agree to any efforts if only they bring about an issue of hatred and contempt toward the Germans. More and more efforts, people, you cannot be defeated! The blood which boils in our veins will not cool until the hour of glory, of my glory and our glory; the glory of the people has come. Be brave, make yourself proud. Your pride is in me, and I am ready. We are maturing in the name of your pride. Inexpressibly beloved country!

(And this is all garbage!)

*25 August
1916*

Love. When the day is closing beyond the window and fades, and is driven beyond the roofs, where mists burn in pink walls like a veil, and the cool and the damp and the inexhaustible melancholy—that, too, is love. When the rooftops of huge cities and the smoke of their smoke-stacks burn as if they were on fire it is a hosanna of eternal life and the life of mankind—it is love. When sunset fires smolder over the ashes of things, it is love, only love . . . So she stood, bronzed by the sun, a charming child, a Tahitian Raragu as the evening city turned pink, all hazily pink and beautiful . . .

7 September

My brother [Leonid] has been killed (1st of Sept.). At dawn on the first he went out with a rear guard of partisans on reconnaissance. Having sent part of the men on a wide sweeping movement behind the German position, he attacked with the rest. They say that a company of Germans suddenly appeared before them, charging at them with bayonets. He quickly ordered a counterattack, but immediately fell, wounded by two bullets. One through the leg, the other through the hip. A machine gunner with his wits about him opened fire on the advancing Germans; he killed them by the dozens and turned the others back. My brother was carried away, but because there was no dressing station or ambulance nearby, and because he did not present himself to have his wounds dressed, he died from loss of blood at 1:30 P.M.

*16 September
1916*

Germany!—confusion in every heart, memories, alarm, hatred. Germany is damnation, Germany is barbarism, Germany is the enemy. In the chaos, vanity, vaingloriousness of nationalistic sentiments: self-esteem, pride, greed, indeed it is difficult to find peace of soul and clarity, and firmness of thought. Only a madman or a saint can lift his gaze beyond your cruel eyes, oh, masses. When you turn vulgar, it takes great efforts not to rejoice with you, but when you become agitated, only an inhuman force of will or depth of intuition can save one from your nasty eyes. You are agitated and who is safe from you? I am neither madman nor saint, and I am not safe. In the seclusion of my notebook, however, in the cowardice of my silence, pathetic, mute, completely inaudible, I whisper a word in protest against you. I say:

Germany is our future, Germany is the only country worthy to exist, Germany has won already or she will win. Germany is the sun of Europe, the golden band on the surface of the ocean, the way of the future. In what political and economic conditions would war not have arisen two years ago? Historically Germany has had only one role in this conflict, the leader of Europe and the revolutionary of Europe's spiritual order. Germany had matured and realized her maturity, Germany had found a way out of the individualistic morass, of religious weakheartedness, of moral blight. Germany understood before any other country the triumph of the technical world, showed it to Europe, led humanity out of the era of realistic humanism, and opened the era of spiritual technology. Machines and masses, stormy energy, directness and solidity of achievement, an immensity of the expanses of thought, the purity and practicality of this thought, cruelty, anger, temperament, pride, arrogance, organization, socialism (only the socialist leaders are blind: Germany realized socialist ideals before all others, having made them, moreover, viable; people are unequal, and for this very reason there can be a viable form of socialism even under monarchy), and finally, their full justification of animal egoism—these are the *qualities* in which Germany surpasses Europe, and which Europe will have to study for a long time to come, with varying success. The flight of the German mind is winged, the ideas with which Germany so suddenly provided Europe were so vital that they were immediately recognized by those who weren't hypocritical, those who knew desire, those who loved life, and who did live. England herself recognized them and realized them with her own extraordinary aplomb, France follows them, Russia strives toward them. To cleanse the world of everything virtuous, soft-hearted, of everything past-oriented and burdensome, to make the world new, to give birth to it again, to save it—Germany was called to this, and Germany accomplished this with exceptional heroism and self-sacrifice. Worthy of immortality, she revealed her soul and bared her heart, and humanity rose up against her will and strength with the hatred and surprise of pitiful mediocrity, not understanding the significance of German organized militarism, or the monarchical socialism of her governing system, or the futurism of her cultural, her spiritual, her moral ideas.

18 September   Should we fight? Yes, we should. We are obliged to fight for the sake of our national life, for the sake of our right to the future. To the same extent that Germany heralds victory, we should show her that she is wrong to consider herself unique; she is chosen, she is called, but she is not unique, since we exist. We exist like a colossus on whose shoulders

Europe will place a heavy burden, we exist from Pomerania to Sakhalin, we are barbarians—a great sea of fire. We should fight, beat, and drive away Germany. We should contend with Germany, and the notion that only Germany has the right to the throne; the nation which does not have a past should have its future. But not in the name of the loose ideals of wasted France, and not for the sake of hypocritically virtuous England—not for the sake of that true bluestocking should we cast weapons. The trampled rights of Belgium, Serbia, what business of ours are their trampled rights? In the name of our life, in the name of our predominance, for the sake of the great futuristic Russia we should bomb the hell out of Pomerania, we should shower the Königsberg forts with shrapnel.

24 September

In general pathos makes one ironic; all the more so if one is solitary, weak, and egotistical. I do not object to irony on the part of my meditations on Germany, especially my shrapnel, my domestic shrapnel, from my office, on the eve of conscription. Nevertheless, and although the German is a decent beast, it must be said in truth that he has caught a whiff of the future. At any rate, the Germans are singularly correct and ingenious at the present moment. The German thought up romanticism, and the German was also the first to damn it to hell. I suggest this is worthy of humanity's attention.

27 September

As to our youth I would like constantly to repeat: develop a sense of duty. Nothing is so looked down on now by our most able youths as the sense of duty.

2 October
1916

Today I spoke with L. Bruni about Charles Péguy* and the rebirth of religiosity. Bruni believes deeply. Genuine knowledge that God exists ties him to God, he says. I make no objection to such "knowledge." Then he finds the path to Russia through Orthodoxy. His genuine humility is evoked by a deep realization of the complexity of life and of the weakness of the individual intellect. Bruni evidently values the ancient Orthodox life experience, which, in his words, resides within us and gives us solidity and courage.

I don't believe it. I don't protest all those vital sensations that are born of the religious state, but I do think it's insanity to project them onto something that stands outside of life. *Life* is God, and God is blind, irrational, impassive. God, Whom you have to take in hand so that he doesn't go playing nasty tricks on you. Pagans used to whip their gods.

Today I would have liked to have had a friend. After all the intense and unceasing work of the past few months, I am tired. Hungry, tired, with socks that are wet down to the last thread, with frozen fingers and a runny, sniffly nose. I came home from the Nikolaevsky Hospital, after humiliation, dirt, and despair of Russia. We cannot win this war, we are not capable of any action, not capable of any measured, energetic, responsible, conscious work. We, the militiamen of the second order of call (the ill and the disabled), were commissioned to appear at nine o'clock at Tsarskoe. I was late. I caught up with my party, since it was already my third time to be called to the hospital and I was used to it. I knew that they wouldn't take us at the hospital before three. They took us at six. We sat in a small dingy room; they led the patients past us. We talked about how we would get situated. (A clerk will take 25 rubles for a short deferment, for a medical smock 1.50. The office is overflowing with twice as many clerks "moonlighting"; you don't see them during inspection.) Most of us have the hope and the ability to get ourselves situated; nobody thinks about the necessity of going to our positions. All the relatives are in the entryway pulling strings; they don't spare even the largest of savings. Deep in each heart there is extraordinary submissiveness, but each one schemes, lies, and buys what he or she can. There is no trust in anyone, no sentiments about the war; just blind submissiveness, animal humility . . . They sell everything that can be sold; a place in line, a necessary stamp, a deferment, a berth.

The more you sacrifice yourself, the better you feel in your soul. Because of this feeling, I don't have the strength to try to rise. I am afraid. I fear that I will be captured and killed; so I always think about my literature and my role, and I seem to myself, in the end, to be very important. I value my life much much more than the lives of a hundred others . . .

I don't have a single friend (my only friend is in Germany).[9] I have no one to tell that I am afraid. And there is no one from whom I might hear heartening words. I'll still try myself . . . I have always thought I was a coward at the bottom of my heart.

A return to Nietzsche. Before returning to him I had to cleanse myself of romanticism. "A dry brilliance is the best spirit." To put it honestly:

---

8   Punin is describing his attempt to get a wartime clerking position at the hospital and the system of bribery which allowed the clerks to earn extra money on the side in exchange for keeping soldiers in the hospital and away from the front.

9   Punin is referring to his childhood friend Aleksandra Korsakova-Galston or "Yuksi," with whom he corresponded all his life (see the Glossary).

Nietzsche was beyond his time even for himself. I have been possessed by strange ideas for a month now, and I can't find peace at night. What to do about Germany? How can one fight against that which saves you, which defines and "liberates" you? The best ideas are futuristic ideas and socialism. Not Marx, but healthy socialism, life. "The transformation of the machine into beauty" (Nietzsche). Only before Tatlin's "reliefs" can you understand how insignificant the world is, how insignificant you are yourself. Scraps of creation, scraps of beauty, scraps of truth. The era of European esthetics. The only way. Let the soul become a "relief." "Relief"—that's the state resembling the true soul. All the instincts of the soul in dry and studied forms. Socialism—Germany—Futurism—it is a worthy triad.

Evening—

The pathos of death, the pathos of war, and the pathos of humility . . . Longing, loneliness. A factory, a factory—my spirit, my tender soul is a factory. At 5 A.M. a solitary and alarming bell, piercing, damned. Heart, begin your work . . . In the damp air and cold, the shadows of night still moan and shuffle, but you are already heading toward your work. The loneliness of the dawning morning, the first tram cars with burning lamps, a returning prostitute, the cab drivers, the drunks—it braces your heart, the chimneys smoke; longing, oh, longing . . .

— — —

The aesthete, the romantic, and the idealist all reside in Nietzsche. For 10 years I have turned a circle around you, oh great one, but in those years, forgive me, I took the three longest of your shadows and escaped into the hills.

The aesthete, the idealist, and the romantic.

6 November

Nikolaevsky Hospital, 2 weeks . . .[10]

Wooden barracks around a small courtyard. They brought us in around 9 o'clock in the evening. None of us had eaten all day. We walked across the street from the main building in yellow coveralls, in single file past the guard at the gate. The second ward— 40 berths, lice-ridden, full of bedbugs, worn-out mattresses, the smell of straw; smoked-out and spattered with spit, it smells of filth, bread. Two lamps dimly burn under the beams of the ceiling. They immediately surrounded us, questioning. After half an hour the bedbugs were already eating us up. Stuffy, insulting, endless squeamishness, disgust, a dis-

10 | In this passage Punin describes his stay at the Nikolaevsky Military Hospital, from which he was eventually released from military service for three months.

gusting piece of bread in your hands. Night. The bitter and acrid smell of stale tobacco smoke, the bitter and acrid smell of a sleeping person, of shoeless soldiers' feet, of boots being aired out; the stuffy and heavy steam of drying spit, uneaten cabbage stew, unwashed glasses, of steaming urine, which the sick, suffering from incontinence, are unable to hold back.

Night. The unceasing clunking of boots, the bumping of people passing through the ward on the way to the latrine, coughing, dry, uneven, penetrating, heartrending, violent with howling. Dry and wet coughs, some with whistles and with rattles; delirium, cries, piercing snores, annoying snores, ringing through the whole ward, in all corners. Night, headaches and stuffiness, legs hurt from hunger, temples pulse, your mouth is as dry and hot as the inside of an oven.

You toss and turn like a snake on the worn-out, rock-hard mattress. The bedbugs bite all the more ceaselessly, sharply, mercilessly, or maybe they are fleas. You scratch your stomach, back, arms, head, groin, behind your ears. You smack and squash fleas on your neck. Someone in the corner shouts, jumps up, waves his arms, and falls back to sleep again. Loneliness, longing, weeping. The hot, dim light of a lamp covered with a paper. I remember my dead brother, the news about his death, the burial services, the march. You dream in a delirium—"Est-ce que nous avons le coeur brisé?" . . . You fall silent. You sleep. Night. The long and loud clunking of several feet, a dull pain throughout the body. *Noir*. The moon is greenish white in the misty window. Rumbling, thumps throughout the ward. You jump up. A person subject to fits is in the passageway with his arms thrown back. His long black beard shakes with wheezing and convulsions. A deaf-mute sits on his legs; two patients in their underclothes hold his arms and chest. There is commotion, running about. There is no medical attendant; he left. The orderly waves his hands—there are 18 people in here now—he comes in, helpers help, the whole place goes crazy. Whispers, opinions, yawns; the serious, attentive, peaceful, kind face of the deaf-mute. One A.M. Unceasing, undying whispers in all corners, the striking of matches, streams of tobacco smoke, laughter, discussion, philosophizing. Oh, this cursed philosophy at night over Rus. They curse the war, mock the tsar, hate the "intelligentsia," harbor dull, envious maliciousness and egoism. God and the holy scriptures. Childish proof, self-satisfied doubts, ignorance, boundless, dumb darkness.

Baseness and boorishness, fear and intrigue, coarseness and sentimentality. The war without exception is not popular in these barracks. There is no understanding, no patriotism. "We don't care whom we serve, the Germans or Nicholas. They say life is better for the Germans." And it is precisely the German emperor who is popular. "Brilliant man, he has every imaginable kind of machine."[11] Arguments and conjecture about who, according to what type, how long and how many will be freed. It gets light. Daytime and loneliness. Still the same suffering, stupid, dark and nervous Russian muzhik.

———————

After two weeks of trials I was freed for three months because of severe myopia and persistent nervousness.

17 November 1916

Verhaeren* †. Too early and before his time. The noise of a theater curtain gathering in folds, the spectacle of powerful sovereigns on the coffin decorated with a branch. Fire, the iron soul, trodden by a thousand feet, the compromise of Symbolism before the sound of Futurism approaching.

A weak poet and a romantic of socialism.

26 November

Evening. Soul-rending melancholy . . . Glory, death, and a prostitute. I left the house exhausted, weakened by unsuccessful work. Nevsky Prospect glowed, moving, rang out, rustling with black skirts, and stirring with the feathers of hats. The sidewalks jumped under my feet, glimmering with the light of lamps in the windows, swinging streetlights, moving, trodden for a thousand nights. Speech, whispers, the touch of hands meeting, the crowd and loneliness. Women in dark coats, beautiful in their exhaustion; women of perfection, adored streetwalkers, stylish libertines, dull, stupid, and shameless; carried along madly, slowly ambling, shuffling in galoshes; and in these faces, the majority of which were hideous, there was, in essence, the single thought of this sex: I am selling myself. The only women brave enough to be sincere! . . . It is precisely for you that I would give my life, my death, my glory . . .

6 December

Miturich is almost inclined to assert that everything which is created "with inspiration" is impressionistic.

9 December

I heard that all the U.S. commodities fell. So peace should be concluded. My mind doesn't believe it. If Germany really cannot fight any longer, the war should still continue; if Germany just wants peace, then peace will be concluded. We have no hope of strategic success.

11   The spelling indicates a vulgar accent.

How Wilhelm contrived to lose this war is still impossible for me to understand. Nevertheless, he lost it in the first month. Diplomatically in England; strategically in France. Austria had no right to oppose our attack. Its corps should have been on the Marne.

Peace. In what position does this put Russia? Oh, Russia . . . Any other nation would have escaped from a government like ours in 24 hours; I am ashamed to belong to a nation that has already been chained to it for a month . . . You have to whip a people like us to get us to do anything sensible. In particular, we should be driven beyond the Urals, so that the rocks and ice might awaken in us some kind of courage.

17 December

Grigory Rasputin was killed in a rout at the house of Prince Yusupov-Sumarokov-Elstone. They are blaming Dmitry Pavlovich. There is widespread but hidden excitement.

I was at Ziloti's* concert at the Mariinsky theater. Rasputin's name was on everyone's lips. After the intermission a hymn was requested by a couple of daredevils. The crowd gave its support immediately, the theater roared; they insisted on a hymn. A hymn was played.

14 January 1917

There is nothing but death to talk about. Do we perish forever, or not? All kinds of spirituality. Man is formal, rationalist, and master . . . and nothing more. What else is there to say?

24 February

The mood is extremely tense. It is difficult to do my own work. On Nevsky from time to time crowds gather, Cossacks are riding. The Duma is procrastinating. The failure of the Ministry of Health doesn't correspond to the tension of the day. By evening rumors of strikes spread through the whole city; the running of the trams was disrupted. People are stocking up on kerosene, candles, water. There really is very little bread; there are lines at the stores; some women cry out from the pain of not receiving any bread.

25 February

Since morning it has been quiet enough, but the trams haven't been running since noon. From the windows of the Mikhailovsky Palace (Museum of Aleksandr III), you can see a thick mass of people on Nevsky, the Cossacks are riding. They say the Cossacks are acting peacefully; in any case, they are not causing the same wild panic that they caused in 1905. There was a moving, disorganized crowd on Nevsky at 4 o'clock: boys, a few workers, city dwellers, women; no flags. The Cossacks flew along the pavement, caught the crowd, dispersed and drove the crowd from Nikolaevsky Station to the Admiralty; they didn't use whips, they threatened the stubborn with pikes; they could hear that there was a bigger demonstration near the Duma, and on the Vyborg side it was difficult to fight one's way there.

Judging by the papers, the government is self-controlled. The problem of the food supply was transferred to the Petrograd city self-government. In the Duma, it seems, there is fierce debate—Rodzianko has placed the speeches of the SRs and SDs under censorship. Oh, these kadets . . . (and others).[12]

Evening

The atmosphere is highly strained. The government shot into the crowd and at workers. There were casualties. No one knows anything about the State Duma. The evening papers didn't come out. They say that the Cossacks are fraternizing with the workers. In one printing house on Vasilevsky Island they drank tea together with the print-shop workers. My neighbor, the owner of the printing house, told me this. Is this a symptom? . . .

26 February

As soon as I got up, I heard shots from the direction of Sadovaya and Nevsky. It's a sunny day and the crack of gunfire is sharp. On the streets there is unusual movement. The trams aren't running, there are no papers. I went to the Obukhov Hospital; there was a crowd. The dead were in the mortuary. A small shed, with benches along the walls, on which there are white sheets with red crosses ⚕. Five people who were killed lay wrapped in these shrouds: three workers, a boy, a woman; the crowd moves, discusses, rebels. They say that they have been shooting since morning at the foundry, at Kirochnaya, at the Nikolaevsky Station.

27 February
Afternoon

There is fighting at the corner of Kirochnaya and Liteyny St. About sixty people, soldiers and officers devoted to the government, have holed up at the gates of the Trust for Wounded Soldiers (of the Army and Navy) and are shooting from where they are. They say that at the entrance to the Aleksandrovsky Committee Building there are wounded, that across from Kirochnaya there is a broken machine gun, that they are pouring hot water on it; they say it froze. From time to time the shooting increases, soldiers run across the street. It appears that the main fighting is on Sergievskaya, from there the shots are uninter-rupted. Along Liteyny St. along the Fontanka and on Nevsky there is

---

12 | Added later in red pencil.

incomprehensible shooting from the rooftops; the sharp clattering of revolver bullets, it seems. Doubtless some of the military have gone over to the side of the revolutionaries. The streets are full of movement on the sidewalks. There are few intelligentsia.

6 o'clock

A provisional government has been formed. Automobiles and trucks filled with armed workers rush past from the direction of Vladimir Square, where the sound of shots can be heard. Huge red flags, shouts of "Hurrah!" and shots into the air. They say that the Arsenal has been taken, as well as the Artillery Headquarters, and its defender, General Mamusov, has been killed; the Kresty, the Peter and Paul fortress is under siege. A whole series of regiments has gone over to the revolutionaries; they are the Preobrazhensky, Saperny, Keksgolmsky, Semenovsky . . .[13] They say the fortress has been taken; it is evening, it is dark, rebelling horseguards just went past with music. Autos race along Zagorodny without cease; they are met with shouts of "Hurrah!" Soldiers and workers shoot into the air, there are few people out, it is noisy and dark; soldiers roam around in groups, smoke, and shoot aimlessly. The revolution has taken the form of a military uprising.

I didn't sleep all night, across the way a section of the city was burning, glowing; isolated gunfire constantly rings out.

Early
morning
28 February

The temporary government has been formed with the participation of the Duma. We just found out that there was a decree on the dismissal of the Duma. After its publication the Duma named itself the provisional government. The Workers' Soviet deputies are meeting in the Duma. The mood is festive, there are lots of people on all the streets, no intelligentsia, the police officers are disarmed; the shots are heard less often, but autos race in all directions. The troops are disorganized, walk around in crowds, a few are drunk, sections of the troops patrol without officers, trying to keep order.

Is it really possible that the creative power of socialism will be realized? My people—are you finally able to become the greatest people?

25 March

In Gumilev's style: there's Vanka-Vstanka[14]—no matter how you knock him over, he gets back up; with Punin no matter how you stand him up, he always falls down. Instability, the lack of roots, inner emptiness,

13   Elite Guards Regiments.

14   Vanka-Vstanka is a Russian children's toy like a Weeble that wobbles but won't fall down.

no activity, just lunges, no convictions, only different points of view, no passion, only temperament, no love, only impulse, and so forth endlessly.

I am incredibly tired.

By the way, there is a kind of survival instinct that tries to construct a soul from all these coffin planks, or at least a coffin for it. With the persistence of strength, nobody surrenders without having tried to die.

————————

Gumilev's remarks essentially mean that no matter how you stand Punin up, he will never be a proper bourgeois as Gumilev understands it.

4 August

Chaos, forces of the century. The train suddenly stopped at the platform between two stations in the Mogilev province. We leaned out the windows, curious. It turned out that a soldier had fallen off the train. He was alive but buried in the dust, and then he ran and caught up with the train. He ran up, young, with a red cockade, upset, confused, out of breath. His face was serious. He walked past me with an unsteady, broken gait. It was obvious that he had landed hard. Back in his coach, his comrades asked him: why did you fall? He was sitting on the platform (having hung his feet on the footboard), became lost in thought, and fell. This is a great people, which falls out of trains because of being lost in thought?

————————

"Socialism in Russia, like everywhere, is not fated to realize its ideas as yet only because socialism is still not official."

"Perhaps Kerensky is very intelligent and kind, but he doesn't have an ounce of statesmanship."

— GENERAL OPINIONS

13 August

How I hate England, I hate it with an animal hatred.

15 Aug.

If I lived out my life, without having aroused a feeling of compassion in any of the people around me, I would think I had lived it worthily.

I love the masses because they don't evoke in me a feeling of compassion, even when they perish.

To hell with individualistic and personal feelings, I want to live only as a collective.

17 August	The Russian muzhik mooches off God.
	—RUSSIAN SAYING

28 August   A night of deepest alarm. The city is deserted, and there's no telling what those thousands of talking, newspaper-reading, whispering, but in the end mysteriously silent people are thinking. Terrifying depth. Kornilov is just outside Petrograd. With 8,000–10,000 men. He's in Dno, in Pavlovsk. In the morning there will be a battle. General Kornilov—in how many hearts in Petrograd is that name echoing with joy, and in how many does it evoke loathing, fear, curses? Oh, how many of us are staring into the night, how many are secretly praying?

—Death to the traitor, the betrayer. It was not for nothing that the Germans let him through. He appears unexpectedly and right away there's a soldier of sorts ready to follow him. The people are silent, strangely silent, won't look a soldier in the eye, yet they still try to guess how many troops are under General Kornilov's command. I'm not sleeping at home with my wife, I am sleeping in my own room (Galya has left town). Getting ready for bed, I loaded my revolver. Loneliness, longing, suffering. Russia . . . I await what might happen in the streets in the morning, anxiously listening to even the slightest rumble—is it a cannonade? The wind howls; today there is a terrible west wind. How many days, hours will I live?

29 August
Morning   Nothing, no news. There is even a kind of lifelessness in people. Are they just waiting, or worn out? Unhappy people, the great unhappy Russian people.

Evening   I saw the Semenovsky Guards Regiment march to Ligovo, in infantry formation, with machine guns. They're a mob, not an army. Gangs. Their faces are ordinary and colorless. They wink, giggle, smoke while in formation, tossing their rifles onto their shoulders; some of the officers smile vaguely, others are intensely serious. These troops wouldn't hold up even in battle with the Ingushes.

By evening the Second Baltic Battalion had already come along Nevsky Prospect heading toward the Nikolaevsky Station. They marched cheerfully, in half-companies, and were accompanied by a crowd, quiet, calm, shouting "hurrah!" from time to time. It appears that all the troops have been ordered out of the city. The city is noticeably deserted. The people wait, wait with absolutely extraordinary and strange anxiety.

In these very days Emperor Wilhelm said in Riga: the harvest is abundant. The lord of hosts has again heeded our prayers.

Neither Lloyd-George nor Kerensky commands such language.

30 Aug.
[whole entry
lightly crossed
out]

So, the Kornilov putsch has failed; not because, in general, it could not have succeeded, but because it was apparently in the hands of a person completely without talent. History will tell of Kornilov's strategic, moral, psychological, volitional mistakes. We, however, shall continue our great deed: to bring into existence one of the commonly accepted ideas of European humanity.

   (In my circles, in quite broad circles even, there was a stir among urban people (not soldiers and workers) of sympathy and compassion for Kornilov.)

1 Sept.

Here it is, the revolutionary city in its time of troubles, hungry, depraved, frightened, absurd, emergent, powerful, and drunk. Some (Fedor Sologub)* assert that it is strangely reminiscent of Paris.

   When you walk down the street, making your way among all these "bourgeois," the unrestrained soldiers in yellow boots, the innumerable merchants who set up shop right on the sidewalk, the prostitutes and brokers—among all these people milling around and celebrating, past the "tails"[15] at the tobacco, meat, and bread shops, past the posters, pasted one on top of the other, you walk, deafened by the rumble of automobiles and the din of trucks, still further, straight ahead, keeping to your own thoughts and will, you sense then, how invisibly everywhere, expanding and contracting, the rumors spread. Rumors about Sweden, about Kerensky, about Chernov, about those "deputy sons-of-bitches," about Germany, about Riga, about the army, about everything that might be on the tips of the tongues of the people at this time. They gossip, "speculate," and laugh nervously. There isn't a social class or line of work that would refuse to be involved in "speculation." You see some petty lieutenants whispering their propositions and prices to an impoverished Jew, you see ladies in white fur capes scribbling numbers and addresses into little address books under the dictation of some kind of insufferable swindler, boys loiter near a group of people at the entrance to a cafe, dandies stroll along the street, prostitutes laugh and tug at the

15   "Tails" means queues.

sleeves of men, and the men, who were, with an elegant gesture, sizing them up like horseflesh with a chuck under the chin, whet their appetite, satisfying themselves and becoming aroused . . . there it is, the revolutionary Nevsky Prospect; the capital of a great people in a time of troubles.

NOTEBOOK TWO

1919 – 1920

Introduction	*The years of War Communism—draconian bolshevik measures, civil war. A world turned upside down. Changes in the arts. The avant-garde close to power. Punin continues work at Russian Museum; Union of Art Workers; "Freedom from Art" movement. Lunacharsky. Punin appointed deputy head of Department of Fine Arts* (IZO) of Commissariat of Education, head of Petrograd section. Appointed to editorial board of journals* Art of the Commune *and* Fine Arts. *Articles on contemporary art. Tatlin. Lilya Brik.*
1919	[first five pages torn out]
26 VIII	Drove around Pavlovsk Park to try to determine my human worth . . .

     Funeral march from Khovanshchina

     Travels of Baudelaire

     Night Song of Nietzsche

     Chopin

     Beethoven

     Chinese songs

     "Vykhozhu odin ya"

You aren't here, never were, with your parted hair, a gymnasium student with brown hair, in a brown dress (Lydia Sergeevna [Leonteva]),* when I was at the round table trying to elicit silence from today's pale autumn light. The way you exited from the gate, tapping the sand with your little boots, which I would have liked to kiss. But I didn't kiss them . . . Windless, the sky is bright, undefiled even by the light— oh, what longing still, it is familiar, everywhere you go, whenever you think. Quiet night, autumn . . . Oh, how I pray to you, quiet of night!

28 VIII

I left my princess there
I couldn't carry the world for you all
The thunder of steeds, the trumpets blare
    Silence

"If a poet is not a giant, does not possess the shoulders of Her-
cules, then he will inevitably be left either without a heart, or
without talent."

— BALZAC

All day I worked intensely, to the point of stupor. I wrote a long article for our journal and the work satisfies; whether my work has matured exactly, or if it's the usual mystification—I find in myself a real and vital strength, and I believe in some kind of new epoch. However, inasmuch as I am widening the sphere of my activity, I am losing my heart. Yesterday, disturbed by memories of Pavlovsk, I was oppressed by thoughts of the weakness of my old emotions. Truly, it's been a long time since I have experienced any kind of feeling. I've been cold, cruel, impetuous. I live like a well-organized machine, and I experience the obligation to love art more than I actually love it. Nevertheless, I would consider it a great misfortune if all the memories of my youth and love dropped from my consciousness; that is, I have sworn not to become just a technical apparatus. Above all, I want to be a genuine, suffering human. There is a deadly silence in the house; it's the fourth day since anyone has been here; and because of this, my whole being is tense. How thickly oiled the wheels are, how smoothly my thoughts flow. There is neither longing nor joy, it all flows . . .

The day before yesterday an inexhaustible melancholy love for Lida [Leonteva] twisted me in the evening. No, it was not my imagination. But as before, words were no help, and I was helpless in the grip of this strange, dull, and unquenchable feeling. It's funny, sentimental, I don't understand it . . .

What wonders the silence works; my heart becomes so full, half-formed thoughts float quietly away, my heart rejoices in this floating. Yesterday and today I still pined for Lida, for myself as a boy. It's sad that I can no longer be like that again. What shy shadows hovered in my consciousness then. Life babbles quietly and strangely as I go on forgetting.

No, I cannot forget; no, I am still alive; I don't want to, I don't want to die so early.

When horses die, they exhale
When grasses die, they dry up
When suns die, they burn out
When people die, they sing songs

[KHLEBNIKOV]

[three pages cut out]

Slowly filling vessels, so that once they have reached a certain level they overflow by their own weight, and then fill up again. That liquid is my despair and my bitterness.

These days are like many bitter tastes in my heart.

Together with lost faith in the revolution, my energy is lost, and here I symbolically cry out over the expanses of the earth.

The world is boundless and so are its spaces. Because they are so boundless, I despair, yearn, suffer, for I am losing faith in giving shape to this world. The world is in a sieve, water in mortar. The space between your fingers is emptiness. This is what I am—emptiness.

31 August   I have returned from Moscow.

All of Moscow is a farmer's market: meat, butter, cheese, sour cream, flour, bread, rolls, meat pies, cabbage, squash, pumpkins, potatoes, cucumbers, beets—everything. Cafes, coffee, cocoa, ice cream, pastries—everything.

Lunch: fish pie, roast beef with trimmings, ice cream, coffee with pies and pastries—500 rubles.

Moscow is boiling, teeming, bourgeois, crowded, and dirty.

But we—Petersburg, as a revolutionary fort—are alone, heroic, deserted, starving. Great city!

[one page cut out]

28 Sept.[1]   My feeling-thoughts are contradictory today. The volume of activity of a man of genius surpasses all the measurements of our world. So I didn't learn to suffer and I am considered flippant, superficial. I am not deep. Since childhood, I have known no terror, nor many sacrifices as far as the fullness and intensity of my creative spark is concerned. (The same feelings even if the words aren't the same.)

---

1   The entry for September 5 has been omitted at the family's request.

In this work, which I do, I am not a unique figure, but I don't belong to the common lot either. I surpass my co-workers insofar as it is necessary for me to become the organizer of their ideas. But a certain tension, an almost muscular tension, demands that I break everything around me, break out, escape. With my longing I can exceed them by a head, with the rhythm by which my heart beats, by my inexorable heat, yet my thought is not free. I don't know if I see further or live more fully than they do, but I love more sincerely and more painfully. At one time suffering was respected, but it should not be respected anymore. Feeling-thoughts that hurt are sick feelings. He who has been suffering so much that he feels older than the earth is not our man of the future. The measure of the world is the measure of our genius, while the measure of an individual is a dead and desecrated fragment of forces that are hostile to us.

These are my evening meditations amidst clear spaces, incommensurable distances from thoughts about the power of suffering for love. All this, is, perhaps, somewhat fruitless, since there is only enough thought to put down in a diary.

[two pages torn out]

. . . throwing back your head, the light tremor of ~~young nostrils~~

"I love to look at you."

There is nothing for me to say but "why?"

"Just that, I love to," and again there is the intense gaze, ever widening eyes, the light trembling of the skin, under which youthful voluptuousness flows, disturbing me, penetrating into me, little by little, and causing my eyelashes to flutter.

"Somehow I saw you this summer in a dream, N."

"How?"

"I won't tell you that."

"And I saw you in a dream, too, distinctly, distinctly, an amazing dream. But I won't tell you what I saw."

The blue and pale banks of the Neva, and in general all the surroundings.

"Where are you going?"

"I'm going home, and you?"

"To the department."

"Where is it?"

"At Isaakievsky."

"I'll go with you."

"Good."

We walk, outdistancing her friends ("I don't want to go with them . . ."). We arrive at the Department, it so happened it was the day of the move from the large hall of the Matlevsky building to the small winter quarters on the Pochtamtsky. It is empty in the halls, we go on through into my office. A mirror. A 17-year-old girl, brown hair in two braids over her shoulders, an animated face, suddenly blushing, flushing, and at the same time darkening. We look in the mirror, I remember Poletaev's words.—"Make her your lover, she is still young and passionate." And I terribly want to take her by the arm decidedly to kiss her hand when we say good-bye. We go into the Department across the yard, into the new offices.

The Department, office, bustle, the new place; Tyrsa, Vaulin, another call, interruption, papers, information. I sit her down in the armchair, I don't want to let her go. I sign things, give orders in front of her, putting it on, flirting—in the little new office in the presence of this wondrous little woman, whom I would like to "make my lover," who is happily laughing at Tyrsa's bullet-holed hat, at my words, business, at all this-half serious work of the Department of Fine Arts.

Having signed and explained, they were dismissed, they left, and I shut the doors. She goes on laughing, singing the "aria of Silva at the table"; "Looks like we've got a bit of the devil in us . . ."[2]

"There, you see, you've kept me so long, and I have to be at the studio by five, and then go home."

"Well, go on then."

She gets up and goes to the door; I come close, her eyes gaze at me and her nostrils quiver, suddenly blood rushes through me from head to toe, my heart beats, my consciousness dims, the darkness, I feel . . . "Ah, so that's how you are, Nik. Nik."

My soul spins, a thought flashes by, and I take her by the hand and kiss it, and she presses her hand to her chest, and brings her face closer. I see her lips, her eyes so near, I'll kiss her now, my heart fills with sweetness. My body tenses along with my male member; the same longing and passion . . . familiar as before.

I hear someone lay hands on the door handle and Director of Affairs A. T. Shakol comes in. She noticed that we were standing too close together and that our faces were agitated: N. in a short skirt, a girl with braids . . .

"Seems one needs to knock at your door these days," she says for some reason, I think, instinctively. I mumble something; somehow I manage, "Nothing special."

2 Quote from Giuseppe Verdi's 1844 opera *Ernani*.

I go out with N.; I show her to the stairs, kiss her hand, which she presses to her lips, and I run, shouting,

"Good-bye! See you."

Returning to the office, not understanding a thing, I speak distractedly, make decisions, explain. Eventually things settle down to "business as usual."

At 5 o'clock Shakol and I step out onto the street. Evening, sun.

"How nice, how very nice it is."

"Nonsense, it's just sun, the most ordinary autumn sun; your emotionalism again."

"You're not the totally iron man you'd like to be either. I've been talking with a man in Moscow, someone you don't know and who doesn't know you, about you and your book. He assures me that it is only intelligentsia repentance, thrown onto a machine. Lunacharsky also took part in this conversation. You don't think everything through."

"Yes, but doesn't it seem to you that this is superficial, this boyishness? I agree that it's not an isolated negative quality; it is also a sign, a psychological sign of that cultural break, which *we, I,* turn into this superficial childishness. We have to, otherwise, we would not be able to work, we would think less, and would understand still less."

"Yes, I agree. Suddenly and urgently quick decisions are demanded of you. I agree this is not an individual characteristic; it is a sign of the environment and the epoch."

"Besides, it is my own most painful and fatal characteristic. I realized this early on, and have not challenged it."

"There's no need to. Let it be so. Go on and be childish."

The train arrived and we went our separate ways.

Evening. I am here, in the study, Galya is in the dining room. Did I betray her? Yes. It offends her—from her point of view, yes; from mine, no. It doesn't have anything to do with her. Again this childishness, why did I get married? I wanted to, had to, it was the right thing to do. But there is no contradiction, there isn't a single contradiction in me, no matter how much my enemies and even my friends might think there is. I am whole. ("I am a little god," etc.) Really, do I love Galya any less than yesterday? No, rather more, because I feel a bit guilty, because I fear her a little. Evening. Military vehicles are dashing past. Battles, the heart of the revolution, Red Petrograd. My body burns from the love in my blood (from the blood, in which there is love), I was overcome with a feeling of love, in which there is the blood of N.

24th	I gave a lesson today. N. acted very poorly; she threw her notes around, fought with her neighbor, made noise, laughed. I had to "yell" at her, and, in the end, I had to seat her separately. I didn't say a word to her. I left; I was dying to see her. I had this feeling, as if she were hinting "I don't love you," that she took no interest in me. A student-"lover."[3] Two ways to relate to one person; how does this work? . . .

All day there was a heavy cannonade from the direction of Kronstadt. Obviously they are beating out the white from Krasnoe Mesto. On the streets there is a feeling of animation, the people read the evening Red paper in groups, as if they were all happy, as if the city were content. Strange. So that means that Yudenich* really is unacceptable to this petty working-bourgeoisie democracy. In addition, they talk of the defeat of the whites even more than before. |
| *24 Oct. Evening.* | N. is far away. Longing and passion. Tomorrow another lesson; will I be able to talk to her? . . . Automobiles dart around at a feverish pace—it's our newspaper, our telegrams, our news. It's obvious from all the autos that the whites have not left, are not leaving, and no one reads about future days. |
| *2 Nov. 1919* | Poletaev was here. During dinner he talked about the Goncourts. He was sorry that we were not writing a diary together. I reminded him of our book. "The filthiest thing in my life," says Poletaev. "The only time in my life that I really stumbled." |
| *14 November* | After class they prepared an ambush for me, N. and her "company." Such types always have such companies. They wouldn't let me out the door, downstairs, on the stairs. Noise and giggling. During the commotion, N. took my hands, squeezed them, and stroked them.

These touches torment and smart. Now, intense longing rose from the very depth of my being. Her touches burned, like love; and were even painful like a fever, tormenting me with its changing fire. |
| *14 November* | The revolution is most wonderful for lack of logic. |
| *15 November* | Took N. from class, took her away . . .

"Why are you so dear?" and we decided to go for a stroll.

"Insanely dear." I pronounce "sane" deeply, as a Pole would pronounce it. She flushed and trembled. We have a meeting next Friday. |
| *18 November* | [two lines heavily crossed out] |

3   Question marks and quotation marks were added later in pencil.

<table>
<tr><td>21 November</td><td>

And those same caresses, those same words
"The hateful trembling of thirsting lips
And the shoulders which have become familiar . . .
No! The world is passionless, pure, and empty!"

—A. BLOK

And I, tormented,
Await the new—and yearn again

—A. BLOK[4]
</td></tr>
<tr><td>

2 January
1920
</td><td>

"Lest Theodorikh, sleeping in the grave
Dreamt not of the storm of life"[5]

The "romance" is developing in the presence of those who started it—N., Shakol, and Lilya Brik—who did not all leave off simultaneously. Spare me the storms of life, let me know once and for all: not for you. No, I am imprisoned among the elders. Imprisonment, my imprisonment. I wring my hands: spare me, spare me this moral torture. I did not want to become Valery Bryusov.* My skull, you are heavy; body-armor, you are heavy; there is nowhere to hide, and it hurts and I am proud. Let me out, let me go, let me fly away. No, never and nowhere.
</td></tr>
<tr><td>

11 January
1920
</td><td>

Went to Lunacharsky's "The King's Barber" at the Narodny Dom. A quite mediocre play. During intermission Lunacharsky was in the wings with his court. Leshchenko, Lourie, Andreeva, Shterenberg,* Altman, Lapitsky, Rapoport, Shklovsky,* and myself. He saw me, stretched out his left hand, and said, "Now here's someone I like a lot; he is the most intelligent man I have met in Soviet Russia. Did you like it? Language, where have you heard such language since 'Masquerade'?" He was drunk and happy. A strange person, I feel sorry for him, to the point of liking him, maybe that's why he likes me. God send him good luck; but the fact that he's a People's Commissar is bad luck in the extreme, at least for him.

And what intrigue surrounds him, and how petty. Melancholy, tender melancholy, because of this.
</td></tr>
<tr><td>28 I-'20.</td><td>

I am really a living person; nevertheless, there is no creativity in me.
</td></tr>
<tr><td>12 II-'20.</td><td>

One quality of the revolution—life gets to be a risk.
</td></tr>
</table>

4   Aleksandr Blok from his poem "The Artist" ("Khudozhnik").
5   Aleksandr Blok from his long poem "Ravenna."

29 II-'20	Father died. Feelings of loneliness. Puni and K.'s flight abroad: lonely thoughts.[6] The wind howls, and the snow flies, Lilya B. is living in Moscow. The house, land, and city have been orphaned, the gate slams shut, the past has leaned against the future, my heart is dead and orphaned.
18 March	There is also romanticism in the fact that you ascribe nonexistent qualities to yourself.
	Met Bely,* and thanks to this his books and his literature seem more interesting.

———

I have been thinking about myself a lot—I don't understand it.

So much has been given to me, but I lack strength: what kind of defect do I have?

Many say that I am abnormally superficial. Solid people around me assert that my will is too weak. I myself feel a weakness in creativity.

And so—I am nothing.

13 April	Excitement (from spring beer)—you want to write, and nothing comes, you either can't get work done, or you are running, but you rewrite page after page, lying there; all of life goes on, flows and rages, modulates in flames that vary from intense to empty. My dear life, dear life, my life, how I love you in the springtime, wind-whipped and crackling, like a splinter in the sunlight. I especially love you, because I have new breeches. . . .

Ahrens

From intelligent comments on the book "Against Civilization"—
"I have never seen a more brilliant defense of more repugnant things."

[1/2 page cut out]

. . . Princess Mary—Poetry. I will go out into the garden, grass, sun, sky—Poetry. I speak, I am clear, calm, kind—Poetry. I trace your dear, strange profile. Something will happen without fail, something new.

17 May	It appears that this is the end of my work at the department. M. F. Andreeva has been appointed Director of the department, and there is news that the executive committee has ordered her to rid the depart-

6 Ivan Puni—"K" may refer to his wife, Ksenya.

ment of "Futurists," which means me, in any case. I'll adapt. Good. Very good, and I'll leave with the greatest satisfaction.

[1/2 page cut out]

Lilya B.

Through her lashes, her pupils darken with agitation. She has solemn eyes; there is something both impudent and sweet in her face, with painted lips and dark eyelids, she is silent and never finishes . . . Her husband has left her with dry self-confidence. Mayakovsky—with downtroddenness, but this "most fascinating woman" knows much about human love and sensual love. Her ability to love saves her, the power of love and the definiteness of her needs. I cannot imagine a woman whom I could possess more completely. Physically she was made for me, but when she speaks about art—I can't . . .

Our short tryst left me with a sweet, strong, calm sadness, as if I had given away my favorite thing in order to preserve an unloved life. I have no regrets, do not weep, but Lilya B. is a living part of my life, and her gaze will long be remembered by me. If we had met ten years ago—it would have been an intense, long, and difficult involvement, but I can't fall in love like that anymore, so tenderly, so completely, so humanly naturally, as with my wife.

What are these short trysts, these infidelities? I scarcely understand. Two weeks haven't passed yet, and my blood is already yearning—bitterly, darkly, and inescapably. Under every pair of eyelashes you look and search, search insatiably.

You seek, not finding, you look, alone. Beauty is not canonical, taking any lively and tremulous form, yet forms of hats are livelier than forms of the face, and dresses are more than the body, more than the body itself. Between the rows, as hungry as I am lonely, I walk past. For a long time, will it be that I walk alone, alive. I walk past alone, incomplete, omniscient about the "new man," and yet myself entirely an old man.

I reread my old letters to my wife, how much love, and now what a page has turned, what a book, from which there is no escape . . . I guess. I keep guessing about the same thing . . . Oh, how well I now feel what it means to live.

If only I could bury myself evenings with my diary.

To feel pain is the easiest way of being alive. If you lose something, if you lose a woman, it is easy to love, to respond, to give. If you lose such a beautiful woman, with such dark and large eyes, with such light steps, with such a sweet tremulous mouth, so sweet and languid, so needed and so unacceptable, as the conditions of the world are unacceptable, then it is easy to start responding to everything and everybody, even those whom you no longer value. Even life is now no longer dear to me, yes, to such a degree that along with it the sweet woman I've lost is also devalued. You stand and think—will life work out, or not, will day come, will there be love, or not? Like a child, so eager to catch every drop, to drink up, you so want to fill your heart and mind, to quench your exhausted, nervous, tense body. And you can't. Sadness, thought, burns, you go to bed, you get up from the bed to the couch, you exhaust yourself, you search and don't find. You pray in solitude. You want her and know that you'll never have her again. You know that her bed, once crumpled by you, is empty. You once again take out a photograph to make sure that she isn't in it, and even if she were, it would be a paper image. You lock everything up and stand in the middle of the room, thinking about where else, what other corner you might search, etc.

But you realize in the depths, in your soul, you realize that it is imprinted, that it is impossible to go to her, that no matter what, nothing would come of it, that it is done, an afterthought, finished, that all that remains is a burning in the heart, and a memory of the body, and that too will soon fade, will soon become ordinary, like a teacup, will be forgotten, and you'll get used to going to the department in the morning, and in the evening going home through the museum park and to bed.

Morning.
26th

I awoke with longing in my heart, like just before dying. And again, I don't know, will there be life, or not? Memories of Lilya B. are rarer and paler; you thirstily grasp at snatches of burnt-out feelings. The heart barely flutters and then again there's the dead swell. Time passes and doesn't pass; empty, chilly, petty.

Evening of
the same day

All these feelings are old feelings. To love until death—that's all that has remained.

29 May[7]

Walked around the Russian Museum.* We must resurrect the "Wanderers." I say: we are returning to them.

31 May

Lilya B. arrived from Moscow.

---

7   Punin's diary entry for May 28, 1920, has been omitted at the family's request.

We saw each other, she came to my place, I went to hers. She talked a lot about the days after my departure. When a girl loves that way, as long as she hasn't forgotten geography, or when a woman loves like that, defenselessly and barely clinging to life, it is difficult and frightening—but when Lilya B., who knows a lot about love, who is strong and controlled, spoiled, proud, and reserved, loves this way, it is good. But we didn't come to an agreement. On the night of the first, I returned from seeing her at the Astoria Hotel, where it was impossible to talk, and called her; she was already alone in the room, and I told her that I only found her interesting physically and that if she agreed to take me that way too, then we could see each other, otherwise I didn't want to, I couldn't. If she didn't agree, then I asked her to arrange it so that we wouldn't see each other. "We won't see each other"—she said good-bye and hung up.

People live for years in St. Petersburg and don't meet. Today I had just left, had hardly stepped out, when I ran into her, didn't recognize her, walked past completely. She turned red and greeted me in passing in a tight voice. We walked past. In the afternoon I went to class, she ran into me on Nevsky, we shook hands and went our separate ways. Theory of probability! "Fatalist." What does it mean?

At 11:00 I went out for cigarettes with Petnikov, got as far as Ekaterinskaya St. and turned toward home. Petnikov went on further, ran into Lilya B. That means I was only a few steps away from her. P. had just returned—he is living with me—and told me how L. B. was in a difficult state, raging, completely hysterical. He had never seen her in such a state (he's known her for a long time). It was terrible to look at her, something was going on with her. Again, what does this mean? Why did it happen this way? I have to find out. Who is pushing us together? What is this, predestination?[8]

---

8   Punin's diary entry for June 30, 1920, has been omitted at the family's request.

NOTEBOOK THREE

1920

Introduction   *Tatlin. Cubo-Futurism. Petrograd. Porcelain Factory. Galya leaves him. They correspond. Concerns and doubts. Hunger in the cities; reports of famine. Crisis of War Communism.*

17 July
1920

This evening I built the "Monument" with Tatlin.[1] We worked on gluing the rods. Bruni, Meerson,* and one other student whose name I don't know were there. [Dymshits-]Tolstaya* worked on her stained glass and cooked kasha.

Tatlin's studio takes up part of the mosaic studio of Svomas* (the former Academy). They eat like sailors and, like the "dregs of society," fight one another for food from the tender's hands, which could break horseshoes from all the work they've done. I don't take part in this, I don't have the strength, and I plead that I am delicate. They eat a whole potful, which again doesn't interest me, but it is merry; as at home in the nursery. They make jokes, as well as they can, with all their might about painting, art, modernism, and so on. If a patch doesn't work on someone's rod, they yell out laughing, "Modernism!" and Tatlin slowly and sternly admonishes, "Doesn't matter, comrades, he got that from the graphic form of 'The World of Art.' Work on, you swine, you'll get better."

"There is no *kind* of art," Tatlin said one day. "Art can go to hell, all art is artistic, that's all there is to it." He had been angered by one artist, who had been going on about pure art. "Meerson and I saw a door in Peterhoff, a simple, white door, and we stood there like dolts in front of this door, white like the surface of porcelain. Meerson was silent the whole day, and in the evening he said, 'I know how a door is painted'—that is also art, but Meerson worked as a painter. I have nothing to

---

1   Vladimir Tatlin's Monument to the Third International was commissioned by the Department of Artistic Work of the People's Commissariat for Enlightenment in 1919. A model of the proposed monument was put on view in 1920 and was very influential in the art world. Tatlin worked on the model for the monument with artists Lev Bruni, Yosif Meerson, Sofya Dymshits-Tolstaya, and Tevel Shapiro (1898–?). Shapiro is most likely the student Punin could not name.

hide, there are secrets enough for my life and for my students." I really want the monument to be finished as soon as possible.[2]

18 July

Today I saw Anna Akhmatova with Shileyko in the park (of the Museum). She carries herself well. I relate to her as to somebody real. I am shy and afraid to see her. I am grateful that she has left the bohemians and Gumilev and that she is not giving readings or publishing poetry now.

19 July

I am absolutely ill. I woke up with dull anemia. I washed with cold water and somehow lingered until midday. I feel a completely unbearable sense of longing, loathing, and apathy, together with a sort of exhausting, hidden inner sexual arousal, which is more in my heart than anywhere else. A lot of work has piled up, but I can't do anything. I go from this to rage and almost jealousy . . . but then there's the longing again, and it exhausts me, exhausts me with woman, childhood, ambition. Sometimes I think it's a contradiction, sometimes a physical illness. Memories, hopes, certitudes, defeats, get all mixed up, beat at the threshold of my thoughts and all the while—impotence, impotence . . . what tormenting longing!

22 July

To escape from this longing I opened Windelband.* I read: "But science and art did not cure him of his dark will to life: in the depths of his soul a passionate striving for turbulent action tears at him, for the acquisition of power, for the development of strength." And further: "This is a nervous professor . . . who is in turn seized, now by the striving for quiet pleasures . . . now by the secret flaming desire for a stormy life." And earlier: "Both moments of this inner antagonism in its fundamental essence Nietzsche himself defined as the 'Dionysian' and the 'Apollonian' principle."[3] I read, ironizing ardently. So this is the same old Nietzschean problem of the "poet" and the "philosopher," and haven't I changed even a hair since 1905? I haven't solved anything or become any deeper. I take up Nietzsche again and read Nietzsche. The form is approximate and amorphous, the ideas elementary and not solid, but the intensity is intransigent and the scope inspires greatness. Scope! . . . How much have I forgotten and compressed from that which defined the scope of my youth, how much has been lost along the way. Once the whole world was full of questions. And I passed

---

2 This entry is an excerpt from a letter Punin wrote to his wife, Anna "Galya" Ahrens.
3 Punin is quoting from Windelband's biography of Friedrich Nietzsche.

through it without having answered them. I know less now about what is day and what is habit than I did then, but I don't pose the questions anymore. I have become limited and petty. Along with this I know that the scope of my talent is equal only to this pettiness and that in order to emerge from this limitation I must kill my talent. The "professional" in me is less than the human being, that's why the human being in me cannot be realized. I lack sufficient form in myself and in a full and self-sufficient work form and content coincide. In the name of form I should limit myself. Hence such a tenacious desire for this "Diary." Here I am more of a man than I am in my life, my articles, or my speeches. Hence my "passionate striving for turbulent activity" and "the dark will to life," the longing, and the efforts to break through into that world, where, it seems form is more complete. The vain efforts to extend form through a romantic mistress, to express oneself more deeply, more definitely, more organically. Futile, for in the Dionysian element I could not find a basis for form, I have no form where I have no profession. And I am always an image, not liberated from the material and immobile as death.

Since I do have some ambition, it is relentlessly painful to "realize" this. (Variation of a letter to Galya.)

28 July

Each of us is alone, in our own peculiar rhythms.

5 October[4]

The lyric is a dark force. In the fall you look to the very bottom of life and are terrified—for your life, ultimately. To go on living just for the sake of living.

A petty formula.

Theoretically: I am complicit in my own demise. I have no interest in the grand gesture or in staking my life on a card. I can't. Yet that is just what I must do, if only just once. Not doing it just isn't enough. There it is, emptiness, weakness, baseness. One walks forever in a half-life.

*29 October
13 March,
1921
[fragmentary
entries]*

---

4   Punin's diary entries for August 30, October 2, and October 27, 1920, have been omitted at the family's request.

NOTEBOOK FOUR

1921–1922

Introduction | *Inauguration of New Economic Policy (NEP). Punin supports government initiatives, but also defends artistic autonomy. Arrested August 2, 1921; never told what charges. In jail a month; Lunacharsky rescues. Book written with Poletaev,* Against Civilization. *Old regime origins. Friendship with émigré artist Puni (Pougny). Plans for 1922 Berlin exhibit of Russian artists, but artists themselves excluded; Punin protests. Birth of daughter, Irina Nikolaevna. Beginning of relationship with Anna Akhmatova.*

[page 1 missing] [1]

[1921]

This works people up, like the decadents, like Dostoevsky. I want to be, and I have to be a civil servant and I have to be "dead" and act and write that way. Otherwise, I can't do anything, nor can you. On this account you aren't in fact doing anything, just making pictures, which are good art, but which nobody needs. Tatlin is valuably, wonderfully needed; he doesn't examine his conscience. He has only one thing to his name and that is: extraordinary taste. I have poor taste. I will always have gray thoughts and feelings, and I won't be praised for that. But I love to work and I can work so that things are done and done clearly. I don't love your art. I'm not interested in it anymore. Now I understand why you have splatters and I understand your traces. It is all for the intelligentsia. You must be useful, useful, useful, even if it makes you inanimate, like a typist, for example. Useful to real people, so that they would immediately understand, so that they would accept immediately.

———

1 | The next entry is incomplete since a page is missing, and it is not clear who is being addressed.

If I myself don't understand anything in art, what then do I understand? The "living" person and that's all. Keep shooting live people, they get in people's way, in the proletariat's way. Keep shooting.

[page missing]

I am indignant because
I have no words to sing
to the darling of my heart
who betrayed me

28 July

These past days—days in which the last thing was taken from me, so that I was completely played out, like someone unsteady walking out into the dawn completely without anything that didn't turn out to be superfluous. Things lit up with good cheer, but not for me, who because of this felt even more purely alone. There is the loneliness of the innovator; he who has quickly lost everything is alone in a different sense. People are alone by the sea, in the field, in winter, under the stars they are very much alone, in the moonlight the loneliness ~~is torment ing like~~ of jealousy. You feel estranged, will life go on, or not, not knowing.

1 August

Bruni said:

What I like a lot in you is your lightness, you leave lightly. (Silence) It's your guardian angel, he is guarding you well. Given your character, things would be very hard for you.

POSTCARD TO EVGENY AHRENS* FROM
PUNIN IN PRISON, AUGUST 5, 1921[2]

VI from cell 32 Punin. Shpalernaya

Have they called my wife? Send more in a basket, including the described items twice a week—Mon. and Fri. It seems it is not possible

---

2 On August 3, 1921, at 2 or 3 A.M., Nikolay Punin was arrested at his apartment and taken to police headquarters. He was held there for 36 hours without questioning or being told what he was held for. He was then transferred to the Depozit prison and placed in cell 32. He was not released until September 6. Punin was never questioned or accused of any crime. His apartment was searched, but police documents show that little was seized except for money, some letters, and his revolver. While in prison, Punin wrote a declaration in which he protested the Cheka's use of investigative power. He conjectures that he was arrested as part of an alleged conspiracy against Soviet power. Punin cites his work for the revolution, the book he wrote with Poletaev, and Lunacharsky's support of him as

to come visit me, but find out if it is possible to give information about health, etc. When sending bread, cut it up. I want rolls and butter, nothing fresh is allowed.

Say hello to the Briks and Shterenberg. The keys for the wardrobe are in the middle table. Use the horse. Please change the sheets—you can write me—write—how is Sasha?[3]

5 VIII—'21

POSTCARD TO EVGENY AHRENS FROM PUNIN IN PRISON, AUGUST 7, 1921

VI Section, cell 32 Punin

7 VIII Shpalernaya 25

Still no real change, I still haven't received a single word from you and this disturbs me—How are you all? As soon as you can, send soap, a toothbrush, and matches. I want cigarettes very much. Greetings to Verun, tell her, that I met Nik. Stepanov. here.[4] We stood in front of each other like little boys. He had the Iliad in his hands, which they immediately took away, poor thing. When you bring a message, get back the vessel in which things were sent last time. Send something in a porcelain container, I have four of them in the left buffet. I have a jar in my things for Pskov. A heartfelt hello to all.

POSTCARD FROM GALYA TO PUNIN IN PRISON, AUGUST 13, 1921

13/ VIII /'21

My dear friend, how are you? Ask for whatever you need, we are sending all but the shoes. I visit Nadezhda Davydova daily. Can I send you books? I already sent one, did you get to keep it? All are healthy and happy. I love Monday and Friday now. All send kisses, greetings. I squeeze your hand.

Your Galya

---

proof of his loyalty, but admits that he is still undecided about his support of the party. Punin is most angered that he is being held without questioning and that such an arrest undermines his authority and the trust of the people and his co-workers. As Punin's correspondence with his wife and father-in-law, Evgeny Ahrens, reveals, conditions in prison appear to have been difficult, but Punin, ever one to strive to find beauty in his life, puts "flowers" at the top of his list of requests for needed items such as bread, butter, and tea.

3   Aleksandr Nikolaevich Punin was Punin's younger brother.

4   "Verun" is Vera Ahrens-Gakkel; "Nik. Stepanov." is Nikolay Stepanovich Gumilev.

COPY OF LETTER FROM LUNACHARSKY TO CHEKA
ON PUNIN'S BEHALF, AUGUST 18, 1921

> To: VVChK Comrade Unshlicht
> Copy to: Dir. of PChK,
> Comrade Semenov

RSFSR
People's Commissariat
of Enlightenment

No 6002
Moscow

On the 3rd of August Comrade N. N. Punin, Head of the Dept. of Fine
Arts, was arrested. The conditions leading up to his arrest were made
known to me not only from the words of his wife, but also from the
word of our greatly valued (by you and me) co-worker, Comrade M. O.
Brik. I myself have known N. N. for a long time. He has now entered
into the service of the Soviets after the revolution and since then has
loyally and productively worked with us, incurring the hatred of bourgeois artistic circles. During his activity, Nikolay Nikolaevich became
ever closer to the communists, and became one of the main transmit-
ters of communism into the Petrograd artistic milieu. There can be no
mention of betrayal on his part. Here we have an obvious and regret-
table mistake. For my part, I ask the VChK to take care of this matter
as quickly as possible and personally provide any guarantee both in the
name of the Narkompros and in the name of my relationship to comrade Punin.

> People's Commissar of Enlightenment A. Lunacharsky
> Certified true copy: Director of business of the Russian Museum
> N. Maik

POSTCARD FROM GALYA TO PUNIN IN PRISON

> 10 – 24 / VIII / '21

We got your postcard, dear friend, today. It came at 7. I personally
sent your greeting to all. Sasha and everyone are fine. Take care of your
health. We are sending all that you ask, write and tell us what you
need. All the family says hello. I squeeze your hand and kiss you.

> Galya.

POSTCARD TO PUNIN FROM GALYA

23–29/VIII, '21

I very rarely receive letters from you, 2 postcards in all. How are you? Change your sheets as often as possible for physical good spirits. I will send a sufficient quantity. I am thinking about asking for an extension of my leave. Papa helps me a lot. He is healthy and in good spirits. Everyone looks after my material well-being. Greetings from all. I squeeze your hand.

Galya.

REPLY TO PUNIN'S LETTER REQUESTING THE RETURN OF HIS SUSPENDERS UPON RELEASE FROM PRISON

Comrade Punin
It appears your suspenders were given to another by mistake.
Unfortunately, there are no others to exchange for yours. As far as the book is concerned, such things are in general sent to the prison library and cannot be returned.
Officer of the VChK
Bogdanovich

11 Sept. 2nd of August I was arrested, locked up in Depozit, where I remained until the 6th of Sept.

27 Sept. There are few who feel their lack of talent as I do.

11 Oct. For me, the most important thing in life is creativity. Other aspects of life can serve it, as long as it is serious and knows its goal, even human life itself, if this creativity is especially great and knows its direction precisely. Human life and its worth are for me secondary. The method of realization of either the former or the latter is love—possessed and frightening in the first case, and beneficent and attentive in the second. This is my last word about ethics.

13 Oct. Today I met Academician Marr.* Remarkable.
He came from N. N. Kuzmin's.
—What kind of revolutionary is he? He is simply a numbed and stifled man, without even a glint of fire in his eyes. I speak to him and he answers: I can't do anything. What kind of revolutionary is this, that can't do anything? If you can't, then let those who can.
Then he began to say very interesting things about language. He discovered a language that we spoke before all the languages known to

us. A language without the designations of feelings and the processes of thought and movement. Where a pitcher and bread meant one and the same thing. (the example is not exact)

door in the sky—sunrise

door in the sea—sunset

dog—a son, a sired animal

They (the scholars) don't understand. Just let him die, though, and leave them this thought, then they will go to work. Just so there is no author of the idea. But now they don't want to.

14th

Nevertheless, we are beginning an epoch of time. Time will gather a tail of three dimensions, demonstrating the life principle moving ever onward.

Stupidity—discussions about the decline of contemporary culture, when the animal is changing, what kind of decline is there? A decline for him who only sees what has been left behind.

In Khlebnikov's "Razin"* the words are already in Tatlin's living space.

26th

Perhaps Raisky is real

(reaction)

[part of stub for 17 March 1922]

8 November

They began the operation with forceps at 4:50. Galya.

At 5:08 a girl was born.[5]

30 November

I dreamt of Lilya Brik, with golden curls.

> *Where deep realism unnoticeably*
> *crosses over into shining spiritualism*
>
> —GLEIZES AND METZINGER,
> *Du Cubisme*[6]

Evening. A Christmas tree, books. The road of life sometimes seems completely meaningless and empty to me, but sometimes, like now.

---

5 This entry refers to the birth of Punin's only child, Irina Nikolaevna Punina.
6 Published in August 1912, this was one of the first books to try to make Cubism more understandable to the general public. Tatlin was not impressed with the book and called it "pseudo-Cubism."

Since my youth I have had an idea. An idea involving attack, onslaught, and war. As if I were always on the attack against the universe or eternity. Rushing wildly into the storm with Schopenhauer in my pocket; a month later the same attack, but linked to the revolution; then the most I had to give was this burst via this woman (L.);[7] but at the same time, it was complete failure.

Then the long and tortuous struggle for and against Nietzsche; a brilliant breakthrough at the front with the aesthetes, with Vera Ahrens and with exhausted religion. And then came the conquest of heaven using logical proofs. (In fact, I was seeking support for the spirit in logical proof.) I am thrown back again. By the mine-field of realism. And yet, and yet, I still have the idea, though it resists being written down.

Where is the word for this longing, this idea? I thought "the Middle Ages" when I gave my paper at Volfil,* but no one understood anything. Which means that I was wrong. Everyone has to understand, with no effort whatsoever; there is no deep wisdom in it; man, all right, but beyond man? Yes; beyond man . . .[8]

BRIEF SUMMARY OF LETTER SENT TO LUNACHARSKY BY SHTERENBERG CONCERNING THE PROPOSED ART EXHIBIT IN BERLIN, 1922

[Shterenberg and others, including Punin, who represented the Petrograd Society of Left Artists, wrote Lunacharsky to voice their concerns over the proposed art exhibit of contemporary Russian artists in Berlin. The works had been chosen by the commissar of education without the permission of the artists. Several artists had been dissatisfied with the choices. The society also wanted to express strong support for having the artists travel to Berlin with the exhibit. Their argument was that without the artists there to discuss their art, the art would be meaningless.]

28/I/'22

Lately, questions about creativity have come up: invention is still not creativity; art is that which is a screen in creation—a sieve.

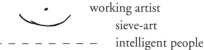

working artist

sieve-art

intelligent people

And form, what then is form?

---

7   Lida Leonteva.

8   Leonid Zykov finds this passage to be Punin's interpretation of a quote by Osip Mandelshtam on Bach.

LETTER TO ARTHUR LOURIE FROM
PUNIN DATED JANUARY 28, 1921

28 I-'21

Dear Arthur,

Now that I am home, I will tell you about us: You are a terribly lonely man. I rail at professors, make scandal for "Art," in general I go around causing scandal somewhere. Maybe these are just knockings, yet are also resolutions. You, however, are irresolute to the point of giving me a frightening feeling that might be called a premonition. To a gothic spire, its position in height, in the surrounding emptiness, might be just as frightening. There is not a single proof that we are right, yet they are not on our level because of this surrounding emptiness.

One could be exhausted and die like a dog, without a ripple. We keep talking about history, but history is a petty and illusory wave, which has as little authenticity as the current recognition of Blok by everyone. The profane don't grant recognition. Yet they will never recognize us, this must be understood. Here's a schema for you. . . .

you

artistic circles

people

We will never get through to the people through artistic circles. They have agreed to organize a huge sieve around you, and we can only pour into it, while it sifts; they won't let us pour directly into the people. This sieve is called art. I, as you know, am not sentimental, but I have such a sense of longing, which urges me to run around to the cafes or houses where there are people, and ask everyone, "Anyone here need us?" So Pushkin belongs to us alone, because they also built a sieve around him, all our complex construction about culture, humanity, is our own sly plan to win back that which by right belongs to us. To reject everyone to the last—this is the excellent wisdom of creation. Only not à la Pasternak, but purely. All who are involved in art besides us—not artists and not the people—should simply be shot. I advise you as a musician to take this in and don't talk anymore about "problems" of culture. They are the offices and fortifications of the structure supporting the sieve. Music, as much music as possible, any music, the very worst is none of their business. Write, write music.

Why is it so hard for us to find the instinct of our own self-preservation? We have encountered such rejection, uninvolvement, emptiness, and solitude that we seem to stand right next to death (providing an excuse to our attackers). The soul grows cold. Van Gogh wanted to stab Gauguin, but cut off his own ear. You understand? Well, O.K. I thank you for your friendship. Let's *create* Pushkin.

Your Punin

6/II

If there were only music, the rest would follow.

20/II

Life is the chaos of the elements acquiring in motion material substance and its qualities. Space is time. Such is one of the possible representations of the universe. No beginning and no end. An eternal flood of elements. Humanity is of those same elements.

21/II

Just to keep waiting. To walk, looking around to see if she is coming. Up to now, I am just going on waiting. It would be inexplicable if I were not certain that only with her (golden curls, golden locks) was it possible to break into those solitary spaces of pure form, where rage is calmed in immortal creativity, leaving form behind. Oh, Mozart, Mozart . . .

Why do I have such a feeling today, a feeling as if now were the time to weep

Love, the power of love. The way to God is woman—the female face, mouth, and the oval of the chin. A woman's mouth—that is the true path. For some reason religion rejected woman. What kind of perversion is this? How can you talk this way about God, the way, and woman?

The songs of women's choirs are especially sweet.

1 March
1922

After several days . . .

It seems possible to divide people first into the elemental type. These are religious people in the long run. In essence they are elementary in form; they just have a strong homogeneity and their inner self does not submit to outside forces; they are tragic, but, as always with the elemental, they are plebeian. These people are always listening to a voice inside themselves, and when there isn't one, then they too don't exist, they are insignificant. Then they are flawed, like everything boring, meaningless, idle; as they themselves say—useful to no one.

The other type is the fighter; they are difficult to define: they are complex. They are intellect, well-armed in form. The Apollonian principle. All means are used. Their intellect can be transparent for the elements that pass through it.

An excellent type of people.

———

Much has been given to me, and much will be asked from me. Nothing can be asked from me, well, how can one ask something of a person who has a "gold mine," but who not only has no carrying bag, but also no hands to gather the gold?

––––––––

Today I was at Matyushin's. All in all a wonderful person. Strong, with an organic principle. After Tatlin it is difficult for me, but M. is better equipped now that T. T. is at a dead end and has been gloomy for two years now. M. is happy as springtime; somehow he foresaw things better than T. Organism.

––––––––

If there were music, all else would follow; I want to study music.

15/III   Not organism (meaning Matyushin), but physiology. Tatlin is organism.

16 March   I received pipe tobacco from Puni in Berlin; I am happy. It's all Yuksi [Korsakova-Galston],* I communicate with Puni through her. I propose peace to you, "émigrés."

17 March   Are the elements God? I don't love the elements as elements.
   Humanity has a goal—immortality. It makes everything permissible, all the "trifles" of the revolution and all the suffering—to immortalize, to save and comfort mankind.
   Humanity has the means to achieve its goal: to become transparent, to release itself of the material. The material was born of the elements, and it is completely elemental in its concreteness, in its givenness. It must be purified so that the eternal, which can be seen in it, might look out gently, might do its work. There will not be time, and there already isn't space. The relief is the resurrection of the past. That too is immortality.[9]

[stub of removed page]

9   This passage may be Punin's reaction to Matyushin's system of extended vision called "zorved" (see-know), which "combined the development of physical vision with that of spiritual intuition. By means of 'zorved' man would be released from the spiritual and physical cage of three dimensions" (from the biographical sketches in Christina Lodder, *Russian Constructivism* [New Haven: Yale University Press, 1993], pp. 251–252). The "Relief" may be a reference to Tatlin's "Painterly Reliefs" and "Counter-reliefs" dating from 1914–1916.

Yesterday after a night conversation with Lourie and Akhmatova, I still felt only the final solitude.

The means of expression haven't been given. The most expressive thing on earth is combustion (Blok). Another way of looking at each artist's creative work is that it is much more *not* him than it is him. "The Martian's Trumpet," while it *is* Khlebnikov, yet it is at the same time a response to our own desire for something concrete, with all its particularities, expressed in terms of everyday life, so that "The Martian's Trumpet" is Khlebnikov's blueprint, but it is not Khlebnikov.

No, no, if only not to be personally responsible.

Pavlovsk. Fall. Dark evenings. The wind rustles, just as it did then, the same; my soul aches, about the same thing, the moon is behind the trees, like a palace with a silver coffin. Does my heart really still ache now?

And even after the revolution? I don't understand.

Help, I don't have the strength for all this. How lonely my heart is.

Who is this unattainable and only one? Dama Luni? No. Perhaps it is the revolution. Yesterday I walked past the former Russian Telegraph Agency on Nevsky, where soon now the "Dominik" will open. They kept painting over the letters "R-O-S-T-A."* Before there used to be agitprop posters denouncing the bourgeoisie in the windows. How angry I used to get and then I felt bitterly insulted. Where did you walk off to? I dream of your blue raincoat.[10]

There are 2 people inside me.

I don't understand anything from all these current citations of Blok; what was wrong with me? It's a disease. I'm recalling that all my life I have been these two people. One is a disease. The yearning to walk off,

10 | A quote from Aleksandr Blok's long poem "The Stranger" ("Neznakomka").

like someone poisoned, near death, close to heaven and at the same time against it, sinful and sinning all the more, and gloomy, irreverent, desperate, enraged, drunken, and ready to get drunk and to dissipate and the other is bright and calm.

But #1 has no intellect or prospect

#2 has no soul

This is all a consequence of the fragmented, unbrotherly state of the world. Disintegration is internal as well as external. Lord, lord, help put the world back together as soon as possible, whether You exist or not.

It's a terrible demise—disintegration.

5 Sept.

She spoke of Arthur [Lourie] after the meeting.

NOTE FROM ANNA AKHMATOVA TO PUNIN[11]

I have a meeting at one of the commissions for the resolution of conflicts. Maybe you won't catch me. Then come on Thurs. in the morning, and until then, work and don't be sad. See, I can give good advice to my friends. And I am a bit sad that I will not see you. Kisses.

Your An.

NOTE FROM ANNA AKHMATOVA TO PUNIN

Nikolay Nikolaevich, today I will be at the "Sounding Shell." Come.

A. Akhmatova

I sat in a meeting at the House of Art when they gave me this note. I was completely moved by it, since I hadn't expected, that An. could condescend to call me. It was even before our conversation about Arthur [Lourie].

NOTE

Dear Nikolay Nikolaevich

If you are free this evening, then it would be endlessly sweet of you to come visit us. Until we meet.

Akhmatova.

Come around 8 or 9.

11 The following three notes have no date, but are estimated to be from September 1922 by Leonid Zykov. The last line was added by Punin.

27th of October

And I don't know why in the dawn
When my strength was already gone
I did not perish, but noticed your face
And begged for your consolation.

2 November

All this divine tension, it is beyond me to describe.

Is it you, finally, my dark, disturbing joy? Is it true that I am living on the last of my strength?

If it is you, then why is there such a fog, and why do you offer no help, beside fear and lies and disturbances?

To imagine a face, and to search for it, is, of course, the best means to justify all the assignations and betrayals of everything that was.

That dear formula of Blok's:

How I love you . . .

How pliant you are, like a stem; lips parting, speaking malicious and destructive words. A pliant fatality, isn't that so? Dear hands, hands from which to drink love. You are entirely like that, something from which to drink love.

And I drink, having forgotten everything.

Evening of the same day.

You're the type who walks by and seems to say: "Come along with me"—and you walk on past. Why do you need to call, and why did you call me? Where am I to go with you, where, homeless beggar woman?

3 November

As yet you do not love; but, believe me,
*You can no longer **not** love.*

4 November

"To my happy dear friend ~~(Anna Akhmatova)~~, that you may cherish and love as long as you live." (inscription on a portrait) [12]

————

What is your happiness and your carefree spirit to me, when I don't understand the deepest part of life? I don't understand it or grasp it with any sixth sense. Is it here, close by, or does it not exist at all, emptiness? And you, black-braided, with the face of a peasant woman, you flaunt your merry laughter before my very eyes. And I am as happy as a

12 "(Inscription on a portrait)" is Punin's own note. It is not clear to what portrait he is referring.

little boy when your feelings touch on this extreme loneliness. Or is it not I who am alone, but you are alone within me, like a candle, like my love for you, like my memory that you exist. My tender joy, don't wait for long-lasting love.

Our closeness is fragile as ice.

You will be sorry for this, little sinner, if you don't die.

Sleep, child, sleep forever, don't wake up, don't understand; my dear hands, dear lips.

8 November.   Picasso and Tatlin

What the French toy with, we convert into a tragedy.[13]

9 November   "Can you make it without me?"

I can't be without you, I can't. I can't remember having felt such disturbing longing. . . . such anxiety.

11 November   My dear blessed friend—my love is difficult only because it must end with the death of one of us—and most likely your death.

Is it too stifling for you in actual fact, or is it stifling for the Russian land and you?

I am so blessed with you, though, and with you I lack nothing, probably I could be like this only with you.

13 Nov.   I have never yet felt the spirit of death so closely, so concretely—not that it was frightening. It wasn't frightening at all, but lonely, and I felt a kind of powerlessness and stifling, as if my breathing had been compressed and so everything was serious as never before in life, and there was no excitement. It would have been simply frustrating if it had not been solemn.

Death is flying past my fate or across my road. I am almost certain of that. Where does this feeling come from?

13   Punin wrote several articles investigating Picasso's influence on Tatlin and comparing the two artists' conclusions about Cubism. In "Conclusions from Cubism," first written in 1923, but not published until recently in the collection *O Tatline*, Punin argues that Picasso's influence on Tatlin was relatively slight and that the two artists drew very different conclusions from Cubism. He argues that, for Picasso, Cubism was always only a method and that the artist himself could not be found in his Cubist works—he would leave them as a snake sheds its skin. For Picasso, Cubism was a fight against the European traditions of art. Tatlin, on the other hand, entered into Cubism as a formative part of life. Tatlin's works are elemental and represent a departure from the traditional artistic search for beauty toward a new task for the artist: to make art a part of life, thus widening the circle of people for whom art is essential, and to synthesize traditional art forms with architecture, applied arts, construction, etc.

It's as if I could even feel the spiritual chill of its flight. My soul is cold, I feel abandoned. Everything that is near me is cold, everything, even lonely and abandoned things.

What is it?

————

I love you . . .

14 November

And there is no dust to dust
And there has been no liberation

"No matter who you are and where you lead me, I love you with my troubled heart and half-shaded memory, and you and you . . ."

18 November

How I love you. You have entered my soul, night has descended upon my life, and praying, I ask it, "Don't pass by."

Life is like night, life where there is so much destruction, where there is destruction most of all. I was somehow pushed toward you, I dimly felt that it could and would be from you and then I rejoiced like a child over a flower that the destruction would be from you. Do you know, or, better, you do know, that when you protect me and guard me, I freeze. You grow older, apathetic.

My bitter death, my dear joy, don't dawn. Don't shelter me in your wondrous dark hair or in your beloved head or in your fearsome heart, don't protect me.

~~I have known for a long time~~ there isn't much more for me to breathe, I don't have enough breath. I didn't get enough of it for life, and life lay on me and crushed me. I differ from it distinctly; it is so much larger than me.

So, if art has not comforted me, then may you comfort me with the final comfort.

————

It's as if I were to kiss death itself on the lips, and death suddenly sheltered me and loved me.

Who then is destruction and where is there liberation from this earth? And will you not liberate me from happiness?

% see preceding p.[14]

14   Notebook Four ends here.

NOTE FROM ANNA AKHMATOVA TO PUNIN:[15]

Of course no one came

I got a migraine in the theater from the unbearable chatter, so that I am still in bed ("in the cold room," etc.)

But the room isn't cold, the stove is burning and even smoking.

Thank you for the letter. You, it turns out, can write like the tenderest of angels. How glad I am that you exist.

Until tomorrow

Anna

And you must nevertheless go abroad. Don't be stubborn. I insist.

---

15   Although this note is not dated, Leonid Zykov estimates that it was written in December 1922.

NOTEBOOK FIVE

1922 – 1923

Introduction	*Close relationship with Akhmatova. Difficult for Galya. Akhmatova's other lover, theater director Mikhail Zimmerman. Akhmatova's second husband, Orientalist Vladimir Shileyko. Large-scale emigration. Criticism of Akhmatova. Eikhenbaum's book. Deaths of Gumilev and Blok the previous year. Party exerts pressure to replace "experts" (i.e., professionals) with Party members. Death of Khlebnikov.*
9 December	"I have this feeling that you are not going my way but are only crossing my road; I thirst for each little feather of your lashes and I fear your closeness as ruin. Therefore I beg for it and wait for it from you, as if my fate were foreordained."
	(from a letter)
30 December	It's finished. I left as easily as usual, not broken and in no way upset. But my heart was weary, as if I had swallowed poison. Life, why are you this way? So you didn't let me dine with you. I am the sixth guest at the banquet of death ~~(poems of A)~~ and all five drank to me, the absent one, but I have the feeling that I will never die. Yet I want to die, I must, it would be horrible not to die. Today I went to see An.; her cold, broken stove, she was quite sick—her heart. I fixed the stove, then we walked in the Summer Garden. She cheered up, began to smile her sweet, womanly smile. We stopped by a bakery. She fed me pastries. We bought a Christmas tree. She walked me home.
	She has been destroyed lately by that shameless and insolent book by Eikhenbaum.
	I have never been so patient with anyone as I have with her. She is amazingly and softly kind ~~(Eikhenbaum came up to her with an innocent look.—He knew about the line, knew at whose table he was eating, and he came with this manuscript, so that she would sanction it, and she didn't say a word to him about the fact that it tormented her)~~. She is lighthearted and happy, but worn out—only I won't say by

what. So empty—not her outer life—they don't bow to anyone as they do to her—but inside her, her life itself is empty, so much so that at times it even frightens me. Besides, no one deserves a simple, naive, guileless, uncomplicated love as much as she herself does; one that is as light-hearted, simple, happy as she is. She is marvelous, has preserved a full living feeling for the *world,* with something (intuition) that is reminiscent of Tatlin. She is often amazed at things to which we are already accustomed. How I love her joyful wonder at a cup, the snow, the sky. She writes quite unconsciously. I was with her, and once again I felt that I have been given very little creativity. I know how one has to go about it, yet I have no real desire for that which is needed, and I indeed have little desire, when I desire at all.

Our love was difficult. Because of this it perished before its time. Neither she nor I could display it, talk about it, free up our lives for it. It seemed to her that her closeness to me would not be forgiven her, and it seemed so to me. Probably she would have been forgiven. Yet everything really did separate us: her situation and mine, our views, everyday life, our generation, understanding of art, the tempo of life itself, our intellectual needs. I still knew how to amuse her, but she never (?) could comfort me. I often felt bitter and stifled with her, as if death were embracing and kissing me. Yet to this very moment, I love her lithe and sharp movements, the lines of her body, and I especially love her face, her mouth, and the sorrowful curve of her smile, her teeth with their little gaps, the oval of her strong chin, her large forehead, and—especially—her soft dark brown hair. Her face is quintessentially feminine. I have always imagined such a woman (to myself), or someone very similar. It seemed to me that my mother had just such a face; the lower part of Yunona's face had the same construction.

A sweet face.

I have sheltered and will continue to shelter her until death, that sweet friend. (So you sheltered her well, did you?—Jan. 7, 1923)

*2 January
1923*

It isn't over yet. My whole "soul" is on fire. Ringing in the New Year, I forgot everything, and then it came, it came with fiery tongues, I found neither place nor peace, and that's the way it is still . . .

3 January

Why did I think it had ended, when nothing has ended, but has only just begun. Today at a concert I was with her for a few steps—everyone who knew us noticed. No, they won't give us any peace.

What am I waiting for, what do I want? I know what. I remember her name, I say it out loud, I burn inside, I call out, I remember her, everything gets mixed up, collapses, she is alone, I cannot be without her. I cannot imagine a worse torment than that life might separate us.

Nothing has ended; looking into one's future is frightening.

————

I have never been so discreet and restrained as with her. What do I fear? Is it fear?

7 January

All day I waited for her, trembling. In the afternoon Tatlin came with the "molecule" (that is what his wife is called) and I wasn't glad to see him. Then I read Lossky*—trifles. He gets out of the difficulties into which "idealism" (substance) falls smartly and not without wit, but that's not the problem. It is very *rooted* in culture, in method. He speaks with such care about truth that you don't believe it, better a lie, if only it is believed, so that life becomes easier to live.

They came by at twenty to nine. She was so light and simple. I was a little heretical. We three drank to Arthur [Lourie]'s world fame. A poor meager evening as a threesome. She alone could have helped, if she had wanted.

Now it is deep night, it is like the soft snow (of a Petersburg winter) because of her.

8/I

I went (with Galya) to Pavlovsk. My guilt before her could be atoned only by love, but there is no love and it can't be done. It's not possible to say that it was only habit; it was rather a love-attachment, but not love, something like the feeling toward a merry and sweet sister. Out of all of this, the most tormenting thing is deceiving her, and the most horrible is tormenting her, and I am doing both. An. understands all this and protects me without parallel. But why? What does she know, what does she foresee?

All day I sensed her presence with an illuminated tenderness, her dark figure in the darkness and noise of the Pavlovsk park. In my love there is veneration. Most of all I am afraid to cause her pain, and I have the constant desire to repeat my words about her appearance: about her face, about her hair, about her hands and how she sits on the floor; she sits like the girl with a pitcher in the Tsarskoe Selo park.

(And this is all rubbish, old intelligentsia rubbish—well, *so,* what then, am I afraid of it?)

[three lines heavily ruled out]

9/I

No, I don't agree with the existing appraisal of Blok. In form he is the closing of the Pushkin age, the end of classical (renaissance, as I would

say) form. You could say that he is that into which Pushkin degener-
ated. In theme: romance, despair, drunken nights, troikas, gypsies, res-
taurants, gray mornings, all the alienated moods of Dostoevsky brought
into an infatuated Petersburg drinking bout; the whole old, the whole
bourgeois world with the delirious image of the Lady, neither quite in
the past, nor in a premonition. The whole old world. And no relationship with the revolution, not a bit. He didn't feel it in any way, or
understand it, and when he finally did feel it, he stopped writing and
died of suffocation; there was nothing, nothing remained of this old
world to breathe. The understanding of the revolution in "The Twelve,"
for instance, is so untrue and superficial. It is also an incomprehensible
distortion of his contemporaries. I'm not saying that he was not a great
man, but his role was not the one they are trying to foist on him now—
he is the end, the past, and the despair.

10/I

For two days An. has been somehow restless, tormented, depressed. I
didn't understand. I thought, naturally, that it was only because it was
Christmas. I myself always feel lonely at such holidays. Yesterday, after
fighting for a long time, she said in a strange voice that was not her
own: I betrayed you (with her husband Sh.). (11 August—Later it
turned out that it was all with the same Mikh. Mikh.) [1]

Then she cried. Would I forgive her?

There was as much pain as I am constitutionally capable of, and I
did not exaggerate for myself any conclusions or any of her confron-
tations. I was completely honest. I felt neither hate nor anger toward
her. (Nothing of the "And I will have vengeance" kind.) Just as I had
betrayed her, she betrayed me—so I felt. I still felt there was no guilt
in the world. It was invented. I cannot conscientiously judge anyone.
There was no sin of that sort which would not have been humanly trivial. And so her betrayal fell somewhere to the very bottom where it
couldn't touch me. I don't know how I was made—was my essence
light or dark, or was it wild and terrible from the beginning?

But today and right now I am very nervous . . . only my nerves
reacted (yesterday my legs and back shook, when she told me, shook
strongly, vibrating like a drum), neither my consciousness nor spirit nor
my heart responded. But I was more gentle and tender, and because of
this she began to cry. I won't say I forgave, but that it was not for me to
forgive an angel. Even if my beginning were light, hers was angelic. It

[1] "Sh." is Vladimir Shileyko, Akhmatova's second husband. "Mikh. Mikh." is Mikhail
Mikhailovich Zimmerman—Akhmatova's friend and lover.

wasn't she who offended in the sin, in the vanity, frivolity, or dissolution, but the angel in her. Her angel has already suffered greatly because of her, but I don't know anyone in whom there has lived such a large and pure angel, in such a dark and sinful body. I love this sweet, terrible body and face because it is the dwelling place of this angel.

Knowing that you betrayed me, I know you *will* betray me, but I don't love you with the kind of love that can be betrayed. And your arms with which, like yesterday, you embraced my neck, saying: my little boy . . . You don't have the power, An., to make me cause you pain—*such* is my love. My dark joy, will anyone agree to drink with me? And I drink greedily, I drink unconsciously, not thinking, I drink my happiness, as if from the lips of life itself. How dark it is, how sweet, alluring, I love it, not distinguishing where you and "it" are. Only I feel blindly that I do not have long to drink . . .

12 January

These two days were magical, illuminated, peaceful, joyful, as I have never known before.

14/I

But through all this there is a kind of impenetrable loneliness, both because of her and all the pain, hurt.

> *"I beat wearily at a man's window*
> *Endless multitudes are knocking there"*

15th

I can't be counted on. Like waves of some sort, scarcely does one begin to take form and you think, "there it is," and a completely different wave comes up and wipes it clean and there is nothing. It is difficult to work in this state. You work but all the time you're looking back over your shoulder, correcting yourself, and you come to think of yourself as a mistake, with regard to humanity and the world.

17/I

(a passionless story) Wednesday

On Friday I asked Anna to "take me with her" Monday to the theater to see Khovanshchina. We arranged to ask Zimmerman for a second ticket on Sunday. She eagerly agreed.

On Monday I warily asked about "Khovanshchina," but she hadn't gotten a ticket. Then we talked a lot, and I told her about "Dama Luni," in detail about our last meeting ("I am not for you, and you are not for me"). She said: "These types of women are always like that, if they aren't in love, then they're sensible and so considerate that there's nothing to dispute, yet if that same woman happens to be in love—

then she'll arrive at three in the morning, disheveled, having overcome a thousand obstacles," she said bitingly.

Anna will always do only that which protects me—my home, my name, even my heart (so that I would never suffer because of her—that was her formula). I didn't say anything but more than ever I wanted to go to the theater with her, and I began to beg her. She didn't say no, yet all the time she kept trying to talk me out of it, and when I said bluntly, "I want to go to the theater with you today," she made a grimace, meaning don't insist, please. I fell silent and it hurt. (She asked— "Does it hurt?"—"Yes." She comforted me.) Soon I got up and left, having decided that I would go to the theater.

I stepped outside, and I so wanted to know whether I would get into the theater that I couldn't walk, I had to take a taxi (it wasn't far to walk), and went to the office. I got a seat (to the amazement of even the management—one alone) in the director's loge. I was hardly able to wait until it was time, worrying, and hurting the whole time. I entered the loge right as the curtain went up, and so I wasn't able to see if she was in the theater.

During the first intermission, I saw her with a white scarf across her shoulders, but I didn't get up or leave and didn't know if she saw me or not. During the second, I didn't see if she had gone out into the foyer; she wasn't among the rows of seats, her seat was empty. I didn't get up or leave. I fought my desire to get up and go to her; I thought: she couldn't not see me if she loves me, she'll come to me in the box. My heart pounded, my body trembled with light nervous tremors. How I longed for her.

Everyone had already returned to the hall and she wasn't there, they lowered the lights, still not there, the action began, the footlights lit the hall, I look through the binoculars: her seat is empty, and I think I've mistaken the row, and count to the 8th row, still searching, but not seeing her. Then I put down the binoculars, then I looked at the stage, then by chance I turned toward the box. Anna was sitting nearby in my box on a chair, in the dark, separated from me by the edge of the wall, in the corner.

For two days after that, when I closed my eyes, I saw her sitting that way—one leg crossed over the other, in a white scarf, in profile. In a terrible state of agitation, trembling, I hid in the corner, in a fold of the portiere. It means she came. Then I saw that the singer Levik came in. We bowed, then Zimmerman, and he stood behind her. Anna, it appeared, had not noticed that I had seen her. I looked at her once; she didn't turn. Again, the same; then she turned—I recoiled, she didn't move, and only much later, when I looked at her again, she suddenly began to laugh and held out her hand. I kissed her fingers, and she laughed. Then she waved her hand, wanting to say something. I leaned over, and she asked in a whisper if I were alone. I looked into her eyes long and agonizingly, at her dear profile, my heart pounded so hard, it was so wonderful and dark.

At the intermission she explained. She had not seen me and had come into the box to hear the words better and was amazed that she had come to where I was, not knowing, and not having planned to. She said that she didn't recognize me when I looked around from the corner of the box, didn't recognize me for a long time, even after having noticed, how (she said) strange my face was ("truly a green color," as she gaily said).

"Well, that's how it always is with me, I'm a bit of a witch."—and she explained that her coming was due to the force of my wish. "Really, I'm not a lunatic for nothing," and again was amazed for a long time that she had come exactly to this box, and not elsewhere where she might have been taken to hear the words better. Then I told her how I wanted to see her in the theater and how I was suffocating from lack of her love.

Toward the fifth act, she suddenly felt poorly, her "solar plexus" began to hurt, she became pale and was obviously in considerable pain. We made it to the end, I escorted her home, visited her for an hour. It was tender, affectionate, the whole time we wondered at the fact that I had a terrible look on my face and how she came to the box . . .

Tuesday I didn't see her.

Today I found her suffering from Arthur [Lourie]'s insult—she had received new proof of his infidelity—she was nervous and (this was the first time) she said a few mean things to me, but then she began to speak about our imminent parting (It was like what Lida [Leonteva] had said). She asked again, "Is it painful for you?" and asked me to teach her how to make it so that I wouldn't be in pain. She also asked me not to hate her and, as we parted, to remember her and said that she would remember me, bright, illuminated. She also said that she absolutely had to leave Arthur's home. I asked her whether she would come live with me if I were alone. She answered: "Then I would come." To the question of why she wanted to part—she answered that she can't: that she had made a mistake, in the verse of Mandelshtam she said, "This night (she pointed to herself) is irreparable, but where you are (pointed at me) it's still light." [2] I walked her to the tram, she went

2 A quotation from Osip Emilevich Mandelshtam.

to the theater, to Zimmerman, I parted with the ~~full~~ certain sense of an imminent break-up and parting. All evening, I suffered torment; it was hard to breathe. Would it were sooner. My heart expanded, enlarged, my whole soul ached. I don't know what will be. I don't know what to want. There's no way out, if she really can't, then there's really no way out. Even if my home were broken up, it wouldn't help. Well, she'd come for a year, but then she'd leave all the same. She said rightly that if she truly loved me, nothing in life could have intervened to destroy it. She doesn't love me. No, she doesn't love me. How to live, what to live with. I (you see), I know that I love her with a secret, deep, true love. This love cannot be escaped soon, if at all. It will last for a long time. And how, in what way could it be escaped?

18/I

But it seems she has the same right to think that I love her very little. I am preserving my home, what love is there in that? So that's all. And I go around the whole time half alive.

19th

The great Russian writers are well fixed! This afternoon I was at F. Sologub's—he'd been spending some time in the northern Russian provinces; evenings at Akhmatova's in sovereign Petersburg.

20th

Tatlin said to me: you need to master only one thing, not to go into ecstasy and not to fall into tragic sorrow. I live in such uncleanness, Anna and I live together in such uncleanness. Can't live like this any longer. That means I don't dare love you. Parting? Can this love really be impure? Then what kind is pure? No, no, something's not right here. Everything is impure, all is a lie, except love.

I sense you with such inexpressible, terrible tenderness. The only thing we can't have is happiness. Only the joy of love or the happiness of closeness makes us impure.

20/I

Tatlin's easy dependability is due to a great extent to his professionalism. It keeps him from wanting to get involved in everything. He says that complex psychology sculpts us all.

Hence my dilettantism. I should simply be a practical man: a merchant today, a political activist tomorrow, a nepman* the day after tomorrow or yesterday. But I still have some basic creativity in artistic form. This ruins everything.

Somehow I need to exterminate all this lyricism and tragedy. Even if it is not genuine and not great, and already such a ready-made ruin.

A. If you've loved the human being in a woman, then you will ceaselessly wait and search for her, and if you've loved just the woman
then on the contrary.

B. In order for a woman to become a man's friend, the two following
conditions are necessary: the woman should be so enduring that she
can withstand constant and sacrificing torment, and the man so
strong he doesn't regret tormenting the woman constantly.

C. Love for a woman, fundamentally understood, cannot be without
his physically mastering her. In those cases where it happens through
the voluntary desire of one of the partners—then the heart and love
dry up and immediately die.

Still, I love An. with a physical love (only?). Nonphysical love, even
with not very emphatic men, like myself, comes only with time.
But it began with what, eh?

The moment of happiness from physical closeness ("orgasm") is always
tainted with those feelings that have laid low and remain from the time
before. If there had been much pain in the relationship the happiness
would also be tormenting. If it had been easy the happiness would be
easy. If it had been troubled or false then the happiness, too, would be
troubled, and sometimes, in such a case, might not even be taken as
happiness but as false languor. When the fragment I have mentioned
has been very prolonged, the difference in feeling is much less tangible.

NOTEBOOK SIX

1923 – 1924

Introduction   *Deepening relationship with Akhmatova. Malevich. Tatlin and*
Akhmatova. End of affair with Lilya Brik. Tatlin on the city of the
future. Punin's appraisal of "the new art." Earthquake in Japan.
Khlebnikov's "Zangezi."* Religion. The "Conversation Book" in
which Akhmatova and Punin write notes to each other, often with
the nicknames "Kotik," "Koty" (pussycat), "Koty Malchik," or "Kotik
Murr" for Punin and "Olen" (deer) or "Akuma" for Akhmatova.¹

3 February
'23

Yesterday I picked up An. to go to the KUBU² to exchange cards for
rations and on the way back I invited her to have breakfast at home
with me. She came. Irina was asleep, Galya wasn't home. I lit the fire.
An. sat in an armchair by the fireplace. She has grown terribly thin
these past months. Why is that so sweet? To sit on the floor and kiss
her hands, where does the sweetness come from? And how stupid these
words probably sound, and how painfully stupid it must all look. But
I sat and kissed her little hands. At the same time I looked at her for a
long time. Desire flitted across her face, and she looked into the next
room—the bedroom—and looked away. What was she thinking? Was
she jealous of G. or was she thinking about us, or was it just by chance?
Then she held her hand out to me and, gesturing in the air with her
fingers (she shook her fingers), said: "No, no, let it be." But I hadn't
asked anything and hadn't even thought about it. All this time An. had
been insisting that I show her my last notebook. In the end I gave it to
her; didn't I really want to give it to her myself? She was touched in

---

1   The phrase "Conversation Book" has been borrowed from Leonid Zykov, editor of
Punin's archives, who in turn borrowed it from Goethe. It refers to the three tiny datebooks included with the Punin diaries held at the Harry Ransom Humanities Research
Center at the University of Texas. These datebooks belonged to Akhmatova and include
addresses, phone numbers, notes, and short "conversations" between Punin and Akhmatova. Akhmatova would write down an observation and Punin would write his reply.

2   The commission for aid to scholars.

some way, and we were already on the street when she said, "I got strong impressions from your notebook." Later I reread it. I don't know, don't understand, what could have made an impression, what she found in it.

Then in the evening I remembered how she had asked, "Are you glad that I came?" (And I answered stupidly enough, "Of course.") I was not glad but happy, with a full, white happiness, so that everything became quiet and pure, like the snow. (An., it is happiness when you are with me—) In my apartment the trees of the garden are right at the window. You can see their branches in the snow through the window. When An. came in she filled the room so that it was as if winter herself had come to visit me, only it was warm. We drank coffee, and for some reason, said little.

Malevich is the study, the arithmetization of the particular properties of pictorial space.

Cubism is the arithmetization of the particular properties of pictorial space.

10 February

Akhmatova spoke of Blok.

The conversation dealt with the ability to wonder at life, with freshness of perception. He is a bit scary. Nothing surprises him, with one exception: the fact that nothing surprises him; just that.

13 February

How lonely you've been, An., since the revolution, how helpless we have been in life, you and I, crushed.

15-II-23

Walking past the cabbies on the corners always reminds me of An.: "You see, I'm always wanting to go for a drive with An. in a cab." Why does a cab always seem to be suggesting love, and by no means weakly? You always keep thinking: why not take her, riding tucked in together in a cab, snuggle her in, and go driving into the snowy dust? What freedom is there in that? It's a Blokovian theme, for which he didn't have a resolution, as usual with him, but only a yearning.

———

One Friday I went with An. to the KUBU to exchange ration-cards. We met Tatlin. I was completely stunned by his "Versailles" attitude toward her. Tatlin was elegance itself! He wanted very much for An. to come see him, assured her that it was warm at his place. To An.'s comment that her legs get cold easily he said, "We'll prop your legs up on the stove. We'll fire it up until it's red hot. Have no fear, you won't be cold." He absolutely wanted to set the date right then. Moreover, An. had already paid him a visit sometime in the fall and very much expected him to come see her. I recall that he even designated a day, but didn't come. Therefore, when he saw An. at KUBU, he immediately came up and said for all to hear, "May I bow before you?" I don't remember, yes, and I can't write down all the "refined Tatlinian forms of address." I was flabbergasted. We agreed on the day (~~Mon.~~ Tuesday). T. invited me too, that time he didn't say anything about Galya. On Sunday we were at the Mitlevsky house at a lecture and T. also invited Galya. I had already told her before about Tatlin's conduct, which had made an impression on me, and about the fact that he had invited me. Neither I nor An. wanted G. to go, since this would cause difficulties for everyone, but that's how it turned out nevertheless. With this in mind, I tried as best I could to talk G. out of going. She was terribly offended and with coldness and anger told me that she would absolutely insist on going to T.'s. And she went. I had already agreed with An. to go by and pick her up, I left the house early, went to An.'s, and arrived with her. Galya came later with Poletaev. At T.'s it was of course difficult for everyone, and for him. When we were leaving his place as a threesome, I took An. by the arm as I always do when I'm walking with her (I have never in my life walked arm in arm with Galya). At An.'s building we said good-bye; An. gave us a general invitation to come see her, but not to the next Tuesday evening affair, to which she had invited Tatlin and his wife. Then endless conversations began, with tears and weeping. Galya berated me for my "baseness." The "baseness" consisted, in her opinion, in the fact that I don't tell her when I go to see An., that I don't preserve any kind of even human relationship with her, Galya (how could she say that, when all my relations with An. are destroyed by my desire to keep G. at home and protect her self-esteem), that I wanted to exhibit my relations with An. by trying to talk G. out of going to T.'s (why couldn't she have said that she, G., had guests, or was supposed to be visiting somewhere?—she isn't always obliged to be with me), that I have been hiding the nature of my meetings with An., deceiving and tormenting her (could I really tell anyone of the nature of these meetings, let alone G.?!—isn't it enough that she knew, was the first to know, even if that only happened by accident? But I didn't deny anything or hide anything then. And what would she say if I had told her, would that really have made things easier for her?), that I am only pretending when I speak of the value of home, and so on, and so on. The blaming, like the conversations, is tortuous, nightly, endless. All day Saturday Galya lay in bed and cried, she didn't even go to the clinic.[3] I didn't say anything about all this to An., so as not to upset

---

3 | Punin's wife was a doctor by profession.

her, knowing how she reacts tormentedly to everything of the sort. Toward evening on Saturday G. said that she had decided to leave me and to move in with Vera [Ahrens]. Yes, I was glad to hear that. It seemed to me that this would be better for her, and that for me it would finally resolve my six months of perplexity and difficulty, and what's more it was what I had really wanted the whole time, tormentedly and intensely—to bring An. home and live with her. I rejoiced, and if anyone's going to speak of my "baseness," then he should do so precisely now, and precisely because I didn't express this joy in front of G. I wanted to tell her, to say that I was glad, that I wanted to live with An. I didn't say anything, but on the contrary began to talk to her about Irina.

That same evening, Saturday, I saw An. and told her about everything. She was angry that I had concealed it until now. She was going to the theater; we got in a cab, it was a freezing night. On Kazanskaya St. the cab knocked a man down, stopped, the man lay there, obviously drunk. Then he got up, looked at us, and said: "It's nothing, nothing, go on your way, my friends," and tried to stand. We went on. I agreed to come see An. the next day, to say whether G. was leaving or had left. Galya didn't leave on the next day or on any other day. On Sun. we went to Mitlevsky House (for my lecture). She livened up and for some reason I seemed tolerable to her, and on the way home we didn't even talk about her leaving. And G. asked in a complicated and delicate enough way whether I was physically close to An. I denied it and will continue to deny everything. This proved to be the deciding factor as to whether or not she would leave. I just don't understand such people. Well, is it really important?

Monday I should have been at the evening gathering at Anna's, to which the Tatlins had been invited. An. asked me if I would be there and I answered no, I can't without G. Galya had already spoken about the fact that An. had not invited her and asked me not to go if An. didn't invite her. I agreed, I gave in. It didn't matter. And so I explained to An. Then An. decided to put off the evening, but because of the Tatlins this didn't turn out to be possible, and in the end An. wrote a note to Galya under my dictation (the note is enclosed here), inviting her.

Galya went. And this I also can't understand.

A lot of horrible things went on in these days, things I cannot write about, things each of us will take to his grave. Now it's a bit quieter, but I don't think it will last.

And so, more and more often I begin to think about how An. would come and live in my home.

I wanted to go to Moscow with her.

But G. decided to go with me when she found out I was preparing to go to Moscow.

Tomorrow is An.'s name day. What a crushed love now. Soon it will be impossible to visit her at home, too. Sudeykina is coming, and then Arthur [Lourie].[4]

I keep remembering her arms around my neck.

16/II

Tatlin said to Akhmatova, "You can still hang around in society, just keep working."

17/II/23

Yesterday I returned late at night. In the garden of the Sheremetev House (where we live) I sat on a bench in our wing. It was quiet, the garden was frosted over, the branches were like nets and crowns strewn over the earth and snow and it was solemn, and so quiet and majestic in the nighttime silence. I remembered An. with a tormenting, fatal longing. How meaningless all my sacrifices seemed, my work, even my gift. None of it is me, yet it is all in that element without which I am not myself. It is not my will to live and think. My single will, my only desire, my own wish for my happiness is An., to live with An. And I can't. Who needs this sacrifice? And what is left without it? Everything, . . . everything, everything.

I looked at this majestic silence, at all these silver night crowns, then at the graying roseate sky above them; it was empty. For the first time in my life I felt in the night, in the silence and the snow before me, and in the white branches, that the world was terrifyingly empty, that there is no meaning . . . no God . . . that the world was empty and without a goal.

But this morning I went to An.'s to tell her how she was talked about yesterday at the Krichevskys, and to tell her about those night thoughts. Anna acted strangely. She began to talk about how she hadn't been sleeping at night, that I kept her from sleeping. She thought about me and about death. She wanted to die, terribly wanted to die.

I was amazed.

This evening I walked her to the theater to see Siegfried (so she said). Approaching the theater, I heard the program sellers say that it wasn't Siegfried, but Onegin, and knowing that An. doesn't like O.,

4 Akhmatova lived with Sudeykina and Arthur Lourie. Sudeykina emigrated to Paris, Lourie to Berlin and later to America. In 1921, Punin got Sudeykina a job in the State Porcelain Factory making figurines and dolls, a job that Akhmatova claimed saved her life, since she was not cut out for any other work in Soviet Russia.

I asked her whether she was still going. She answered yes and darted into the entrance.

I wasn't surprised. I had had the disturbing feeling that she wasn't going for Siegfried, that she didn't go to the theater for the theater. I didn't start thinking about it.

When An. said she didn't sleep nights and that she thought she didn't sleep because of me and that I "pushed her toward death," her words seemed very strange. Then we sat on the couch, An. got confused and started to rush around, talked a lot right away using tender words, which she doesn't usually do. And then she asked: do you think I am true to you? I answered that I thought she was not true, but that I didn't trust my feelings in this. And then I understood everything immediately. Then for a long time she talked on in an anguishing state of conflict, and then refused to talk, led me on, and then retreated, the whole time asserting that she couldn't deceive me, an innocent man.

She wanted to show me some kind of letter, but then changed her mind. I insisted that she show it to me, although in essence it was already clear. The letter was just what I thought it would be, from Zimmerman, and the following was written in it:

"Greetings to you, dear Annushka"—and then it said that, in place of Siegfried, Onegin was showing, and also Z[immerman] asked whether her pain had passed. Obviously An. had lamented to him too about the stomach pain that had been bothering her lately.[5]

––––––––

––––––––

How can I go on loving you, An.?

20/II

Three days—all about this, I am sleeping poorly . . . Oh, Lord, how tired I am.

21st

I can't say, as I did then, that love was not touched . . . she shook it from its roots to its top, so that I walked and lived as though in some kind of strange earthquake: it tore, broke, and destroyed me, and nothing was left untorn, unbroken, undestroyed. And the most painful thing was the fact that nothing was left unaffected . . .

Yet she is not guilty, and is indeed more innocent than I or anyone

5 Mikhail Mikhailovich Zimmerman was sometimes referred to as Mikh. Mikh. or Misha.

else. It is inexplicable but I know that it is precisely true: her essence is angelic. She is an angel, an angel. What is to blame is just that my love was not enough for her.

See to it that you don't hurt her because of your egotism. Work on your love, make it pure, make it pure.

Still, there is one terrible thing; because of him, her love seems like a desecration of love.

Don't reproach her, even in your thoughts, for her sinful body.

The same day   The sun is already warming up. I went out into the garden — sky and snow. It's a lyric that sings of love. I love my world with you, An.

23 February   This afternoon I took An. to the doctor. Then I was at KUBU at a meeting and at Krichevsky's (on account of the poster). I wanted to know what the doctor said, and I called from K.'s to Shchegolev's, where An. should have been (it was St. Valentine's Day). She wasn't there. Possibly, she was upset and didn't go to Shch.'s at all. This evening I went past her house. I went on purpose, to stop in and see her. I got up to the building and didn't want to. And it seemed that in essence there wasn't any love.

I don't have enough love, it won't suffice . . .

Emptiness in the soul. And I thought, if Galya were not still at home, if she had really left, then what a terrible, desolate emptiness there would have been.

In the afternoon An. said: still, you love me a little bit. What does that mean, "a little bit"? It means that I am not capable of great love.

Yet it is also possible that she did not evoke great love in me. Am I guilty or is she?

Yes, I am a bit cold.

Did I expect this and ask it of her? (There was only one thing left for me . . . a pathetic power to incite her unsatiated womanly blood, to arouse her animal passion.) So she did not enter into my life at all, and maybe, if there was no life there, she couldn't.

It is also possible that there is no other love than animal love, or that horribly peaceful brotherly love. If only it were simpler. Romanticism will never fade away. And so I plod along, to put it simply. But my nerves are scattered across the sky in a fruitless fever.

Good Lord, the burden! Pull my life together. I despair of doing so myself.

If only I had lived without biography, in work and my essays.

That would have been better (biography destroys). Does a Nekrasov-Mayakovsky still reside in each of us?[6]

An., I love you nevertheless. I simply love you. I love you like Galya, and you too will be mistress of my house, a little more original than Galya, but therefore also unfaithful . . .

I really don't want to live. I don't. I just want to work; books, yes, and essays; yes, books.

I remember her hands, like those of "la cruche cassée." Much of the best in me was given when I met you; much was also squandered. The first time so much was squandered that I understood it was squandered, so I feel old and weary.

Only you are not to blame. You covered everything with your sufferings long ago.

Go, Warm Intercessor, and give her peace, bless her from your height (cold and empty, like the sky between the stars), bless her head, which I so loved to hold in my hands, which I would have held in my hands forever. If there were such a thing as forever.

Be gentle with her, Lord, as we cannot.

> Why is it so painful, because of what?

5 March

Dear, I remember, do you?

TELEGRAM TO AKHMATOVA FROM PUNIN

12 March
1923

I suggest Saturday. I await your telegram.

TELEGRAM TO AKHMATOVA FROM PUNIN

13 March
1923

Come without fail.

[telegrams unsigned in original]

20 March

Yesterday I returned from Moscow. I stayed with the Briks. L. B. said that her feelings for me were still alive and talked about how she had "howled" a lot back then because of me. "The main thing," she said, "is that I didn't know at all how to be with you; if I was more active you would tense up and leave, and when I became passive, you also

---

6 Punin wittily combines the names of two famous Russian poets, Nikolay Alekseevich Nekrasov (1821–1878) and Vladimir Vladimirovich Mayakovsky, both of whom used their lives and in particular their love affairs as subjects for their poetry.

failed to react in any way." But she doesn't know one thing; that I have fallen out of love, that in general there can't be anything without being in love, no matter how she, Lilya, acted. The fact of the matter is that something remains in me after love which women take to be evidence of infatuation. L. B. up to now still thinks that I am not indifferent, that I am not a mere stone now in my relation to her. She stroked my hand and wanted me to kiss her. I remembered An. and didn't kiss her. And it was not because I felt An.'s presence. Since the 23rd of Feb., I have felt her presence less and less. I only feel her presence on certain occasions and then it hits me suddenly, like the dawn, everything blazes up, streams out in flames onto the world, and it's because of my feelings of duty toward her. When I returned and came to see An. she was terribly overjoyed, but felt like fate and torment awaited her. I had indeed already made a decision to see her only once a week. I want so badly to work, and she sensed this. She became strangely angry. We didn't say good-bye. Today she said that for the first time she had felt pain because of me, and that something had happened inside her, something irreparable. Everything was over, she knew that relations between us were over.

I think so too.

I know that I don't know how to organize anything, that if anything remains it is the feeling that I would soon pay for it, two or three times over. I know no measure.

I lack measure—that's all there is to it. And the ability to grieve, to which I relate, as I do baseness. Strange, I don't understand anything.[7]

[three pages out]

For other people sex is connected with feeling, for me it is connected with the head. That's the way I was made.

It's just that I feel only with my nerves—that is terrible. Or so it seems to me.

This is a terrible thing, horrible.

I live on the periphery and with my mind. My nervous system isn't integrated. Only my mind. I lack the most real, the most important, genuine, aspect of personhood—the elemental feelings: instincts, faith, love, the spirit. I only have a nervous, sharp mind, which you can't even say is a great mind, because it lacks a foundation, a mission. It acts in purely logical space.

H-O-R-R-I-B-L-E.

7 Marginal note in Punin's handwriting: "It was the other way around with her."

LETTER TO AKHMATOVA FROM PUNIN,
DATED 21 MARCH 1923

21 March 1923

Anna, truly, something irreparable has occurred. I don't have the strength to understand and I don't want to think about whether you "substituted" me, as you claim, or you suddenly saw something that you had not seen earlier, but your confusion, your, as I see it, totally inexplicable sudden frenzied talk—under the scrutiny which I give to all that concerns you—is terrifying. I know, too, that you speak honestly, that there is something important in this, which might be called the beginning of the end, or destruction, if not the end.

Always and from the first day, I felt an as yet untested sense of reverence and tenderness, of love, of joyful purity in our relations. Partly, I rejoiced that in these relations there were no longueurs or dead days and meetings. Everything was terse, always the same intensity, pure to the point of transparency, like time created by the fingers of angels. The whole winter was like Winter itself. How I still love all that was experienced by us: I tell you that I will not ever allow myself to be sad about it, because I feel that it would be insulting and petty. It is base to be sad about it.

If I were still an aesthete, I would of course have to write (and would have written) a parting letter and end it all at once. But I don't want that, I don't, I don't. Anna, dear. Our love was tormenting, for me extremely. It was "a dark joy and sweet destruction" as I always called it. If, truly, the end has come—and I also sense this—then I only have one wish—to suffer this end with you. I don't want to preserve anything, to save, to admire anything, but I want to live it through to the end. If only I could live it with you to the end, even, if it is necessary, to the point of sheer boredom with one another, to the point of being oppressed by one another, so that no desire remained any longer, no memories, nothing. I loved you and still love you, no matter what you said. I am almost positive that you said it because of your own fatal love, so I don't have any (or almost no) killingly selfish feelings toward our relations. As much as I could, I tried not to cause you pain and tried to protect you. If nothing else, I agree to accept all the blame for your suffering (from jealousy, perhaps, or from my impudence). If I can no longer torment and protect you, I agree to accept all the blame for this before you, before everyone. Even if I, all the same, love you less—I also want this "love you less." If only there were something, even if not for long, and if only nothing else remained of the experience of our union on earth. This is all I want of you. There is only one thing I don't want—parting—you know that. I write you this, understanding very well that the important thing is not me, you are suffering, our meetings have become difficult for you, therefore only you can decide matters. I would never, in thought or action, find grounds to admonish you for our love in its beginning and its end. I endlessly, blindly believe in the very foundation of your feeling, your instinct to discern the necessary from the false. I'm not making this up. I do feel this way. In our love you alone were and remain correct, not in chance meetings and conversations, but in your very being. There is something deep there, giving you that right forever. My endlessly dear friend, do you feel this way, too?

I have written you everything that I could, after our bitter farewell in the garden under the stars to make things better for you, as you know.

As far as the form of our meetings—perhaps you are expecting precisely this and this is most important to you—take it as you like, but what I said to you was as it should be. I cannot prove to you that it had to be that way, but it had to be, believe me, I can't be otherwise, and forgive me if you can.

I kiss your dear hands and hair. Although I didn't want to torment you, it has happened. Dear hands, how I will always remember them.

25 March

Tatlin was here today.

He spoke wonderfully and with great scope about the culture of the future.

Among other things, he spoke about the relationship between the city and the country. We can't put the countryside on the back burner, we must electrify it. Today's type of large city is the unstable type produced by a dying era. It doesn't make sense to fill a city with private life. These are places on our earthly globe for workers. Once space has been conquered people won't need to live in them. Instead of having their private life there, they would fly in, say, from the Crimea, to work or for business. In this way, our countryside would preserve its human meaning.[8]

---

8   Tatlin's ideas about the new city and the new life of the worker resemble and may have been influenced by the ideas of his contemporaries Aleksandr Vasilevich Chayanov (1888–1937) and Velemir Khlebnikov. Chayanov's short story "The Travels of My Brother Aleksey in the Land of the Peasant Utopia," written between 1919 and 1920, describes among other things a new city in which people worked but didn't live, traveling instead by plane to work. In his prose work "Ourselves and Our Houses," Velemir Khlebnikov also described such cities, where people flew everywhere, so that the rooftops of buildings became very important and the streets were hardly used at all.

26th	The epigraph to everything that happened with regard to An.:
	"Feeling-thoughts, from which stem painful feelings."
28th	"You are as solitary as the night, looming enormous over everything that lives."
30th	I just returned from An. Lord, what closeness. What tenderness I feel toward her! It is inhuman. What is it? What's going to happen?
5 April	Terrible longing for her.
	I saw the Russian Museum with the Moscow Vkhutemas.* What a fresh and light eye they have.
	The history of Russian art is tragic.
	In the craftsmanship itself there are such tragic moments: Ivanov,* Fedotov,* Vrubel.* You could prove that Vrubel and Fedotov lost their minds because of this and Ivanov was split like a log. It is a stifling history, where people suffocate because there was no culture anywhere around, either in traditions or in the artists themselves.
Night of the 8th	Kh. V., An.[9]
17 April	What can I say about Anna?
	Those who want not to be at fault in anything are at fault in everything.
18 April	Terrible days have come.
	An. has become dependent on me, the affair has overflowed the bounds of love, has become my human affair.

CONVERSATION BOOK — NO DATE

We need to talk about how long we haven't seen each other. Of course I was completely alone. I would have come, if it had been possible to speak freely!

You'll break yourself of me in 24 hrs. What garbage! [Akhmatova]

---

9   "Kh. V." is the abbreviation for "Khristos Voskresen!" (Christ Is Risen!).

1923

Restaurant Fedorova
Some kind of writer is sitting behind us. I remember his portrait. And the lady knows me. Is it [illegible name]?

An., dear, little night, I can't take it anymore.
     Promise me, that you'll never again go to the M[ariinsky] theater and see M. M. If you can't—write me. [Punin]

I agree not to be unfaithful to whoever you want, only don't *think,* that this *is the end.* (K[otik] M[urr])

Now I can agree or not agree with what? With whatever you want. (A[khmatova])

It's Alyansky's brother. Koty, cheer up, if I feel that you love me—then nothing else is necessary. [Akhmatova]

Anik, it's not even worth discussing, that nothing in love has changed, but I have lost the belief that we will be together. In this we are both equally to blame. [Punin]

3 June

An., I am calling you.

4th

If you look at the world rationally, it is the equilibrium of two unknowns, one of which is time and the other is space.

5th

An., again, I am calling you.

3 July

Finally, warm days.
     Galya has gone to Lipetsk. The equilibrium has come to rest on a knife-blade, but it would seem that we are both such that we could live on this knife-blade for years. Life has strangely struck and crushed me. Galya is undermined forever.
     Lebedev* said of ~~An.~~ woman: woman is always tall, with long, straight legs, a face that is like a little fireplace beastie, catlike, thin and feminine, without a look of intellect, but penetrating, knowing, and predatory.
     How different love is. An. reminds me of my love for Dama Luni. Sometimes, I need her so much that I would crawl under a rock to see

her. It is a mindless love. Whatever I might have said or written about her, I can't finish, until I have put into some kind of words that I often long for her and call her by name, calling out into empty space, into that eternity which I feel with torment and suffer from with the aching feeling that they are both one. Life is a confused and troubled thing.

8 July

This is how it was today. An. dined at my place. At six she had to call Zimmerman. His father had died. An. feels very sorry for him. I took her to the museum to use the telephone. A short conversation. Isolated words reached me as I stood in the corridor. Among them, the word "tomorrow." Immediately I wondered if she would ask me to come to see her tomorrow evening as she had asked me yesterday and as we had already agreed in spite of the fact that it would be very difficult for me to come.

She left around eight and I went to take her home. When we were saying good-bye (it was already ten o'clock), she asked me as usual: "When will you come?" I answered, "Whenever you want." An. said, "Well then, tomorrow," and then, as if remembering something, "No, tomorrow, why don't you work a little for God's sake. Come on Tuesday, O.K.?" She knew, I had told her, that tomorrow I can't work, that I would barely have been able to come see her after ten, but even if she had forgotten, doesn't this very forgetfulness show a lack of love?

I smiled, "Between three and four on Tuesday." . . .

She doesn't love me and never loved me. What's more she cannot love, she isn't able to. And a terrible thought occurred to me: she needs me *only* as one more display, moreover, a display of a particular kind—Punin—the innovator, the Futurist, the threat to bourgeois philistinism, our number one scandal-maker in the city, the uncompromising.

Tomorrow evening I will go see An.—she will be with M. M. [Zimmerman].

Don't do it because of _ _ _ _.

12 July

So I went to see An. M. M. was with her. He left almost immediately, although he hadn't known about my arrival.

All this doesn't prove anything, it is terribly stupid.

Today An. went to Shchegolev's for his name-day.

An. wore a dark blue cotton dress sent to her not long ago ~~by Arthur~~ [Lourie] from abroad: a simple dress, but on An., it looked festive. How I love to look at her head. The night-time in her hair, and that isn't literature. And it's not a warm July night, like the one outside the window now, but another kind of night-time.

Went with An. today to the islands. A hot, sunny day and a strong wind from the sea. From Novaya Derevnya to Kamenny Ostrov, we floated along the Neva in a boat. It swayed lightly on the blue waves, An. sat in a linen dress, suffused by the sun. The arrows of her lashes rarely fluttered, the wind made her frown, but a wonderful satisfied glow shone in her eyes. There was so much animation in her words and movements. It might be called childlike, if all her feelings were not being held in, like a person who already knows a lot and is weary. She reached out toward the sun with her arms; arms that remember how many they have embraced. This memory of life ran through her whole body, and along with it her friendship with the sunny air as with a brother, her submissiveness to his soft and living caress. At Antekarsky An. rejoiced at the sea, and we went out on the wooden platform that reaches out a few yards into the water.

The wind whipped and flapped her dress against her, a few little strands of her black hair wisped across her face, the water splashed between the rocks at her feet, and the strip of sea on the horizon was blue-black. An. pointed to it with her finger: "I know that strip, I know it well. It was always like that," and she reminisced about Khersones. You could sense that it was very hot, but because of the strong wind the body didn't feel the heat, yet our faces and hands burned and chafed. She was happy, she felt light and simple. She reminisced a lot about Tsarskoe Selo. Lately An. often laments that we were only distant acquaintances for so many years. Again she lamented.

Then we walked around the whole shore. She was tender and trusting, her arm and shoulder pressed to my arm. Insatiably I admired her animated face on which the sun played, across which shadows and wisps of hair ran, revealing her high forehead. An. doesn't like it and was constantly straightening her bangs and covering her forehead with her hand. In her eyes there is a craftiness, a mocking laughter, irony, and a calm slyness approved by her mind. My heart was light. To the north thunder rumbled a few times.

On the way home we drank tea in a tea shop across from the ferry in Novaya Derevnya. The tea shop reminded us both of Blok. At the counter, the owner wound up some kind of music box from behind. As we were leaving we stopped arm in arm in front of an oleograph by Klever. An. had seen it many times in childhood. The oleograph cheered me up. I liked how the fires in these huts burned so warmly.

And in the evening that same day I was again painfully jealous of M. M. We talked and tormented each other until five in the morning. M. M. told her that she treated him like a dog. I felt sorry for him again, I felt guilty toward An. Out of jealousy I said to her that recently things between me and Galya had revived ("gotten better"). An. was hurt. We parted exhausted, with frayed nerves, reconciled, but only after the sun had already risen. The six-floor building on the Fontanka across from the Cinizelli Circus was bathed in rays of light, the six rows of windows blackened in the sun. A cool constant wind reached me from the Neva. My heart was light. It's good luck to be in love.

NOTE ON BLUE PAPER FROM AKHMATOVA TO MIKHAIL ZIMMERMAN[10]

Dear Mikhail Mikhailovich, don't send me a ticket today—I will not go to the performance. It so happens that we no longer need to meet.
Farewell.
Akhmatova

LETTER FROM AKHMATOVA TO PUNIN (NO DATE)

Our Koty
I completely forgot that today Mishenka was coming for me to take me to the doctor. On the way back I'll come to you. If I can.
Olen (kiss)

17 July

Since morning I wanted to see An. I knew that in the evening she would be reading at a "closed session" of the "Union of Writers." In the afternoon Abramov called to invite me to go with him to it. We agreed to go at eight o'clock. The whole rest of the day I lived in expectation of the evening. I was at Abramov's by eight. We waited for Zamyatin,* who was supposed to come for us. At ten o'clock Zamyatin still hadn't showed. We decided to go on our own. We arrived during the intermission. An. had already read and had left.

During the course of the whole evening, while Zamyatin read his article and the "discussion" went on, it was terribly painful. So this is reciprocal love, and I felt as if I alone loved. I raised my head and with open eyes saw her face in the air.

After the reading I went with Abramov and Zamyatin to have dinner at Palkin. Zamyatin's wife spoke of An. a few times. I think she was interested in our relationship. After dinner I was walking with the Zamyatins along Liteynaya St. past my house and suddenly thought

10 | This note was apparently never sent.

that perhaps I could stop by to see An. It was 2 A.M. I knew that on that day Kuzmin was with them, and that, in general, they had guests. My heart began to pound, I walked past the building, as if walking the Zamyatins home. I said good-bye to them at their building on Mokhovaya St. and ran to the Fontanka. The gates were open, there was light in all the windows of An.'s apt., which meant the guests hadn't left yet. I knocked at the back entrance. I carefully walked through the first two rooms. In the third An. lay on the couch. The guests had already left, except for one, who remained with Olga (Sudeykina) in the other half of the apartment. They were keeping her from going to bed, so An. was dozing there on the couch.

"When I saw you, I thought I had lost my mind," she said.

We talked for about half an hour. An. was very tired. It was wonderful to hear her and to see her. It grew light. Olga burst in, undressed, saw me, cried out, and yelled at An. to go to bed in her bed. An. was very distressed that Olga had seen me since she would inevitably tell her "cavalier" about it. I was also uncomfortable because of this "decameron," and was sorry that I had come.[11] An. didn't want to sleep in Olga's bed, said that she would sleep on the couch. I said good-bye, kissed her hands, my dear hands. Outside the window birds began to sing.

2 August

There is a love for which there is everything: meetings, hands, drinking tea together. You part, and it passes, but you can't live half a day without being together. There is another love for which drinking tea is the same as dying, frequent meetings are terrible, and partings are desired. Today there is a terribly chaotic wind, it tears at the leaves and whips across the puddles. I have trained myself to hide the pain of her meetings with another. Is she only sorry for him? I will not know or find out whether it is really true that she loves me. But my heart remembers that she loved more. Its memory is more persistent than that of my mind. It would be simple to live if one were given the mind (*ratio*) alone. It is painful. No, fruitless laments are senseless, and there is nowhere to go . . .

I have not learned silence.

11 Reference to Giovanni Boccaccio's *Decameron,* a book of short stories narrated by ten noble men and women who pass the time out in the country by telling stories. The stories are often of erotic intrigues, thus relating to Punin's fear that his tryst with Akhmatova would become fodder for local gossip-mongers.

I could do nothing the whole day because of the pain. I walked around and lay down. Here's how my feelings-thoughts went: An. asserts that she has sacrificed M. [Zimmerman] for me, yet her meetings with him are more frequent and last longer. If I ask her to stop seeing him and she agrees I will cause an innocent person to suffer undeservedly, and, according to An.'s stories, a good person, and I will bring pain to her, An. If she doesn't want to part with him, then either I will have to resign myself to this or we will have to part. In the first case An. will again comfort me, which will calm my heart, but only until the next "incident," and with every new "incident," new pain and new comforting—a senselessly tormenting life. If I part with her that means I am the one who did not love, not she. Then why am I suffering, or do I suffer because of masculine vanity-jealousy and not out of love? I love her, so I cannot part with her, and even if I part with her because of the pain, out of fear of the pain, from egoism, then how bitter everything will become—this love, and the memory of her, both for her, An., and for me. And what will I win, gain, if I part with her out of pain? Only losing her before it was time, and I would darken everything we lived through together with my guilt. Is all that's left for me to do to watch this new love grow and not even lift a finger? If I fight for her love systematically and tirelessly—and that is the only way to fight—then why would I need this love, won only by force and will? Who needs it? What is there to do? I saw there was no solution. When I realized so clearly that if their meetings really were more frequent and prolonged there would be no solution; I could either leave her or stay with her—my throat constricted painfully. I couldn't understand how this happened, that she, not I (as it was in the winter), turned out to be the one leaving, and I knew that I could neither tell her nor not tell her about all this. But what I would say or what I wouldn't say, I didn't know. Then I felt how painful it was for Galya. I was tormentedly yearning in my impotent, senseless doubts, which somehow had increased tenfold. And truly, if An.'s love for M. were growing, then I had no option. I would have to stay to understand it and survive it to the last, until the moment when she said: "Don't bother me." That's the way it is for all those in love. If you don't consider torment and violence there is no way out, but that isn't even love.

And suddenly, in the evening, after tea, all my thought-feelings took shape differently, and I stopped suffering. I didn't allow doubts to creep in, and didn't know whether I could be as I was before, and I don't know how, but I ceased to suffer. Everything settled into a simple schema, and there was no yearning, and it became calm and bright.

Here is how I started to think: if she betrays me or will betray me, loving me, then I must forgive her. I should have been a poor lover if I could not forgive my loved one.

If she were on the path to betrayal, or if she betrayed me without loving me, I should not lament, for there is no power that can force someone to love. Nor did I lament any longer. That's the way I am made. I can't be forced to suffer for more than a day . . . it's funny, troubling, and perplexing.

But even now it seems to me that M. will be An.'s lover, that she herself does not yet realize this, that she can't leave him.

Well, let it be—I don't feel superficial saying this. No, by all my right, by the depth of my life, by all that I have lived through to the end, the "I" within me says: let it be so. And any human being who knows a lot about life could only say the same. And it is really a great "yes" to the world.

6 August

This was how today went.

I slept late. While dressing I felt an unhurried morning ease. I decided not to go out until evening, and as I had dressed, I sat down at the table to work. I remember well that suddenly almost from the very depths of my being there came a familiar feeling—the desire to see An. again and again. I convinced myself not to go see her, but this feeling still remained, like water in the Neva, and rose in waves. I thought: why does it hurt so to want to see her mornings, from the morning on? And a bit later, I thought, how strange that today, not as usual in the morning, but there is still a feeling of jealousy in this desire. I didn't understand. As I figured, An. should have been at home. She was planning to go to Volodya Sh. (her husband) for lunch in the afternoon. Why was I jealous and so troubled? I tried to talk myself out of it and couldn't. I went to buy cigarettes and decided to stop by An.'s for 10 minutes. In the garden they gave me a letter from Galya—a horrible, tormenting letter. I was completely shaken, I felt helpless and powerless. I needed to see An. even more, to question her, to tell her about the letter.

I arrived (it was ten minutes to one). An. was not home, she had left to go to Volodya [Shileyko]'s about ten minutes before, and she didn't say when she would return. She had hurried, had even taken tea separately.

And my first thought was: how strange that she hurried, when she never goes to see him that early. I left, not knowing myself how I turned to the right, how I got to the Summer Garden, how I entered it and walked faster and faster along the path, then ran across the parapet. Then two inscrutable silhouettes appeared, I went past them, some lovers no doubt, and I came out by Peter's Cabin and on the bench across from it I saw An. sitting. Alone. She was waiting. An. laughed. She held out her hand to me. I don't remember at all what I said to her or what she said. I only remember that I quickly told her everything, and she was happily (not angrily) struck by my impetuous appearance, and that soon she got up and led me from that bench further toward the gates. We sat there. Presently all the details of this meeting and these relationships became clear. M. M., actually, was supposed to meet her at 12:30 and take her to Volodya's. We were both amazed at the strange feeling that had brought me to her. There was nothing strange about the fact that I was happy to be beside her again and that I believed her words. But it is strange that she really is to blame, but not at all for what those who might read the story of this meeting would blame her.

25 August

In the "new art" there is not a single element of form that wasn't there in the old, but the new art is really a new sense of the world: (the form is not new, the content is new)

26th

The world is given to us in happiness and is architectonic. The sense of the connections and the relationships of its parts is also the feeling of happiness. The feeling of happiness is somehow very close to the feeling of wisdom. The loss of the sense of the relations and connections, its destruction, is suffering. Ruin is suffering, the occasional sense that life is illusory, as a dream is a sign of suffering. Loss of the relations, the connections, the sense of the architectonic nature of life, evokes a sense of the illusoriness of life that is suffering. All this relates to form, to the formal in the sense of happiness and suffering.

CONVERSATION BOOK

> Don't look at me like that—my head swims. We will
> be together, if only together.[12] Now, now, Koty, you'll
> see you'll quickly fall out of love with me.
> 29 Aug. 1923 [Akhmatova]

---

12 This sentence was written by Punin. The rest of the entry is Akhmatova's.

1 September Today I had a dream: An. gives me a hand mirror, similar to the one she has, falling out of its frame, so that you have to hold it supporting the glass, but the frame is different, walnut. I look into it, it grows bigger, now something like a bathroom mirror, and I see that the mirror reflects everything around, but it doesn't reflect me, as if I were transparent. I see everything that is behind me, but I don't see myself. Amazed, I show it to An. and tell her about it.

In the morning I went to see her. Yesterday I introduced her to Poletaev and she told me her dream: it seems that either I or B. V. (Anrep)* was showing her a piece of paper on which her picture had been drawn, and she says: I don't see it, you see, I am sleeping, I have my eyes closed . . .

The dreams are the same in that both of us didn't see ourselves.

CONVERSATION BOOK

5 Sept. '23 **Don't come see me until the 5th of Oct.**
Absolutely amazing . . . I can barely smoke . . .
[Akhmatova]

8 September Seems like such a long time since I've written. So many things have happened! One big thing is the earthquake in Japan. I sense in this retribution for Tsushima, this should even have boundless significance for the formation of ideas in the time now gathering.[13]

The thought of any organization, of government, is destroyed. Organization is violence. Politics cannot be *not* base.

The signs of our Middle Ages are all the more distinct, almost omens. I believe in its inevitable formation. Its image is "Zangezi"—the most exhausted, dark sighs of mankind since the times of Gilgamesh. It is also a very weary epic poem, only young, like the first despair of youth. "Like a butterfly that has flown past." I know nothing more weary and quiet: everything within me becomes quiet and closed when I read it. It is like a whisper through death, a whisper in death. Lines of dream and death. And the endless, eternal solitude of man, locked in a web of dream and dust.

Dama Luni came—as always upset and noisy, although aging, seeking closeness again for some reason . . .

13 In 1923 an earthquake and subsequent fire almost destroyed all of Tokyo. Punin sees retribution for Japan's slaughter of the Russian naval forces during the battle of Tsushima in 1904.

I am with An. daily. My tenderness is impassioned and deep. She has marvelously pliant hands and across her face the wing of the other world constantly passes. The shadow of changes in the governments of Eternity is on this face and the course of Eternity's struggle with death. There is no other face like it on earth.

This face is between me and heaven, like a path to heaven reflected in the face. I won't say it is the face of an angel, but the face of an angel's wing.

It is of little importance to know everything, to experience, to think things through. An. perhaps knows less and has not yet thought things out—but what is important is born in this deep, weary purity. Life experience is insignificant in comparison with the fact that there is a soul.

I am happy with her, but unhappy that I cannot be with her forever. It has already been a year since we have been together, if it is possible to call these hours and days torn from life a year. Will this also pass and fade away?

I don't remember my past. Could I compare this with anything in my past? Is there anything in my past to equal this?

L. (D. Luni)—just seems like romanticism, just a love of the imagination. I almost didn't see her, and when I saw her, if my notebook can be believed, I didn't love her. There was more of me in it than of her. It is much more difficult for me to say that I did not love Galya. Because of that it is so difficult for me to leave her, and will I leave? Two worlds are fighting here, two different elements of life. How oracular! . . .

12 September

I was at church for mass not long ago. At first, as always, I disliked everything: both the tasteless church and the theatrical priest with his pathetic speech. I even thought: yes, his manner of speaking is just like a communist agitator at a factory. He is just as incompetent and just as hypocritically insincere: brothers and sisters (= comrades), our beloved teacher (= imperialists of the Entente, or as one said today, at the porcelain factory, yes, and none other than a member of the executive committee, "working masses of the German working-proletarian class"), and so on. I absolutely hated it, but then I began to think about why others liked it, not many this time (there were hardly any people in the church, although it was a holiday), the ones who remained, those people standing there. And suddenly I felt a sense of customary everyday life, a deep ancient sense of the way of life, and such an everyday need for prayer, churches, and clergy. And I thought that for them this is an accessible, simple spiritual life, for which they themselves are not responsible. How many times better they are, better than the crowd that only criticizes. And then I understood that the priest, even if he is a hypocrite or incompetent, is still beneficial, and that what is important is not what he says, but that he exists. Then they opened the gates of the iconostasis, and I saw the candelabrum behind the ceremonial table—red icon lamps—and I was filled with such tenderness and humility.[14] I thought: my lack of goodwill is from pride, from the blind and stupid belief that I know it all. Enough already of criticizing and intellectualizing. I thought "teach me faith," and I approached the cross not thinking of anything, only feeling the drops of holy water on my forehead.[15]

13th of S.

Without religion there cannot be a comprehensive world view. Perhaps a world view, more often a viewpoint on the world, but a full sense of the existence of the world is not possible without religious feeling.

15 S.

There is no wonder in my soul and that is why I have no faith. I am totally structured around the relationship of "cause and effect." Every feeling immediately alerts my intellect and while it sorts things out according to the method of "cause and effect," the feeling disappears, and only the memory of it remains, and the resolution of the intellect. My life is a chain of events without wonder. I pray to the emptiness for a sense of wonder! . . .

17th

Yesterday at the Association Tyrsa was talking, remembering the Dept. of Fine Arts and how at one of the Moscow conferences the participants voted by a show of hands for or against space (the business at hand concerned the introduction of spatial paintings [counter-relief] into the program of the as yet "free government workshops" at that time).

Also its own type of "jeu de paumes."[16]

21st

An. told me her dream.

She sees she is going somewhere and the dream goes on, as a dream. Then she is lying down and it seems to her she is lying on her own bed in the bedroom. The window lightens, either from the sunrise or the

---

14 The Russian word for table here is *prestol'*, indicating a special table used in the Orthodox service for Communion.

15 The Russian actually reads *kropilo* or brush rather than "drops" since the Russian Orthodox Church uses a brush for splashing the holy water.

16 Literally, game of tennis. The expression refers to the oath of the nobility giving its support to the estates general in the French revolution of 1789.

moon, and she has a pain in her side as if someone were pressing on her and she sees a tall thin man she doesn't know standing over her. He has a blunt knife in his hand and he is hitting her in the back with it, but the knife doesn't cut. He presses it in and says: "Remember that you are only mine," and gradually this man dissipates away, leaves in wisps of smoke, and then it becomes an ordinary dream again.

A month ago I had this dream: I am sitting with An. on a bench either in a corridor or in the very last room of a row of rooms; to the right there is a window, beyond the window moonlight. I look out the window and I see—beyond the window in the moon-shades blue shadows float past. One of them flew up to us, came in the room, lit it up slightly, and left, and we both felt that it was reaching us, touching us, and because of this our bodies grew cold, as when the wind from the river carries in the fog. Then another shadow also passed through us, and again we felt its cold, but then suddenly the window is no longer a window but a door and in the doorway stands an unknown tall man. And he looks at us heavily. The door is barely open, this man raises his hand, and in his hand is a revolver. He doesn't see me—but aims at me—and shoots, and I feel a warm fire along my arm from his shot (the revolver flashes in his hand). Then I think, and as it were whisper to An.: "The main thing is not to be afraid, don't let on that this is terrifying." And I think, we have to overpower him, otherwise it'll be bad for us. I stand up and say something authoritatively to him, but he shoots again and misses again, and I take his hand sharply by the wrist and force him to turn it together with the revolver onto himself. I feel the curve of the metal trigger on my finger, I squeeze off a shot, and the man falls. An. is terribly afraid that he has been killed and runs to him. I approach calmly, turn his collar and the shoulder of his shirt, and show An.: look, there is blood on the shoulder, he is only wounded, don't be afraid. Then An. takes him in her arms and carries him across the entire room, down, and down below it's like a sick bay. An. carries him onto a glass balcony and wants to step over the railing, and I think, why is An. doing this, she'll fall over the balcony with him, and I say: there is a staircase over there, why have you brought him here? . . . I have such a feeling of love that I am afraid to tell even An.

As soon as we part and she goes away—especially when she goes away—I begin unbearably, longingly to miss her. Later this longing gets weaker, but just after parting I almost cry. I get tears in my throat, and I'd like to run after her, to stop her.

Before I always knew that nothing would happen to me if the one I loved left me, but now I don't know, I am not sure of anything. I love her with a terrible, heavy feeling, and in this feeling there is little happiness, although I see and know that she loves me very much and tormentedly.

An. has stopped writing verse. Why? What does it mean, here it's been already a year and scarcely a single poem? She says, it is because of me . . .

29 Sept.

After a reading of "Gray morning"

> *To drive somewhere into the body of centuries*
> *the cold of an insufficient life.*

————

What more do you want from me? What kind of heart? What kind of emptiness in it? Isn't everything yet humbled before you, to the very end?

> *I pray to God to free me from this love.*
> *For how long, how long, the pain . . .*

1 October

I've just received a little book of Khlebnikov's verses that was just published.

In relation to our time a classical Pushkinian pathos (a high spiritual level) sounds almost indelicate (like "bad taste"). Life is so open, so revealing, that pathos is almost tactless. Khlebnikov, on the other hand, has great tact and no pathos of any kind.

If this high level saved the classical poets—it was almost poetry itself—then Khleb. is saved by a wondrous purity, unknown to us.

—Dawning . . . you could say of him

Ancient—also.

————

6 October

I am so struck by her now that I don't even sense her love.

Is it by her love?

16 October

This year there is a warm, soft autumn—like the fur of a fox. The day before yesterday there was such a sunset that the next day the whole city talked about it.

An. was just here and had tea with us. As I recall, when she used to come I would get so anxious. I remember that for a long time I couldn't get used to her. But just now she sat there, laughing so, as if there were nothing simpler than her in the world. An. brought me an apple.

30 October	Today snow fell—now it is quiet outside, like underground. I took her to the Marble Palace. Since the day that she wrote the "parting letter" and returned the cross to me I have felt that all is lost. Not that she is lost, but everything, the whole world, my life. Today I stood over the Neva, watching how the snow fell. The Neva is cold in its bare granite banks (by the porcelain factory), and I thought that it was like us, falling, forever. How strange it is: war, revolution, all the life around us.

We said good-bye, and I sensed how we were both standing in the snow, thirstily, for a long time, I kissed her hand (taken away) with inhuman tenderness. How I love that hand. And at home in the garden, snow again, branches, and the emptiness of the night above them. And her, everywhere her. We survived again till snowfall . . .

15 November   She said, "If you loved me more, or were a less decent person, you would have been with me long ago."

January 1924   I feel that an individual doesn't exist as an integral consciousness. There is only a series of situations in which a person finds himself as the bearer of certain qualities.

There is no organic whole which in all situations would preserve even one of its traits.

There is no good man, but one and the same person can be good and can under certain conditions also not be. There is no honest person, but there are, there do occur, honest acts . . . etc.

What an antireligious thought, and something is missing in it.

Contemporary thought!—not without irony.

Does this mean there is no soul?

That everything is reflexology? [17]

It only means that I have no soul; that is, that I don't feel it under my attributes.

Besides, I have no soul as an individual spiritual form or as substance, but I have always felt that the soul, as a part of a uniform human life element, is not material. It is immaterial in the sense that in the cur-

---

17   "Reflexology" most likely refers to the discovery of the conditioned reflex by Ivan Petrovich Pavlov (1849–1936), a Russian physiologist and experimental psychologist. In 1904, he received the Nobel Prize for his work. The discovery of the conditioned reflex was made accidentally during an experiment on the digestive system. His famous experiment, in which laboratory dogs were conditioned to salivate at the sound of a bell, has had great influence on behaviorist psychology.

rent state of things there is no way to measure its meaning. One cannot make a judgment about it, it is unknowable, and only comprehensible. Only the qualities through which it is revealed are knowable, but whether it reveals itself completely in these qualities . . . we don't know.

[page out]

2 February

The night is empty, the snow white . . . another night and your hair, my Deer.[18]

4 February

Yesterday she came here without me and wrote her letter (A) on the wall downstairs between the doors.

I saw it and kissed the letter.

————

In our time one must also have a special courage, to have the right "to feel."

18   Deer is Punin's nickname for Akhmatova. This name may originally have been coined by Akhmatova and Sudeykina's occasional maid, who said Akhmatova would wander about looking like a deer. Akhmatova had long, dark hair that many found beautiful.

NOTEBOOK SEVEN
1924

[three pages cut out]

12 May Not long ago Anna was at Glück's Orpheus . . . Today, looking at an old building, she said,

"When I think of or see the 18th century (or anything approaching this century), I always feel that all this carelessness, frivolity, and *joie de vivre* is just for appearances; they wanted to be full of life and happy but they were not so at all. For me these little lambs and shepherds are inseparable from revolution, and the wigs always have and still do remind me of the wigs on those heads on stakes, and that's how we know them."

All this that An. said is very characteristic of her and isn't at all the product of a gloomy world view but of her sense of morality.

She is essentially a happy, even a very happy person (as long as she is in good health), but her moral sensibility, her sense of responsibility, is so deep and so thought-out (serious), that she can never, not in any state of prosperity, forget that the suffering of the world is insurmountable, and nothing can lessen it. Her whole system of relations to people and "politics" is built on this. I am always amazed to what extent her art, born in an atmosphere of pure estheticism (Gumilev, V. Ivanov,* and others) is moral through and through, moral in the sense of seeking the inner justification for life.

Troubling how this somehow and somewhere forces one to think of Dostoevsky.

[one page cut out]

[no date]

There is nothing in the world that does not arouse her interest. Completely weak-willed by nature, she tries to subjugate everyone and everything with her personal "I," but at times is purely femininely stubborn and simultaneously cannot live without personal feelings which do not depend on the idea of mind and will. Tries to be true to herself, fair, and as a result becomes weak. To rule, to be above everyone, is an organic demand of her soul. Strives for the very great—endlessly adapts herself to new failures, disillusionments, and views them as tests of her strength. Everlasting youth. Fights with pettiness and baseness. Cannot be alone and cannot be simple, clear, beautiful. She sees an ideal in the appearance of will. No bounds to indignation, once it appears. Scorns, makes fun, and reveres, all at once.

> Graphologue
> Montov-Gakhyanin

exhibit
summer '24

CONVERSATION BOOK

26 May

We were in Pavlovsk in 1924.—Anna

9 June 1924

**We sat in the Summer Garden the first warm day.
[Akhmatova]**

And I felt as if you were the end of the earth and there was nothing else.—K[otik] M[urr]

And I was amazed, that everything around was so green and fragrant. My Koty!

A[khmatova] or Olen

[1] Akhmatova mentions this graphological analysis in her conversations with Lydia Chukovskaya.

First show at the M[ariinsky] Theater I will take
Koty.—Anna Akhm.
Signature: *don't make fun*
10 June 1924
And a forfeit?

15 June

The whole western sky is in flames of lightning. I walked with An. along the banks of the Neva—dark, as in July.

23 June

Today I was at the editorial offices of the "Russian Contemporary"* for a long time—it was a painful, tormenting experience. They trade. With literature. Akhmatova always felt as if she had a "knife at her throat" after she'd been talking with Tikhonov.* After a short conversation with him Shklovsky would go on feeling all day as if he had just "gulped down a cup of very black coffee." I always feel somehow offended after a conversation with him. But why? No one quite knows. Today at the editorial offices there was the repulsive A. Tolstoy.

A nephew or grandson of Druzhinin's brought some items from the archives and Druzhinin's notebook, some indecent poems of Nekrasov, Turgenev,* Loginov, of Druzhinin* himself. Korney Chukovsky* read aloud, everyone laughed loudly, I didn't understand and it pained me. We should weep over the 1860's. These poems and this archive should be burned. Oh, not to be with them! Never to have to be with them. I can't, I don't have the strength for it.

Shklovsky said to Tikhonov: "You are a shoemaker in philology, what do you understand?" and "You are like welded iron, A. N." Today Tikhonov gave Shklovsky full freedom to write what he, Sh., wants. This is all very well, and maybe necessary, but I don't understand why one's essays have to be stuck in a foreign journal. I would rather serve as a clerk in the State Porcelain Factory.

_____ _____ _____ It is stifling from all this, as if the earth were not a sphere in free space. As if the sky were not the endlessness of space . . .

5 July

I had an interesting conversation with Tatlin. It is difficult to convey the conversation, especially one that was so sharp and lively, as sometimes happens when there is a great and genuine man among the participants. Tatlin is fascinating, completely unconveyable in writing. He speaks with a wonderful, childlike, and passionate intonation, sincere and always with some kind of great thought—a wonder-child—a man of immense stature.

Among other things, he spoke of the airplane, on which it seems he is now working.[2] He sharply criticized the construction and exterior of existing apparatuses, pointing to their complexity and to the fact that the evolution of their construction is extraordinarily misguided and not organic. Of the instruments existing on the modern flying apparatus he said: "Why do they drag a whole office with them?" and also, "They are flying with entire sovnarkoms."[3] According to Tatlin, all of this has come about because they are "flying by means of science" and not by means organic to man and the senses. They don't know or they don't want to know how birds fly, and still they all act wise. T. says, "I don't believe in them as a source of instruction. I will fly in my own way, no matter what, as I breathe, as I swim. My means of flying will always be more perfect than their apparatuses that rely on air suction" (referring to the new English jet airplanes).[4] Tyrsa, who was present during the conversation, tried to synthesize technology and the organism, saying that an apparatus was an extension of the body. Tatlin didn't give in, and I had the impression that T. really had the impulse to fly with his arms. "Air is also material," continued T., "and if we study it organically, then we will master it, like stone, iron, or water." T. is obsessed by this idea.

In the conversation he sharply contrasted China and Russia with Europe and America. Among other things, he believes that we have entered a primitive stratum of culture, like the archaic. He views form as the result of the senses and of the designation of the thing. Decoration is the disorganization of form. In passing, Tyrsa said of Malevich that he also did what the decorative architects did (the neoempiricists-

2 Punin is referring to "Letatlin," a personal flying machine that he built along with the students from the Higher Technical Institute of Art or Vkhutein from 1929 to 1932, although from this entry it is apparent that Tatlin was interested in the idea much earlier. "Letatlin" is a pun on the Russian verb *letat'*, meaning "to fly," and Tatlin's name. The machine was made primarily of wood and organic materials. It was designed to be a personal means of flight that could be propelled by one person alone without any engines. Letatlin was to be designed simply and inexpensively enough that the average Soviet citizen could have one. Tatlin called his invention an "air bicycle"; although it was never truly successful, he tested the machine, and it was displayed in the Pushkin Museum in 1932. Tatlin was not the only artist of his generation to be interested in flying machines. In fact, fellow Constructivist Petr Miturich created a model called "The Flyer" as early as 1921 and as late as 1930 was still working on other methods of transportation, all relying on undulating motion and therefore called "volnovniki."

3 "Sovnarkom" is the acronym for the Council of People's Commissars.

4 Punin may be referring to English experiments in jet propulsion, since in 1924 there were as yet no jet airplanes. The first jet-propelled airplane to fly was a rocket-propelled tail-first glider flown in Germany on June 11, 1928.

renaissance—and the whole World of Art group—Lyalevich, Peretyat-kovich, Fomin, Shchuko, etc.) with the only difference being that they decorated facades, and their work was easily scraped off, while Male-vich decorates form. This was just as much estheticism and the destruction of form. An., dear An., at once brought to my attention the fact that the old Petersburg buildings, falling apart and devoid of their cornices, windows, balconies, pilasters, are still architectural, simply as an architectural mass in space. They stand, "like Roman ruins." "But scrape away these new facades, and what is left?—clumsy, empty boxes." In general, An. has an amazing sense of architecture, of spatial form in general.

Then Tatlin showed us his suit. To me it was simply esthetically pleasing. In spite of Petrograd State Clothing, it would be so great for Europe if people arrived from Russia in clothes of Tatlin's cut instead of short Parisian jackets. What independence from Europe, what firmness of approach there would be in this simple and essentially completely attainable act! But these idiots and scoundrels only know how to be shot for their theft and bribery . . . In form, Tatlin's clothes have something about them of shoulders and movements of the archangels of Russian icons (of the Holy Trinity for instance).

I always feel a sense of despair after such conversations. Why do I get so mixed up and exhaust myself when so much is much simpler, when there is so much needed to be done. And I always think about the fact that a good half of me is still in that old world, that I am entirely on the boundary-line, and that's what makes it so difficult for me. That's why everything is so mixed up in me.

CONVERSATION BOOK

13 July 1924

Tsarskoselsky Station
Koty is leaving for Podolsk. I remain here.—Akhm.

25 July

Nemirov-Podolsk

On the 29th of June, Galya and Irinochka left with Zoya and her daughter for the Podolsk region. It was a risky trip because they went first to places unknown to us. We were to spend the summer with Malevich, Matyushin, Mansurov, and others. But then after Galya had already arrived in Nemirov it became clear that none of them would come. No one met them and nothing had been arranged for them, not even a place to stay. From the very first day of their departure, I was worried about them (Galya and Irina), or it was the indistinct recurrence of emotions of some kind, and I began to long for them, almost with a physical longing. In the evenings I missed them so and was in such pain that I couldn't do anything. Subsequently this anxiety turned out to be justified in that beside a difficult three-day journey with night stopovers at stations, Irina fell ill with dysentery. I promised to join them for two weeks in mid-July. So here I am, the one to whom the freedom of solitude and the freedom always to be able to see An. had been given, and suddenly, secretly, I start impatiently counting the days until I could go to my family. An. inevitably noticed this. And could not help feeling the strain of all this. Those were burdensome days which exhausted me, and I began to want to leave even more.

The eve of the day that I was to depart was the name day of Pavel Shchegolev. I don't like it when An. goes to Shch.'s — they drink a lot there and the people are too free and easy — there is something in everything they do that causes pain to my feelings for An., and I asked her not to go to Shch.'s. Moreover, she didn't express any special desire to go there. But then, at 10 o'clock that night, when I had agreed to come see An., she wasn't home. Zamyatina had come for her, and they had gone to Shch., for an hour, Olga Sudeykina told me. I started to wait, and I waited a long time. I left. I walked down the Field of Mars, came back again. It was almost one. Anna wasn't there. Wild jealousy boiled and raged in me. About one o'clock I left again and set out in the direction of the building where the Shchegolevs lived, across Troitsky bridge. On the bridge, I stood and looked at the water and tried to decide whether or not to break up with An. *today.* I knew that one doesn't break up for such a reason, and I secretly prayed that it should all be like a miracle that virtually asked me to break up. There was pain, a pain I knew well, only more unbearable than ever. And I was amazed because the past days had dragged on, and I wanted so much to go to Galya. Finally, I met An. She was walking arm in arm with Zamyatin. She had flowers in her hands. Zamyatin was drunk. I, with some inept but probably expressive speech, asked Zam. to leave An. to me, on the understanding that I would take her wherever he told me to in half an hour. Z. cowered and after making some kind of clumsy motion with his hand quickly "drew back" (precisely that) to where the others who were left behind were, as it later turned out, to Fedin * and Zamyatina. I went with An. I don't remember what happened first; it would seem that my first act of valor was to seize and tear to pieces the flowers in An.'s hands and to throw them in the Neva. Then I began to ask her about breaking up, or to suggest breaking up to her, I don't know which. We went down to the embankment; Fedin caught up with us, and the two Z's; and Lyudmila (Z.) noticed that An. didn't have any flowers. It all became clear to everyone. But I remember that sharp feeling that flashed like lightning down my whole spine, that feeling of pleasure, when I tore up and threw away the flowers, and there was also a feeling in my fingers when I took the flowers. And I heard the crunch of the stems in my ears. It was a white night. There was blood on my fingers, probably from the roses; the blood stuck. And I got some of it on An.'s hands.

We got to An.'s. I cried and the whole time asked her to give me the baptismal cross on a gold chain I had given her a year and a half ago. And An. cried, her cheeks were wet. She became angry and cried.

We didn't break up.

But I was leaving the next day with a heavy tormented feeling of separation. An. kept frightening me with it the whole time, saying, "There, you're leaving, and we'll never see each other again."

I left, she took me to the train. Asked when I would write her, I said, when I felt like it, probably from Vinnitsa. She didn't like my answer. I asked her whether she would write. She didn't promise, but it was obvious that she would write, at least she thought so at that moment. I wrote her even from Tsarskoe, then from Vitebsk, Kiev, and Vinnitsa. All the way I longed for her to the point of extreme pain and was sorry that I had left, and when I was in Vinnitsa I even wanted to go back. I couldn't "be without her." Especially in the evenings. I cried into my pillow in the coach.

Now I am here.

27 July

Now I am here. My meeting with Galya was tender, then disturbing, then tormenting, all the more tormenting by measure of my longing for her, which had grown so. Yesterday after a short conversation Galya finally wrote a letter to her father telling him that we were separating. But this letter wasn't sent. I have it. Galya has asked me to send it when I leave since she is afraid he would be upset by her letter and he is now alone in the city. She is afraid for his heart. This letter will not be sent, of course. Still, it is important that Galya wrote it.

But there are no letters from An. Whether it is because I am leaving soon, or in general because I have taken about as much as I can, I am no longer suffering.

So, we may not be together any longer. [Heavily crossed out]

Evening

Because I will not be able to hold your hands
Because I betrayed your salty, tender lips.

I must await the dawn in a dreamy acropolis
How I hate these weeping ancient fragments.[5]

CONVERSATION BOOK

6 August
1924

Summer Garden
Koty returned from the country—Akhm.

8 August

Font[anka Embankment] No. 2 (in bed).

An excerpt from a morning *conversation*
K[otik] M[urr]: Why are you so attracted to
M. [Zimmerman]?
Me: I am not in any way attracted.
K[otik Murr]: No you are attracted. Answer or I'll
make you (I still can!)

Honi soit [qui mal y pense]

10 August

Petrograd
There is no whole and no parts. Parts exist when there is a whole, and
vice versa.
    Therefore there is no organic world view that assumes the whole
before the parts, nor an inorganic (mechanical) world view that con-
structs the whole from the parts.

CONVERSATION BOOK

15 August '24,
in the
morning

Sheremetev Palace *Fountain House*
Last day alone together Koty. Koty just now refused to
live in the same house with me. Is he right?—Akhm.
    Koty. It was after the "night of burning intoxica-
tion," etc. [Punin]

15 Aug. 1924,
4 P.M.

State Porcelain Factory
Yesterday evening I saw the eclipse of the moon from
the Field of Mars. I couldn't imagine what it was. A
singular and terrifying event.—Akhm.

5 | Quote from Osip Mandelshtam.

16 Aug. 1924	*Bank of the Strelna* We were in Strelna. Swam. Brisé.—Akhm. Koty—and here he kissed Olen on the forehead. [Punin]
1924. 18 Aug.	This evening I was at M. Ts.'s. On the way home as M. was walking me back I met Koty-Malchik on the No. 2 tram at the corner of Sadovaya and Nevsky.
19 Aug.	K. M. rowed me in a boat up to the seashore—by the Yacht Club.—Akhm.
20 August	I strolled along the Fontanka, at the circus Olen took the comb out of her hair and combed it. It was a hot day. 4 o'clock.—Koty
	Before this we looked around the Palace built by Schluter in the Summer Garden. The comb thing is rubbish. It's not worth writing down.—Akhm.
21 Aug. 1924	*Restaurant Daryal* We were at the Hermitage for the first time in the newly reopened halls. Tomorrow G. G. is returning.[6]—Akhm.
23 Aug. 1924	K. M. is jealous. He just said if you go to see M. [Zimmerman], tomorrow I will come with Galya (that is, to Fedorov's restaurant). Hail Koty!—Akhm.
8 September	I rowed An. in a boat on the silver sea to the point of exhaustion—it was 58 degrees. Then we had dinner at Fedorov's. I learned from An. that the palace that is across from Elagin was built by Quarenghi (really Bazhenov [acc. to Olen]). The next day Anka disgraced herself (note by [Koty]-Malchik).
15 Sept. '24 *St. Pete.*	Koty said that he has become so rooted in Sherem[etev] House that he wouldn't exchange it for anything (i.e., for me).— Olen
	I didn't say this—K[oty Malchik]
23 Sept. *[no entry]*	

6 Galya Ahrens, Punin's wife.

NOTEBOOK EIGHT

1924–1925

Introduction *Akhmatova's letters to Punin from the summer of 1924. Continued notes from the "Conversation Book." Flood of September 1924. Censorship tightens. Punin's deepening disillusionment with the Communist Party. Lossky. The theory of relativity. Malevich and Tatlin. Fedin's* Cities and Years. *Antireligious campaign. G. V. Plekhanov's prognosis.* **

LETTERS FROM THE SUMMER OF 1924[1]

Letter (front)

Dear Nikolay Nikolaevich, I spoke with L. Ch. on the phone. She begged me to come see her, and you, when you return, should join us. If you don't want to come, call me.

Anna

Letter

Nikolay Nikolaevich,

As soon as we said good-bye I realized that we would no longer be together.

Very often you tell me that if I fall out of love with you and leave you it won't be hard for you to stay away from me.

I remind you of this, I remind you also of our last evening when you yourself asked so much for us to end "this evil game."

It would be good if you could live in the country a bit longer so I could leave the city before your return. I ask about this not out of fear of our meeting, but because I am very tired and I am not up to explanations. Good-bye, don't think badly of me.

Akhm.

---

[1] Enclosed at the back of this notebook are a collection of letters from Akhmatova to Punin during the summer of 1924. Most have no date, but must predate the first passage in the diary and therefore have been included here at the beginning.

Letter Dated "27 July, St. Pete."

Dear Nikolay Nikolaevich, how annoying it is that I cannot visit Kiev this summer. O. A. [Sudeykina] still just lies there, the publisher still isn't paying a cent. And this summer she threatens to end it all every day.[2]

K. Petrov-Vodkin* came to say good-bye, by now he is already on his way to Paris. I am posing for Natasha; I read the Bible and Grabar and await the return of my dear friends.[3] How are you vacationing, how's Kiev, and when do you come home?

Your Olenik

Letter

Dear friend,

Thank-you for the letters. I have already received four (from Tsarskoe, Vitebsk, Kiev, and Vinnitsa). Tomorrow I await the fifth. All is as it was here: Olga [Sudeykina] is sick, she's not a bit better, "Petrograd Publishers" doesn't pay anything, Mishenka [Zimmerman] was in Odessa, Volodya [Shileyko] is getting ready to go to Moscow, he came to say good-bye. Actually, he is heading for Paris.

I am well, I rejoice in the wonderful days, in the evenings I read the Bible. I like thinking that you haven't walked on pavement for a whole week, haven't so much as looked at the damned Fontanka, and are breathing air that is almost southern. Get well, and don't rush to return to the city. Please say hello to Anna and Zoya Evgenevna [Ahrens] for me and kiss both the little Punins.

Your friend and sister
Anna

Letter

26 August '24

Siverskaya 63, Republic

Dear friend, your letter (the fourth) I received just today. The Shchegolevs went to the Caucasus, and I am living in their dacha with Lyudmila Nikolaevna. Come see us when you return to the city. How

---

2 According to Roberta Reeder, Akhmatova spent the summer of 1924 looking after Olga Glebova-Sudeykina, who was ill with peritonitis. Sudeykina emigrated to Paris when she recovered. See Roberta Reeder, *Anna Akhmatova* (London: Allison and Busby, 1995), p. 173.

3 Natasha is Natalya Danko.

is Ira? Poor A. E.[4] How hard it was for her in the country with a sick child. *Still*—it is good that you went to them. Thank you for the letters, for the stars, for everything. I am well. Things are fine here, Anna.

Where is Bukhan?[5] Bring a pillow and sheets for yourself. There is a blanket. A.

DIARY 1924[6]

23 September I woke up late (12 o'clock). The branches outside the windows were swaying wildly. I went out into the wet garden; a boy from the building excitedly told me that the water was very high in the Fontanka. The water truly was six inches up the embankment. They were shooting from the fortress.[7] From time to time the wind whipped past from behind the bend of the Fontanka beyond the Anichkov bridge and lifting turbid yellow waves drove them in ripples and spray. The spray covered me as soon as I stepped out of the gate of the Sheremetev House.

On Nevsky there was the usual, perhaps a little less than the usual number of people. It was very wet and the wind interfered with walking.

2 o'clock

I had been considerably delayed at the editorial office of "Life of Art." It was close to 5 o'clock when the editorial meeting ended and they had started shooting from the fortress every three minutes. As I left a boy ran up and said, "Leave quickly, the Catherine canal has overflowed its banks." The wind whipped and tore along Kazan Square, and because the rain was churning and because it was slippery and difficult to walk, the wind carried me off the sidewalk. In the region of the square the canal was still within its banks but there was a thick fountain of water shooting from the hatches that are by the rotunda of the cathedral. Movement along the Nevsky was visibly disrupted, the trams had stopped and there were more people walking than usual. They walked quickly, some ran, driving the crowd forward. I decided not to go home,

4 | Galya Ahrens.
5 | "Bukhan" means the bogeyman; this was also the family nickname for Akhmatova's second husband, Vladimir Shileyko.
6 | This entry gives an eyewitness account of the great flood of 1924. The flood occurred 100 years after the last great flood (and 200 after the first!) in the capital city, which was immortalized by Pushkin in his long poem "The Bronze Horseman." According to the memoirs of Valentina Shchegoleva, Akhmatova was at a special service honoring the poet Aleksandr Blok, who died in 1921, and showed no fear that she had to return home on foot, soaked by the flood water and whipped by the wind.
7 | Shots to indicate the flood warning and level of the water.

but to An.'s. She is now living in the Prachechny building, which is on the corner of the Neva and the Fontanka across from the Summer Garden. And I also ran, afraid that I wouldn't make it to An.'s. I ran to the corner of the Engineers' Castle and Sadovaya when they came rushing toward me from above. First, draymen on unharnessed horses, then pedestrians with faces that were both alarmed and animated, and finally came the water. It splashed along the cobblestones at the edge of the road, swelled with the wooden pavement along the middle of sidewalk, and in the distance along all of the Field of Mars it poured out into a wide yellowish-gray lake. Here, too, the wind carried the spray far and ripped at the trees. It was senseless to go along Field of Mars. I turned, hoping to get to An.'s along the Fontanka.

Basically I had already grasped that I wouldn't make it to An.'s and it became painful, and it was bitter not to be able to be with her on such a day (tears came to my eyes). When I ran out onto the Fontanka there remained only a narrow strip by the barracks along which it was possible to walk out onto Semenovsky bridge. From the bridge I saw that the gates of the Sheremetev House were closed and the water was already level with the rails along the bank, so I had to go home by Liteyny Prospect.

Galya was home, everyone had their coats on, because every minute they came out to take a look outside. I wanted to call, but the phone wasn't working. It grew dark, the wind roared. The tree in the garden was leaning along the wall of the wing of the building and banged against the roof. I put on high boots and together with Galya left to try to get to An.'s from the direction of Sergievskaya St. I learned from Galya, who had just returned from An.'s, that she and Olga (Sudeykina) were home and that when Galya left the embankment was covered with water. It grew completely dark. They were shooting constantly. The clouds hung unusually low. It seemed like they were swirling, grazing the tops of the trees. We came out onto Liteynaya, along which the trams were still running. People crowded on the sidewalks. When we reached Sergievskaya we turned onto it toward the Fontanka, but it was impossible to go further than Mokhovaya. There was standing water, and soldiers from the former Artillery Unit of the Arsenal were not allowing anyone past. Further along Sergievskaya there floated a boat. We turned back along the Liteyny bridge. People crowded on the parapet of the bank, laughed gaily, joked, caught a hat that had fallen in the Neva, tried to gauge the flood level.

The Neva was threatening. Huge waves whipped right up to the parapet, splashed on the people, fell back, foaming. The whole embankment rose to the surface, paving blocks creaking moved in a thick mass along the surface of the water. Nothing was visible in the distance and this made the clouds seem still lower. A wild, violent wind whistled on the bridge. I will not forget that whistle, it cannot be described, a whistle shrill and predatory, tearing under the clouds right above our heads. It would quiet down for a few minutes, flying off somewhere further, and then it would fill the whole horizon with its roar, as if carried by some kind of gigantic wires. They began to shoot again, more often. A few times the wind jostled so that we had to hold onto the rails of the bridge. It was frightening because of the darkness, the insanity, the immensity of it. The faces of those few passersby who happened upon the bridge grew solemn. At that moment somewhere not far above us the gray-blackness tore open for a minute and through the darkness of night there shone a yellow light, then everything clouded over again, and began to swirl and whistle. The rain poured. The sound of the shots was muffled. They didn't seem so prophetic in this crashing, whistling, and roaring.

We jumped onto the last tram driving to the depot and returned home. The courtyard at the Sheremetev House was covered with water, the stack of firewood had floated away. It must have been about 7 o'clock. When we got to the apartment the electricity was out and the water wasn't running. It was obvious that the flood was immense. We went outside again around 10 o'clock: one of the people who had come in had said that the water was receding. Truly, half the courtyard was already free of water. We headed down Liteyny on Sergievskaya again. The sidewalk of Sergievskaya was free of water almost all the way up to the Fontanka. The wind began to die down. I said good-bye to Galya and went in the water, since I was wearing high boots, on the Fontanka Embankment. By all the gates where the sidewalk broke off, the water came up to my knees. In the courtyard of the building where An. lived it was above my knees, but it was quite warm, and the wind became warmer, it even felt rather pleasant when my legs got soaked. A boat lay across the walk, almost right at the gate of the building. When I got to An.'s it was 10 o'clock. Everything was fine there. An. was very agitated.

CONVERSATION BOOK

As is well known, there was a flood. K[oty] M[alchik] came to see me knee deep in water.—Akhm.

24th	I didn't sleep all night; I got up at 7 and went out to look. It was a wonderful sunny, warm day. The sky was blue and there wasn't a single cloud, the wind didn't even tug. Petersburg looked pretty awful. The edge of the flood ran from the Liteyny bridge across Sergievskaya at Mokhovaya (Mokhovaya hadn't been under water), Pantaley-monovskaya, just behind the church, Semenovskaya almost to the bridge, Nevsky, almost up to the Anichkov bridge, across Gorokhovaya (somewhere near Kazachy), having touched the square by the Tsarsko-selsky Station to the square of the Technological Institute and further. The height of the water everywhere was lower than the flood of a century ago by 6–8 inches. On the pavements, where there had been planks they were washed away. The benches had been carried from the Field of Mars and strewn amusingly and surprisingly. In many places on the banks of the Neva huge barges stood on the broken parapets. In various places on the streets you could find boats lying on the sidewalk or on the tram rails. There was a frightening emptiness in the Summer Garden. Here a stream of especially strong surge-waters of the hurricane had obviously run. Since it had made a sort of cut through, all the trees were broken in this place. The roadways were horribly smashed up along Millionaya, where the wooden frames under the wooden paving blocks had been pushed up and carried away. The telephone, electricity, and water were not working. On the street there were lines for the weakly running water taps that usually served to wash the streets. There were lines at the kerosene shops.
Evening	The city, as in '19, is empty, dead, and dark. In the papers they write that the flooding is the legacy of tsarism.
28 Sept.	Art is the only human activity that doesn't darken the earth.

CONVERSATION BOOK

4 Oct.	**An. broke the promise (see 10 June '24) and went alone to the theater to see "Salomé."** K[oty] M[alchik] **cannot forget this.** [Punin] **K. M. took her there and was very hurt. She felt bad, bad!** [Akhmatova]
10 Oct.	**Yesterday K. began to write** *this* **book.—Akm.** [Akhmatova]
11 Oct.	**I am lying ill for the second day, reading Dante.** **Koty, dear . . .** [Akhmatova]

"Examining the relationship of the whole to its elements (or parts), it is possible to assert that the elements are the *original* form of existence, and the whole is something *secondary,* the elements are the *basic* thing, and the whole *is made up* of them . . ."

"Such a whole and such an understanding of the whole we will call *inorganic.*"

"An organic understanding of the whole directly contradicts the inorganic. It consists of the assertions that the whole exists *before* its elements, that the whole is something *basic,* and the elements are made up . . ."

Lossky, *Matter in the System of Organic Philosophy,*
Petersburg, 1922, pp. 6 and 7.

One cannot imagine a whole that doesn't have parts, and vice versa. Where could one get a conception of the whole if simultaneously one could not imagine it separated into its parts. There is no whole if there are no parts and no parts if there is no whole. They are completely relative in relation to each other.

A whole without parts is only an idea. That is, a purely rationalistic fiction. And the other way around.

Neither a truly organic or inorganic (mechanical) doctrine of the world can therefore be true. Both are rationalistic fictions. Those inorganic doctrines which assume that the element of the world is the inanimate atom, i.e., materialistic doctrines, are false because they think that existence, the whole, is made of elements, of matter. They consider the atom the *original* form of existence, and the whole *secondary.* But obviously there is neither an original nor a secondary form of existence. Existence is unified, in it there exist simultaneously both original (according to the mechanistic doctrine, the parts are the atoms of matter) and secondary (in accordance with this doctrine, the whole is the world). Only mentally, rationalistically, can one admit existence as something original, atoms of matter. Such an atom is pure fiction. Also false are the organic doctrines that admit the existence of a whole, of a "superworld being, of God" (Lossky p. 7) which is earlier than its parts, animate or inanimate pieces of the world. Such a God is also a rationalistic fiction. The world, or what in this case is also life, is whole and unified, but not in the sense of its reduction to some kind of original—whole or parts, but in the sense of a process. The world is a whole and unified process in which there are no beginnings or endings.

". . . universal space is finite, but not in the previously indicated, ordinary, literal sense of the word. It is finite in that a circle or spherical surface, or in general any closed line and closed surface, should be called 'finite.'"

Khvolson, A. *Einstein's Theory of Relativity,* 2nd ed.,
Petersburg, '22, p. 8.[8]

The universe is a closed curvature, crudely speaking, a sphere. And we are in the universe, as though closed in a sphere. There is the whole and simultaneously the parts. The beginning and at the same time the end. We and the universe are connected in a great, and for the mind, strange, unity: we can neither be separate from the universe nor can the universe be taken from us. The existence of the universe brings us about and our existence brings about the universe. Moreover, this unity does not depend on whether we believe in ourselves as spiritual beings or consider ourselves just mechanisms.

We and the universe are one, therefore we cannot get beyond the bounds of the universe. We cannot escape this sphere which is the universe. No matter how boundlessly we move forward, at the same time that we move forward we remain in the universe. The end of the universe would be where we could no longer move forward, but precisely because of this end we could not be aware of or even imagine it.

Absolute emptiness is that on which none of our powers formed in the universe can act. What is inaccessible in the universe in particular is absolute emptiness. The latter is only a logical concept obtained by reason, having only been conceived as something which is the direct opposite of fullness. It is a purely rationalistic fiction.

Inorganic materialistic teachings are false, but this in no way solves the question of the soul and of God; first, because organic teachings, asserting that the whole is God, are also false (for reason of its metaphysicality among other things), and second, because the possible materialistic teachings were developed in the spirit of this unity (a unity of process and of some founding principle) as mentioned above. That is, to put it another way, the universe as a sphere, without beginning and end, can be materialistic as a whole and in parts, can be understood as pure matter, as a mechanism (Lossky's definitions don't make any sense mechanistically, for a mechanism cannot be something in which the parts exist before the whole—Give a man all the parts of a Diesel motor, and, if he doesn't know what it is, he cannot make one from these parts alone).

8   For more on current scientific theories and their impact on Russian avant-garde art, see Linda Henderson, *The Fourth Dimension and Non-Euclidean Geometry in Modern Art* (Princeton, N.J.: Princeton University Press, 1983).

The universe as unity of process understood materialistically cannot have within itself any kind of animacy. According to this concept our subjective sense of our own animacy is only illusory. A materialist should also consider that he is himself inanimate. In general he cannot distinguish living from dead matter. I grant the possibility of such a conception of the universe, knowing, however, how little true it is. The universe is so constructed precisely by virtue of its finiteness that a purely materialist conception of it cannot prove to be in contradiction to experience. Whoever rejects the existence of the spiritual does not sense it; whoever does not sense a soul does not have one.

Further I don't understand. It seems strange in that: why can there not be a whole without parts, whereas matter can be without a soul and fullness can be known, and absolute emptiness cannot?

26 October
[P. noted
mistakenly
26 Sept.]

I continue.

There where A is, there is also not-A—such is the law of logic. But this is only the law of logic. In life, in reality, this law can only be formulated: there where A is, not-A can exist only where the forces cognizing A remain the very same as those for not-A.

I call this law the law of sufficient basis for oppositions. In fact, if we have a shaped force for the understanding of the universe (our conceptualizing activity: outer and inner feelings, reason, memory, imagination, etc.), able to act only in that there is a universe, then it is understandable why we are not capable of knowing that which is not the universe—emptiness. Such is the effect of the law of sufficient basis for oppositions.

As far as the interrelationship of the soul and body is concerned, the matter is much more complex. First of all, is the soul really that which is not the body? This must be well thought out and understood. Moreover, the falseness of a purely materialistic conception (body) does not mean that it contradicts experience, but only that it does not exhaust experience, that it is less than experience, and that it is only on condition that experience would produce (or apprehend) a man who doesn't reject his own animacy. For the consistent materialist the universe really is materialistic, but it is materialistic only for him and for those who are of a similar mind, those who reject their own animacy. For such people the soul or God is uncognizable, since cognition of it or Him is conditioned by the law of sufficient basis for oppositions.

I believe that God and the soul are given to me in experience, and I feel them to be something that is not the body and not the corporeal universe.

I conclude.

I. The universe is one not in the sense of its reduction to a single principle (or element) but in the sense of its unity and the limitlessness of an enclosed process.

II. The world cannot be understood either materialistically or ideal-istically, but no other way than realistically, attaching to this term no other meaning than that in which it usually consists; i.e., as something which in reality exists. In this way the most we can now say about the universe is: it is real and this has long been known.

III. Our studies of the world have always been only studies of its forms and have always been less than that experience in which the uni-verse has been given to us, since in those cases when they are not dis-cussing precisely which forms of the world they are studying, these studies are no more true than any rationalist fictions.

IV. Can we ever have true knowledge of the universe as a whole? Only if the number of its forms were limited. Then, having understood the forms and laws of their interaction as a whole, we should have understood the universe. Yet it would seem that there are an endless number of its forms!

Note: in speaking of knowledge, I speak not only of rational sci-entific knowledge, but also of intuitive: religious, artistic, etc.

CONVERSATION BOOK

29 Oct. '24

**Today K. M. finally offered me a "constitution":
(to see each other Mon., Thurs., Sat. evening).
The suggestion was accepted.—Akhm[atova]**
All untrue, Olen, all of it, you yourself know it.
[Punin]

4 November

The first cold days. The whole sky is full of stars now, twinkling. Today Anichka moved to the Marble Palace. A little scary.

Why are she and I in different bodies? We should be in one body.

I didn't sleep all night. I thought a lot and morosely about her.

5th

She was with me. What a worried woman. How can such a person live . . . ?

———

I carry the weight of the past in the form of its unresolved doubts.

———

The most characteristic feature of modern times is that no one doubts anything, that there is no time to doubt, yet one of the signs of the culture of the mind is the presence of contradiction, the more contradiction in consciousness, the more intense the culture of the mind.

Creative work is invention, always in a known measure an exhausting contradiction—in this sense it is in opposition to culture.

To what extent are such indubitable inventors as Filonov,* Malevich (Matyushin), and even Tatlin little cultured. It would be a mistake to think that creation is only invention.

————

Marx and Engels are helpless philosophers, but does Marxism give, as a theory, a basis for the production of a Marxist philosophy?

————

Lebedev is a clothes-hanger, dressed in a person.

(A.)[9]

CONVERSATION BOOK

8 November

I came to see An. at the Marble Palace, An. is in a terrible *state,* but out of perniciousness doesn't want to move in with me for 5 days. [Punin]

————

Koty, I love you, things are bad for me. Now go home, tomorrow I will come see you my dear—Olen

10 November 1924

K. M. suggested: come with me to the Commissariat and register. Then he would rent a room for me in his name and return himself to live here. Koty, you are insane. [Akhmatova]

10th

Social mores alone are a stable basis for cooperation.

12th

Stepping outside on a foggy morning, Irina said:
 Mama, where have they heated the samovar?
 Irina has a dog whose eyes are sewn-on boot buttons. Today she looked at this dog for a long time, then with perplexity and uncertainty said: "Mama, does she have buttons for eyes?"

9 | Punin is apparently quoting Akhmatova here.

14th	It's already been ten days since Anichka has been living at the Marble Palace—ten days of sheer meaninglessness, and even in sleep the pain doesn't abate. No good comes of this love . . . !

CONVERSATION BOOK

15 November	**Anya has a cruel heart, although She is also tender.—K[oty] M[alchik]**
The same day	**K. M. has a cruel heart and wild temper.—Olen**
16 November '24	**We went to a film for the first time. We are close!—Olen** **We cried! [Akhmatova]**

18th of November	Today I saw A. for about 40 minutes; snow had fallen outside, we walked around Millionaya. At the Pavlovsky Regiment barracks she said, "I love you very much, and that's not good," and explained that it is not good to rely so much on one thing, you can't have only one point of reference, a person should spread herself out somehow. I, however, always thought the opposite and everyone thinks the opposite. It is precisely the characteristic of love that it relies on one person. That's the way it has to be. The "heavy tension" of my feelings for her is precisely because she thinks it immoral to rely on one person, or to lean on one person.
19th	Nonobjectivity in art is also an object. The depiction of an object is not objectivity, it is pure nonobjectivity, notorious illusoriness.
1 December	I cannot forgive you, said An., that you passed me by twice: in the XVIIIth century and at the beginning of the XXth century. How did it happen that we didn't meet in Tsarskoe when we were still at the gymnasium, and how did it happen later that I was at An.'s about three times (at the Gumilevs), and I passed by? I was rarely there because . . . In the fall of 1890 we might also have passed each other by in prams in Pavlovsk Park. We were living there then year-round. An., if she calculated correctly, was brought to Pavlovsk about then, and they lived there until Christmas. She was a few months old.

21st of Dec.
12 A.M.

Marble Palace
I am lying ill, and K. M. came to see me, with a clean
copy of *Lef.* He said that I don't understand what
"dynamism" is. In general he reproached me for drab-
ness. I decided to quit writing because of this.—An.

Fine, if she decided it, then she decided it!—K. M.

26 December

Ira just said: "Papa, I don't want me not to exist."

CONVERSATION BOOK

31 December
12 A.M.

K. M. greeted the new year without Olen—it was
very painful, because he didn't believe we would be
together another year.—K[oty] M[alchik]

2 January
1925

A quarter of the new century. I didn't think I would survive it . . . so
ingloriously.

From recent events: Fedin's novel *Cities and Years.* The novel is so-so,
one of the average; to an advocate of the psychological novel it seems
naive. The motivation is especially poor. Bolsheviks in the form of
students of the institute for girls of noble families. He couldn't shoot
Andrey. Mary is like Rita, Rita like Mary, and both are the tenth edition of Edward and Countess Asya. Not one character managed a single
day without mentioning the "leaders." It was as if for Fedin they didn't
exist. But it is the best of novels of this type. I give it a "C." It is talked
about a lot in the "circles."

In the last issue of the *Lyre* there was the wonderful poetry of Aseev;*
how the censors let it pass, I don't know.

———

If only I could open a bakery!

13 January

No one has ever drunk as much as they do now. Even the most unfor-
tunate person drinks upon receiving 30 rubles. They drink everywhere.
You can't not drink, you become wildly bored when you don't drink.
Desperate time!

18 January

Yesterday I had to buy galoshes. The Gostiny [Dvor] looks like a provincial market. There is no way to buy anything that is well made. All
the goods are of second- or third-class quality. Before these kinds of

things were bargained for at the Aleksandrovsky market. There are quite a lot of people, but if you look at their faces, they are pale and exhausted, old and gray. In the Passage black marketeers whisper in the corners.

Above all there is boredom.

It was a sunny, warm day. 37 degrees, a west wind blowing. There is no winter yet. It's like April days. Almost every day lately there has been high water in the Neva. For the third day, day and night they have been shooting, the water has reached 5 arshins higher than normal.[10] When the water rises, faces come to life, they don't fear the flood, they await it as some kind of event which might be able to dispel the boredom for a time. People have never been so bored.

In the evening I was at a party at a certain house. Again conversations about the flooding. Someone in the corner says: "Why are you all so happy about the flooding? It won't wash away the bolsheviks in any case." A general sigh of regret: "True, it won't." For the past seven years their authority has not acquired a single new partisan. If someone joined them, that someone also left. On average, in the circle which I frequent, the opposition has become more solid, strong, and significantly better based. There is no doubt that Plekhanov's prognosis was correct. No one is interested in political problems at all, they all think something like, "There just are no leaders." They are somewhat ironic toward Trotsky.

In the institutes there are unheard-of squabbles and intrigues, everywhere there is chopping and changing. All kinds of "administrators" keep being dismissed, and their places are taken more often than not by some kind of person who "says nothing." For the most part they appoint communists, but these too leave quickly enough due either to some sort of incompetence or because of their "impurity." At one meeting Marr said with his usual passion and an accent: "I have a birth, I need a midwife, and they tell me to be sure to call a communist." Hack work is unchecked and overflowing. There is self-serving speculation on Marxism and Lenin. Making a bust of Lenin or drawing him lying in state is most profitable. Even here, though, you need connections and acquaintances. One fairly well-known artist said while emigrating: "Yes, I am leaving because the corpse doesn't feed me anymore."

[half of this page is cut out] . . . not a single artistic work produced, in any way significant. In our circle L. Bruni is more cheerful than others, perhaps because he is a religious person.

10 | An arshin is 27.95 inches.

So it is throughout Russia. Russia isn't working. That we must manage with our own raw materials and pay with our own manufactured goods—that is the only priority of the present day.

CONVERSATION BOOK

I miss An. a lot like the first year, but only more terribly and desperately. [Punin]

NOTEBOOK NINE

1925–1926

CONVERSATION BOOK

2 Feb.
Marble
Palace

Yesterday we agreed not to see each other (1st time since Podolsk), but K. M. still came to see me. Now he is sleeping.—Olen
And again at 12:30 P.M. K. M. came to see me

8 February
1925

In terms of our political situation we feel as if we are beyond the end, that the end should have been long ago, but it still hasn't come. Because of this there is emptiness. In terms of our culture, we have been thrown back 50 years. We are suffocating because of this.

The censor Bystrova marked out an uncensored word (three letters) in some citation of Pushkin. The publisher went to her assistant Vasilev to ask about the restoration of the text. Vasilev sent the publisher to Bystrova herself. Upon returning, the publisher said: I am not comfortable speaking with her about such a word. Vasilev said, "Why would you think that I would be comfortable speaking with her about it?" There was nothing more for the publisher to say and he had to give in.

18 February

There is no snow, there wasn't any, and probably by now there won't be any. This whole time it has been 35 degrees, 45–46 degrees in the sun. During winter it wasn't ever below 40 degrees. Snow fell, but it didn't stick for even a full day it seems. In our garden the paths are already completely soft, the light grass is turning green. Today it was partly sunny. Dark snowy clouds passed by to the north, but there was neither rain nor snow. Anichka was just here. She said Shchegolev-Tolstoy's play "The Empress' Plot" was banned by the censor. Tolstoy is totally devastated, the more so since Zamyatin had great success with his "Flea." This Tolstoy is awfully pitiful. An., after much fuss, received some aid, the pitiful sum of 25 rubles, from KUBU. Tomorrow Krasin* should come to visit, and the word on my trip to Paris should become clear. [Tamara] Miklashevskaya really wants to set this trip up for me. Today I saw Chekhonin,* who energetically urged me to go. He himself is preparing to and probably will go. But I don't have the strength to overcome the triple net of intrigue necessary to go. It is all disgusting to the point of horror, and the more I penetrate into the depths of these administrative hierarchies, the more stinkingly horrible they are. The rapacious and stagnant mass rots and stinks. That is the administrative apparatus.

I want to go to Moscow, to see Bruni and Miturich. Although Tatlin and Malevich and Filonov are in Petersburg now, it still seems that the rest of life is nevertheless in Moscow. Tatlin made a new model of the "tower," but in his wild and blunt rage he is again unable to do anything. The day before yesterday he smashed some doors in the museum and he pounced on Malevich in a frenzy. Nothing is "moving" anywhere, everything stands still, a dead swaying. There is something evil in the dead calm of our time. Everyone is waiting for something and something certainly should happen, and nothing does . . . this can't really last until the tenth anniversary, can it? Things have become terrifying because of this uncertainty, people are thrown into despair, and in despair they become corrupt. There has never been greater corruption, greater despair, in the whole of Russia's history. There was the time of Arakcheev, of Nicholas I, and of Aleksandr III, but that was despotism, oppressing the people with the 300-lb. blows of "backward ideas." But now it is not despotism, and not even petty tyranny, but the rot of some kind of deposit that has settled on young and living skin. This deposit will have to rot away and completely destroy what it clings to, and therefore everything that is fruitless now is even more fruitless than it was under the Arakcheevshchina* or Aleksandr III.

We are not suffering as we suffered for example in 1918–1922 (the suffering of those years was undoubtedly fruitful), but we are suffocating, we are withering and drying up, rotting and writhing in deadly convulsion, but for some reason we all know that it is not fatal and that death will not come. Still, we will not become like Spain. L. said, returning from abroad not long ago, that in the West there is full opportunity to work but that the material is very poor. We have wonderful material, and no possibility to work. This probably is true.

We were together in Tsarskoe.—Akhm.
3rd day of winter sun in the park, like Gondla, we
spoke of how to live together here in little rooms.[1]—
K[oty] M[alchik]

21 February

Tamara "coughed it up." I just called her. She said that Krasin couldn't arrange anything but a visa, which he, perhaps, might be in a position to send me. We'll see. Tamara fears me because of my counter-revolutionary speeches. Well, so what—war is war.

Today I was with An. at Tsarskoe. It's the third day in a row that a light powdery snow has fallen. 18 degrees Fahrenheit. Sunny, transparent high sky. The Tsarskoe Selo park is covered with snow, there are almost no paths, trails have been made through the park, along the shortest route to Sofia. It was empty and because of this it was still more majestic and splendid. The sun mixed with the snow, gilded the glades, tree trunks, and burned in the air. It seems strange that people still live in this town. How do they live? How can they live in such peace on the remnants of such a past? This town, tacked onto the giant palaces on the edge of the park, dead, half ruined, recalls the dwelling of a grave-digger in some kind of immense cemetery. I got the same feeling that I had experienced in Chufut-Kale. Walking through the empty streets you remember the rows of carriages with drivers and lackeys in red livery. In the days of the tsar they stretched from the palace itself to the lower stables. English half-breeds rushed about with shorn heads and blew whistles. Along Srednaya, past the building where we lived, the tsaritsa used to ride past almost daily at 4 o'clock with her children in a wide barouche pulled by a pair of horses in Russian harness with a fat coachman on whose soft chest gleamed a colored row of medals. All the households were familiar to us as well as the daily life in the houses: the lackeys who opened the doors, the stairs covered in red velvet runners, the vestibules, ballrooms, boudoirs—the footsteps and the ring of sabers and swords, the bald spots presented for kisses, the children in wide trousers and short jackets trimmed with astrakhan fur, in hats of the same fur, or in the red hats of the Levitsky school, with their governesses and tutors. And the other life; the gymnasia students in light blue caps and light blue scarves pulled out of light gray coats, students in cabs, balls at the Ratusha [the old town hall], splendid balls, where everything was as it was in "court society," but where that "society"

1   "Gondla" is an epic poem by Akhmatova's first husband, Nikolay Gumilev.

would not recognize anything as its own, returning as it did with the last train from Petersburg, swift rides home on one's own horse past the silver-plated cast-iron electric street lamps. A sleepy maid without cap and apron. The dining room where cold tea and snacks had been set out on the sideboard, etc. The dead town sleeps, the palaces sleep and the park sleeps. Irreparable, irrevocable . . . But through this deep, terrible, white death-sleep the past looks out, completely apathetic to what has happened. Whether it itself has this power or whether eternal art, for some reason never able to die, has given this power to it—I don't know. But, like a former sun or a dead star, the past gazes through this city of graves in total silence with a wise face, all-seeing and knowing all. Or is this also life? My feelings today are like those that occur when you look through a telescope at the craters and fields of the moon . . .

Anichka stopped by Gumilev's house hoping to find N. S. [Gumilev]'s old papers—there was nothing. They were probably burned by the inhabitants, the house having changed hands more than once.

CONVERSATION BOOK

27 Feb. 1925

Marble Palace
Today K. M. leaves for Moscow (8:30).

> *"Not to part while we still live*
> *Not for work, nor for play*
> *Love won't bear it, takes revenge*
> *Love will take its gifts away."*

(Z. GIPPIUS)*

Somehow we managed to part and not snuff out the flame
K[oty] M[alchik] leaves completely tortured with [illegible] [Akhmatova]

6 March

Marble Palace
Yesterday K. M. returned from Moscow. He says that I have somehow changed. How? [Akhmatova]

Probably Olen was unfaithful and that's why she's like that.—Ni[kolay Punin]

Well, all the same, yes. [Akhmatova]
14 June 1925. Fountain House

LETTER TO AKHMATOVA FROM PUNIN

2 March 1925

Moscow

Oh, An.—today I am especially thinking of you—tirelessly, along all the streets of this city, which so little resembles you. I had to go to the Museum of Aleksandr III, but I went there secretly hoping to meet with Bukhan and asked for him. Yes, he was there. I just needed to be close to what was yours, to what had been touched by your hands—those dear and pure hands, my love.

I am already tired of waiting for our meeting and like this summer, the nearer that moment, the farther it seems, as if it will for some reason never be. Yesterday I had a chance to go to Chulkov to hear some paper by A. Bely, but I was afraid and didn't go.

All my business is almost done. Today I read a paper, tomorrow another, and will receive money. Wednesday I leave. I will be with you Thursday morning and if you don't chase me away, all day until the next morning.

I am bringing you a portrait by Levka for publication in Petrograd.

Where are you now (5 o'clock)—is everything going well for you—is your heart light, An., ah?[2] How I love your angry heart, tender, despairing. God's gift to me. I'm a little tired, the weather is wet, and it is twilight, but because of you there is triumph and light as if you were the light that could change the world. I am happy with you and triumphant and comforted. What more? How far away you are.

I kiss your hands but not tomorrow or the day after.

Koty

7 March

I was in Moscow.[3] Moscow resembles an Asiatic camp settled on "seven hills." Moscow is immersed in everyday life. They don't talk about poli-

2 Written in pencil above this by Akhmatova—"Koty, now, now!"

3 On March 11, 1918, the Russian capital was moved from Petrograd to Moscow, ostensibly for protection against enemies during the civil war that followed the revolution. But once the bolsheviks were firmly in power, the capital remained Moscow and was not moved back. This was protested by many of the intelligentsia, who saw themselves as vanguards of the revolution and who were based in Petrograd. By 1925, when Punin was writing this passage, St. Petersburg's name had been changed again to Leningrad in honor of Lenin, who died in 1924. There has historically been a rivalry or tension between the two cities, and we can speculate on the reasons why the new Soviet government would want Moscow to be the capital. First, it is indeed easier to defend and further into the heartland of Russia. Second, it is less associated with the imperial aspect of tsarist rule, which had used St. Petersburg as its seat of power since its founding in 1703 by Peter the Great. Third, by 1925 the Soviet government was turning away from internationalism toward "socialism in one country"; St. Petersburg, with its "window to the West" and European architecture,

tics (I didn't see a paper the whole six days that I was there) and you don't feel the government, as if it didn't exist. This last characteristic happily sets Moscow apart from St. Petersburg. The local Moscow government has been squeezed, as if flattened by the Union powers, and in essence has no influence whatsoever, while the All-Union powers still put on a show of being "cultured" to some measure in order to pass as acceptable. In the administrative organs with which one must do business in Moscow half the people who sit there are "ours"; that is, "intelligentsia" with "connections" and this is a godsend . . . There is no real work, but they go on working out of some measure of loyalty. It is not exactly appropriate to speak of flourishing, but art is not crushed. Its professional characteristics are still recognizable. Orthodox religious currents seemed especially strong and active to me. In these circles, which I cannot name, a great culture is actually ripening and is being worked out. Without any hypocrisy, free from mysticism—a powerful, vital, truly free and strong religious consciousness. Their attitude to me was kind and loving. They forgave me.

In Moscow they don't talk about Trotsky either. In general they regard him as a stupid phenomenon, of no practical use.

I saw Brik—he too is in opposition, but couldn't sustain it either. Mayakovsky is habitually rude, his new works are completely insignificant. Favorsky made an amazing impression on me. A powerful man. My heart lit up with his spirit.

Miturich is very angry with Bruni because he didn't acknowledge Vera Khlebnikov and didn't "allow her a visit" with Nina (Bruni's wife). For this he put him in the 8th category on his chart. Both Miturich and Bruni are drawing beautifully. There is more money in Moscow and it is better secured there. It is as if Moscow had prepared for a long-term cultural hibernation, its strength having been turned inward and been at work there. Outwardly, everyone is loyal, "it looks very easy." They are sitting it out. But no one knows for sure how long they'll have to sit.

---

was seen as more western and less Russian. Finally, Leningrad was a stronghold of the intelligentsia, with whom the government had an ambivalent relationship. During the 1920's, the government actively moved many of the major institutions such as the Academy of Sciences to Moscow; in general the New Economic Policy period was one of loss for St. Petersburg, as those who were looking to benefit from the opportunities for private industry moved to the more trade-oriented Moscow. In the early 1930's, the Soviet government began massive building projects in Moscow as a way to reinvent the city as the Soviet capital. For more on the relationship between the two cities throughout history, see Katerina Clark's *Petersburg, Crucible of Cultural Revolution* (Cambridge, Mass.: Harvard University Press, 1995).

They told me about An.'s acquaintance with Count Vasily Komarov-sky.* Count K. met Gumilev somewhere and paid him a visit at the house on Bulvarnaya St. (where Gumilev lived then, having just recently married). An. wasn't home. When she came in, Kom[arovsky] stood up, bowed low, and, approaching her with his heavy gait, bent over An.'s hand and said, "Now the fate of Russian poetry is in your hands." Naturally, Vasily Aleks[eevich Komarovsky] didn't attach any serious significance to his words, he simply wanted to be extremely elegant.

An. remembers this meeting and told me that it embarrassed her greatly and that in general she was very shy of Komarovsky when she first met him (but not for long). Later he wrote her poems and visited the Gumilevs often, and it was not without pride that in his own time he told me about it.

[Note at bottom: "At this time, Komarovsky didn't yet know that An. wrote poetry." In one of his acts of madness he told An. that she was a Russian icon and that he wanted to marry her. Auntie Komarovsky (as Aunt Lyuba was called) was afraid of Vasily Alek(seevich)'s friendship with An., thinking that they might fall in love. She feared an "affair with the bohemian."

As is well known, Komarovsky wrote a novel entitled "To Tsushima," but didn't publish it since he didn't want (his words) "to fight with the dynasty."]

CONVERSATION BOOK

Pressed flower with the inscription—snowdrop from Podolsk region. 23 March 1925

Anichka is sick for the third week in a row. When I arrived from Moscow she was already feeling poorly. The whole affair that played out with Alyansky* had a profound effect on her.

—In a conversation about art An. said: in any Italian fisherman there is more art than in Anatole France's* head—these words made a stunning impression on me, as to what a great extent An. *felt* art. Oh, with how much knowledge of life she has been gifted. I often feel like a pupil before her . . .

—Yesterday I reread Huysmans* with tenderness, trepidation, happiness.

Who else knew so much about the soul?

25 March

More on Komarovsky—

Komarovsky was a very kind person. The tramps, of which there were quite a few in Tsarskoe Selo, sniffed this out. Komarovsky knew that they were drunkards and hooligans, but nevertheless he always gave them spare change. During his walks these types lay in wait for him at every crossroad. All this confused him, and he said with affected agitation: "These scoundrels have made me their tsar."

CONVERSATION BOOK

26 March
1925.
Marble
Palace

Today, 26 March, K[oty] M[alchik] for the first time acted around me so that I understood that he no longer loves me.—Akhm.

The same day

K. M. said: "To hell with you, go live with Bukhan!"
Hail to the USSR!—Akhm.

Half an hour later all was taken back.—K[oty] M[alchik]

31 March

Marble Palace
Today—anyone you like, only not me.—Olen

31 March

The more I am tormented, the more often I realize with amazement that the people around me have all been tormented for a long time. I didn't know this and I was aggressive with them, and because I was aggressive, they are afraid, they judge and hate me now.

It is impossible to comprehend that you have a soul if you don't feel it inside, just as it is also impossible to understand how tormented people are if you yourself haven't been.

————

Mercy, mercy!
How can one instill mercy in a 17-year-old Komsomol* member?
—And how was it possible to instill it in you six years ago?

CONVERSATION BOOK

9 April 1925

Tsarskoe Selo, Moskovskaya 1—
Today it is exactly a week since I have been living in Tsarskoe. This afternoon I was in Pavlovsk Park with K[oty] M[alchik]. It is spring there.—Olen

I went to see An. in Tsarskoe. On the way a tailor who was a bit high preached to the whole coach, but the Red Army recruits, of whom by chance there were many, only laughed. He said:

"They are turning to the countryside . . . they are flirting with the peasantry, and why are they flirting?—because they need bayonets, they need to be supported by bayonets . . . It used to be—Mr. Worker, sir, what would you like, Mr. Worker, sir? But now no, there is a bond with the countryside. Last year about this time you saw slogans like: Sir workers, if you are sick, or if you are tired, please go take a vacation in the Crimea. But now it is: peasants, please, go to the Crimea. You think there won't be an International, but there will be, without fail, there will be, only not according to the theories of Marx, it will be our people's International, when we kick out all the scoundrels" (and so on).

I'm spending almost every day with Anna in Tsarskoe Selo. The weather is bad.

—

As is well known, our time prides itself on its anecdotes with Soviet themes. The sheer number of them is striking. Every day you can almost be sure to hear some joke about an event that just occurred. In a word, people are cracking jokes. The day before yesterday, O. Mandelshtam came to see An. and said, "I've thought up half an anecdote. Help me come up with the second half." An. gladly agrees to help. O. says: of course the substance has to do with that important event, the anniversary of the death of Ilych, during which all passersby on the street were supposed to stop where they were during the gun salute. (It must be noted that up to 10 anecdotes are circulating on this theme.) They stop. Two Jews. One stands still, the other runs around in a circle. "And what happens next I can't think, but I feel that a good anecdote should come out of it . . . "

Anichka constantly has a temperature, has gotten thinner.

CONVERSATION BOOK

Today we walked in the park. K[oty] M[alchik] took my picture at "the Girl." We talked about the Society of Tsarskoe Selo at the beginning of the century. We are close!— Olen

I have never before been fated to her as I am now when she is in Tsarskoe.—K[oty] M[alchik]

Yesterday morning I went to Tsarskoe with a camera. It was a warm sunny day. I went to the park with An., took a picture of her at the [statue of] "the girl with a pitcher." We spent the whole day together and I stayed overnight at her place. We spent the whole time talking about life together, about how to rent two little rooms in Kolomna (in order to be further away from people) and to live.

It feels so good to think and talk about it, could it really not be fated to be?

People think that life knows two extremes: suffering and happiness; they may not be right. There are other extremes, for which suffering and happiness are only the shading. I would never assert that A. does not torment me, or that in general she *cannot* torment me. The truth is that it is closer to the other way around, she can and does. But I can breathe when I'm with her, and this means more to me than happiness. Galya might not torment me, and I have suffocated because of this in our life together. There was already no such life by '19. In '19 it had already become mechanical. And now I can't even imagine how to explain it to Galya. With An. I breathe life in so easily and with such full breath, and I cannot survive without her . . .

Tatlin came by, very depressed by his material needs, and said: "If I croak, I will burn and tear up all my things, I won't leave anything to them; you know I have become enraged."

How is it that we've all come to grief? Will we ever understand it?

CONVERSATION BOOK

Hospital
**K[oty] M[alchik]! Don't forget that tomorrow at 2:30
I will wait for you on the new bench in the hospital
garden.— Olen
If it rains, call me—I will hear it in my room.**

Irinka always mixes up words in sentences that she is learning from poetry, for example.

The day before yesterday she showed me a book with pictures, and in one of them there was a drawing of a ladybug. Irina, pointing to it with her finger said, "It's a buggy lady."[4]

4 This is a play on words. The Russian for ladybug is "god's cow," which if reversed is close to "Cow God."

2 June 1925

Hospital
Take me to our homeland . . .

Home.
25 May
Old Style

A little dream, a little nightcap . . . Yesterday we fought but I don't believe it is bad for us. K[oty] M[alchik] grumbles ceaselessly that I made him suffer with my illness. I am lying ill for the fourth month. It's time to go into the woods.—Olen

Yesterday was the 11 of June (the day of my birth new style) All day I lay ill. At 10:30 P.M. I went with Tanya to see K[oty] M[alchik]. He asked: Why'd you drag yourself here!—Akhm.

Shelley, my dear Shelley, how can you write about me that way? And you? [5]

23 June

A rainbow across the whole sky!

24 June '25.
Marble
Palace

Day of my birth in the old style. I promised K[oty] M[alchik] to go abroad with him in the spring of 1926 if. . . .—Olen
But only 1/10 of Olen is left. She is tired after only 10 min.—still a queen. Her dear little elbows are the same.—K[oty] M[alchik]

27 June 1925

Boat LGO
K. Kh. Nb. Elagin Island—Summer Gardens— Another year has passed and we are again on the island. Hot. They are repairing the Strelka. What for? The water is almost white. And in another year?— Olen

5 July 1925
beyond the
gates [of
town] at
Danko

We are sitting on the same bench as a year ago. We sent a letter to Olga [Sudeykina] in Paris. Peonies, roses, the Zephyr wind blows: Is this bad!?

---

5   Possible reference to Percy Bysshe Shelley. Akhmatova was always interested in this author and even wanted to translate his play *The Cenci* into Russian. She never completed this project. The play centers around incest and murder.

From the dictionary of the future:

Volynsky, Akim Lvovich (his real name is Flexer*)—simultaneously a well-known activist of the revolution and a counterrevolutionary.

Wed. 1 o'clock
Sheremetev House

The fourth day of hot, blue days (77 degrees in the shade, in the sun 100), Galya and Irina left last Tuesday for Kursk Province (Borisovo).

Today An. stayed on, to spend the night. I put her up in the study and all night long I could sense her presence in the house even in my sleep. In the morning I went in to see her; she was still asleep. I had no idea she was so pretty asleep. We drank tea together, then I washed her hair, and she spent almost all day translating a French book for me. It is so peaceful to be with her constantly.

In the evening, Gessen came by (A. I.—An.'s publisher) to invite her to the country where his family lives. An. became confused. We think G. invited An. because he is not in a position to pay her the money he promised her. We also talked of events and the break of relations with England, which is apparently inevitable.[6] An. (and I) want war, not seeing any other way out of the suffocating situation we are now in. G. is afraid of war; how characteristic! As a private publisher he is oppressed by the existing situation no less than us, but obviously he fears reaction and the possible restoration. His mood is indicative. That is, it bears witness in the end to the economic ties of the new bourgeoisie with the existing government. It is not insignificant that he is Jewish. It is impossible to determine in what circles and to what extent the Soviet power is the most accepted of all the possible powers. "Nepmen" in any case are not the opposition, it is possible to define

6   Although England's economic ties with the Soviet Union had been renewed since 1921 and the first Labor government extended diplomatic recognition to the Soviet Union in 1924, the "Zinovev letter" and continuing Soviet agitation for communist revolutions on the international front sorely strained Anglo-Soviet relations. The letter, supposedly written by Communist Party leader Zinovev to the British communists, called for a forcible overthrow of the government. Although it was later identified as a forgery, it hastened the downfall of the Labor government and further weakened Zinovev's position in the Soviet Union. Stalin's idea of communism in one country gained influence, and the Zinovevites were thrown out of Moscow. In 1925, a British team sent by the League of Nations went to survey the Aland Islands, which the Soviet Union had wanted to remain neutral. The Soviet Union used this as propaganda, claiming that England really wished to occupy and perhaps arm the islands in preparation for war against the Soviet Union. See the *Pravda* article "Angliia ukrepliaetsia na Baltiiskom more," August 2, 1925, and "Novaia ataka" in the August 9, 1925, edition of *Izvestiia*.

their attitude with the phrase "just be patient" or "it's bad, very bad, but we have to live through it, to stick it out." This is how Rybakov views it more or less—a typical "nepman"—all from fear of restoration.

But it is disturbing, very disturbing.

Deep blue night, the zephyr wind floats through the window.

But there is little hope of a better life.

It will all get worse and worse . . .

CONVERSATION BOOK

9 July—
Sheremetev
Fountain
House

Yesterday I was at K[oty] M[alchik's] for 28 hours. I read and translated "L'art français sous la révolution" and we looked at the "Yusupov Gallery" by S. Ernst. It was very quiet and cool. In the evening Gessen came by. Then the evening service—completely moving. We parted and said good-bye at my place in Marble Palace. My heart was heavy.—Akum. [Akhmatova]
—I wrote this 9 July at K[oty] M[alchik's]

13 July

3rd Anniversary of Lourie's concert-"feast" at the Hotel Europeysky. What does Euronedespo mean?

13 July—
Marble
Palace
at my place

With this I allow N. N. Punin to have one child with any woman.—Anna Akhmatova

15 July '25

I promise K[otik] M[alchik] not to see [Zimmerman] from this day on.—Anna.

Marble Palace—When I am no longer here, may rebellious thoughts not come to you, you know, how parting with you is *always* bitter for me. Why is it so?—Anna.

18 July

The lyceum students were shot.[7] They say 52 people; the rest were exiled, their possessions were confiscated right down to children's toys

7 As Punin notes, this incident was not officially made public, but the *London Times* ran two stories on it, one on July 23 and another on August 6. According to the *Times*, fifty-eight people were arrested and executed without a trial on or about July 3. The victims were associated with the Aleksandr Lyceum and the School of Law. No explanation was given for the executions except for the suspicion of counterrevolutionary activity.

and winter clothes. There was no official announcement of the shooting. In the city, of course, everyone knows about it, at least in those
circles with which I have contact: among the members of the intelligentsia who are in the service. They talk about it with horror and disgust, but without surprise and without any real indignation. They talk
as if it couldn't have been otherwise . . . you sense that they will soon
forget about it. . . . great torpor and extreme exhaustion.

CONVERSATION BOOK

21 July 1925

The lime trees are blooming. For a long time it has
been quiet and not frightening. Tomorrow I leave for
Bezhetsk. This morning at Fountain House it became
clear. "A roaring by the wash-basin."—Olen

*The Same
Day*

K[oty] M[alchik] said, "The dear one with whom I
lived for three years will still cry."—Fountain House.
The next two pages are our correspondence at
Nik[olaevsky] Station torn out at K. M.'s request—A.

22 July 1925

N[ikolaevsky] Station—coach
Dear, why have we both been *this way* these days. In
parting, *this* could grow into misfortune.—Olen

*26 July
1925—
Fountain
House*

Today I returned from Bezhetsk. K[oty] M[alchik],
gloomy and sad, is silent.—Olen

*29 July 1925.
Siverskaya
Feldmarch,
No. 63.*

Nikolay [Punin] came to see me. We expect a thun-
derstorm. I showed him an article about Annensky
and the Baratenev Pushkin. Did she forgive?—It
would be good if she did.—Olen

31 July

It has become a dry yellow summer. There hasn't been such an exodus
from Petersburg since the revolution. No one is here, I haven't heard
anything from anyone. The streets are scorching hot. Some things are
under repair. Mainly they are painting the buildings. This work is
under the direction of "Old Petersburg."* They are painting the buildings well. The plaster decoration of the later buildings ('60's–'80's) has
been removed, as a result it is less ugly. They just painted the Academy
of Sciences built by Quarenghi. They are painting the Kunstkammer

by Mattarnovi. On the corner building next to the Stock Exchange they are removing the pilasters, which were probably stuck on during the reign of Aleksandr II. I don't like the Exchange, it is somehow complicated.

CONVERSATION BOOK

1 August 1925   11-year anniversary of the war.

2 August '25   We went to the Ethnographic museum. We looked at shamans and northern regions. We have never been so close! We walked around to look at the Prince Vladimir Cathedral. The clergyman said that they adhere to the new style and therefore people don't come. The belfry is nice. We were at Belkin's. Then at Tuchka. They are painting the Library at the Academy of Sciences. A golden day. I am sleeping at K[oty] M[alchik's]. We drank wine in the study. Talked about Dama Luni; I read about a church of the XI century that was discovered in April of 1910 in Kiev (the year and month of my wedding to N. S. [Gumilev]). We are close!— Olen

What inhuman closeness. Whose predestination is this?—K[oty] M[alchik]

2 August   I am endlessly close to An. We are together whole days at a time.

Today we were at the Ethnographic Museum. Anichka especially liked the Tunguz shamans. She spoke of their clothes, that they had such amazing, wonderful taste. They really do make a huge impression with the organic wholeness of their look. These insane old men possess an unheard-of, highly cultured taste for iron and skins. It would be interesting for Tatlin to look at these shamans. The skin on them looks like tongues of fire, and iron appears somehow especially ironlike.

I also liked very much the people of the northernmost regions. In the work of the utensils and clothing from other regions there is a great sense of taste, culture, etc., but always anything from these regions is just a well-made thing, an object of material culture, and it is only in the northern regions where it is not simply a thing, an object of material culture, but also some kind of epiphany, some kind of glorification. I think the northern provinces are more organic and the role of nature in the works from these regions is more powerful, irrevocable. And perhaps the sense of nature itself is fuller and more synthesized there.

Everything is a pearly meditation on the world, everything—
is a swan's sigh . . . Inexpressible beauty . . .

— — —

An. looked at the Ukraine with disgust: she really doesn't like
Ukrainians.[8]

— — —   — — —   — — —

Yesterday An. said: "you sometimes feel closer to me than I feel to
myself."

CONVERSATION BOOK

3 August—
The garden
of the Smolny
*Convent**
over the Neva

**I haven't been here in 23 years. Nothing has changed.
Elizabeth's lime trees. But girls are swimming, shouting. Komsomol students play soccer. Again a golden
day. The cathedral is like in a dream.—Anna**

**An. very much rejoices in the garden and told how
everything was and what was there. We stood on the
colonnade and looked at the Neva and swimmers.
[Punin]**

**And in the evening we went to look at the Mining
Inst[itute] (both for the first time). V[asilevsky]**

8   Anna Akhmatova (then Anna Gorenko) spent her childhood summers at the Crimean
resort town of Khersones on the Black Sea coast. Many of her poems about the sea and
memories of being a "wild child" stem from her experiences there. In 1905, Akhmatova's
parents separated, and she went to live in Evpatoriya (also on the Black Sea coast) with
her mother. From then on, Akhmatova had mostly unhappy memories of her life in the
Ukraine. In 1906, she lost her sister Inna to tuberculosis and entered the Fundukuleev-
skaya Gymnasium in Kiev. There she lived with the family of her cousin Marya Zmun-
chilla during the school year and with other relatives during holidays. She did not get
along with her relatives and found her violent and foul-mouthed uncle unbearable. In
1907, she entered the Kiev College for Women and remained in the Ukraine until her
marriage to Nikolay Gumilev in 1910. Presumably, her dislike for the Ukraine stems
from these unpleasant early experiences. In her conversations with Lydia Chukovskaya,
Akhmatova had this to say about Ukrainians: ". . . I didn't like prerevolutionary Kiev. A
city of vulgar women. It was full of wealthy men and sugar refiners. They lavished thousands on the latest fashions, they and their wives . . . My 17-and-a-half-stone cousin,
waiting at Shvyster's, the famous tailor's, for a new dress to be fitted, kissed the little icon
pendant of St. Nicholas around her neck and said: 'Make it a good fit'" (*The Akhmatova
Journals*, 1:40). Akhmatova did, however, recognize the beauty and history of Kiev, even
writing an early poem about the city, but maintained that the city was "spoiled by the
19th century" (*The Akhmatova Journals*, 1:19).

O[strov] is wondrous, coastal, quiet. Full moon. Sailing boats. Creaking. Very sad. One can never leave here.—Akhm.

Yesterday I went with An. to the Smolny Convent. By chance we succeeded in getting beyond the front gates. We walked around the church and went out into the garden. An. was in Smolny for a few months as a young girl and remembers this garden. It is abandoned, wonderful. In the depths of the garden there is a colonnade, there are windows with bars looking out toward the Neva. Near the colonnade are lime trees (Elizabethan). A girl of about 16 was swimming in the Neva and she admonished us for looking at her. We walked around the church. The church was locked, the glass was broken in many places, and the colors were faded and peeling. Silence and emptiness. People who looked kind of communist live in the convent. Young men walk along the paths with "ladies" in red scarves. It is neglected, and there are traces of destruction everywhere, but there is no peace. The kind of peace which lies, for example, around the old, no less abandoned Novgorod churches. The church flows, grows, and is disturbed, exactly as if it is not we who walked around it, but rather that it walks before us; unfolding again and again folding its stone forms. Then all evening I heard the captive voice of this ghost of white nights. I especially like it from the side of the apse: it is a kind of stairway of white angels streaming, rustling, sad, and blinding. We walked around for a long time, all the while looking upward. Then we walked out onto the square, which was overgrown with chamomile. "Where they executed people before daybreak," said An., and we went through the rebuilt entrance to the Quarenghi Building.[9] An. showed me the window where their dormitory was.

We ate dinner at Fedorov's, from there we went to the Mining Institute. We sat on the steps above the Neva; it began to get dark, a red moon rose in the cloudy fog, on the far shore smoke rose, a factory of some kind. Twice a tugboat steamed past on the Neva, its wake ran up to the banks and noisily splashed on the stone steps. The portico of the institute loomed at our backs, heavy and silent, sinking into the darkness. An. looked at it a lot and for a long time. She grew sad; it seems she wanted to go abroad very badly. She remembered Olga [Sudeykina], and how they had said good-bye to Arthur [Lourie] three years ago.

---

9   Akhmatova is quoting a line from Innokenty Annensky's poem "Petersburg," first published in the journal *Apollon* in 1910.

We are doomed.

In the last two years we have often thought that of ourselves.

"We are surrounded by enemies and there is nowhere for us to look for help, except from Her, the Heavenly Intercessor."—from one of the sermons of the All Night Vigil on the holiday of the icon of Our Lady.

. . . Speaking of all that had passed An. also said, "when every man around us is like a wound."

I should go to the Kursk Province [to join my family]. It is terrible to tear myself away from her and to see her image at night, stretching across the sky . . .

6 August

We were allowed to "plead for" some of the students who had been condemned in the lyceum case, among them Valerian Chudovsky. He forbade anyone to "plead for" him, saying that if it isn't possible for all the students, then he didn't want it for himself.

The capture of the Aland Islands,* Esel and Dago, by the English depressed everyone, as if everyone knew that their sons and the husbands of their daughters would someday pay with their lives for these islands . . .

CONVERSATION BOOK

*9 Aug. 1925,
Sunday*

The eve of autumn. At the new lions. Strelka. Tomorrow K[oty] M[alchik] leaves me. If only we will meet again on this earth.—Akhm[atova]

*The same day,
across from
the Marble
Palace at
Tishkina's
floating
restaurant,
10:30 P.M.*

I scare Nikolay [Punin] with parting: Conciergerie, etc.[10] He says: I don't have any premonitions. And I am glad. On the islands we talked of the Pushkinian temptation.

An. is deerlike, bends her neck toward the Neva, but more chattery than I have ever known her. It is love— only. Just now the guy next to us said: I worked in the GPU and he worked for Trotsky. [Punin]

*10 August
1925,
Nik[olaevsky]
Station, at
the Buffet*

**Good-bye, dear Joy, don't be sad, I am with you—
Anna**

10 | The Conciergerie was a famous French prison.

Borisovka
Convent

Lightning lit up the sky in the south like the sun. They just rang the bells to come to the All Night Vigil; the girls from the forestry have brought the evening milk. This is the second week we have been living in the ruined convent. The convent is not old. It was founded by Boris Sheremetev, whom Peter addressed as "min hir." The walls date from the beginning of the 19th century.[11] Even five years ago it was a clean and prosperous dwelling place, accommodating up to 900 nuns. The nuns lived in separate attic-cells and evidently had a relatively rich and free private life. In any case they provided their own food and lived on the income from their handiwork: they made cloth and filigree for icons, wax wedding flowers, etc. I live right in one of the cells; a light little room with four windows surrounded by a closed gallery. There are little curtains on the windows. The floors are painted; near the room there are all kinds of little closets, 5–7 feet in height.

Now there is death and destruction here. At first they drove off the nuns, but gradually they gathered here again and now live in their cells, like private citizens, paying for their dwelling according to the wages of the free professions. They live under the same direction as before and have many of the same rules as before. But the churches are closed, the crosses have been torn off the churches, and every kind of violence has been committed. At the gate right by the entrance they built an open wooden latrine, justifying this by the fact that the road passes by it and it is necessary to have a public lavatory on a thoroughfare. They have put members of the Komsomol in the former convent hospital. They mock the nuns in every way, and not only the nuns . . . it is a den of thieves with which the local organs of the people's Commissariat of Enlightenment struggle in vain. The church's utensils have been looted and anything that could be sold has been sold. They tore up the gospels and handed them out to children for "kites." I came upon two broken and hanging kites, made of pages from the holy books. They cut out the eyes of the icon of St. German. A certain one-legged, 80-year-old nun who had accepted the arrangement was carried out of her cell and sent back to her native place with a convoy. The Mother Superior

11 The Sheremetev family was one of the wealthiest of the nobility in the nineteenth century. Count Boris Petrovich Sheremetev was one of Peter the Great's commanding officers. He was also instrumental in bringing the arts to Russia, in particular ballet (through his own serf ballet troup) and painting (by having his serfs trained as artists). The Sheremetev Palace in which the Punin family and Akhmatova lived also belonged to the same family before the revolution.

had been arrested countless times and now lives 15 miles away in the countryside.

A huge majority of the nuns are peasants from the Don region. They have their reticent and peaceful dignity. They are cordial and not angered, but they do bitterly lament and touchingly long for the past. In the evenings they love to talk long and lovingly about their convent. They don't believe in an impending fall of Soviet power. They trust that the laws will be softened.

We live in a cell, one of four in a wooden building. Under us live the nun Margarita, an older woman of about 50 or 60 years, and the nun Slava (Svetoslava?) who is still very young. Both are devout and humble and obliging. They fast daily; on the day of Communion they put on their holiday dresses, amazing dresses with very high waists and long trains, skirts with heavy gathers. They wear white scarves with special ties at the back of the head. I wanted to take a picture of them, but it wasn't so easy to persuade them to let me.

Since I started to write, it has grown quite dark. The lightning flares up. Irina just passed through the street-side courtyard to go to sleep. She said a bee stung her on the mouth. An unfinished coffin stands by the convent below. Irina climbed into it with Lev's children and said it was a boat.

The convent is located on a mountain; below is the city (sloboda) of Borisovka. There are three churches there, and the nuns go there for services. They descend the mountain heights in the evening with lanterns, since the descent is winding and follows the banks above the ravenous Vorskla river. Now dogs bark and songs of some kind are carried up from down there below, and fires twinkle in the distance. And now they are ringing the church bells again for the "Worthiness." [12] Soon the nuns' lanterns will twinkle in the black night as they travel up the mountain. I love to sit on the veranda to watch these forsaken souls pass by; here some come already, stepping with the heels of heavy boots and conversing in whispers. You can hardly tell them from the night. How did they get up here without lamps? . . .

20 August   Today I saw a nun who, so they say, is 105 years old.

22nd   In two days I am leaving. I have begun to miss An. painfully. At night I wake up and think of her, very disturbed. During the day her image

---

12 Part of the Orthodox service held when a new member of the clergy is ordained.

will suddenly appear before my eyes, for no evident reason, even when I'm looking at water flowing from a pipe.

The longer it has been since we parted, the stronger my memory of her. She somehow gathers around her all that does not belong to the material, to the everyday mundane. Here again there are two worlds; the illusory life-world of the day and the long night-world of inexpressible words and unfinished thoughts of her.

25 August

Today we leave. We wanted to find out something about the trains, when and where and what transfer and at what time we are arriving in Moscow. We went to the station, but it was impossible to find out anything there. The "one-armed guard" knows only the hours and minutes of the arrival and departure of the trains via Borisovka. The director of the station is out hunting, the head of the State Political Dept. is drinking beer at the bar next door, the cashier, although he isn't sleeping, drinking, or hunting, knows only what the one-armed guard knows. The railway-car coupler knew more than the others, but even he could only say that if the Borisovsky train weren't late, then it would meet with the Lgovsky train at Bryansk. "I myself have ridden it," added the coupler. "And did you run late?" we asked. "Ran late," he said and then he added, "It is always late," and waved his hand as if to say that not to run late in life was in general impossible, and that this was something one didn't talk about. So we are going as if to Alaska, knowing only that we leave from Borisovska Station at three in the morning.

Today is a clear cool day with a light wind from the northeast. My memories of An. are purer and lighter than they have been these past days.

From my travels this summer I've gotten a general impression of provincial Russia. Most of all from conversations in the country (leaving out the local nuns), which are about wolves, and in the towns and cities, about mad dogs. Rabies, according to statistical evidence, has reached unprecedented proportions, and moreover occurs throughout all of Russia. The whole way people complained about the wolves and told of all kinds of terrible things. Of political conversations the most witty were the religious and academic ones. With well-known reservations, it is possible to say that Russia is stricken by a struggle between the principles of faith and the principles of knowledge, precisely a struggle, because they confront each other.

It is material poverty, of course, that lies over all this, especially the lack of manufactured goods. In Borisovka, for instance, it was most difficult of all to obtain needles, tin ware, iron in general, roofing-iron in particular, paint, etc. And there are about 30,000 inhabitants here; in the outlying areas of Borisovka many hundreds of acres of forest (oak) have been cut down. Because of this, the Vorskla, once a splendid navigable river, has become just a ditch.

Of art—not a word; from no one, nowhere; it doesn't exist . . .

15 Sept.

Vile "jubilee" (Academy of Sciences) [13]

20 Sept.

A world view is above all, if you like, a method; and method is a matter of skill and habit.

Even in original and broad world views, habit plays a greater role than people think.

21 Sept.

O. Mandelshtam told me that at the jubilee ceremonies of the Academy of Science a certain English professor said: "A country that has a hotel (Hotel d'Europe[1]) like that cannot be entirely lost."

In any case one of them, either the professor or M., if he himself made this up, really hit the nail on the head. It wouldn't be possible to characterize all the vileness of that which was in the Academy of Sciences more precisely or more fully than that.

----

1) a separate hotel especially for guests of the Academy (actually a part of the hotel) [Punin's own note at the end of this entry]

24 Sept.

Life is so fragile and frightening that no state of anxiety with regard to it would be too much.

PICTURE

[front] "Portrait de David, par Lui-Même" (1794), Musée de Louvre
[back] To my little Nikolay on his birthday in remembrance of our work this summer and fall, 1925. "notre père Davide" Anna

14 November

This is what happened today.

An. (Akhm.) came to have dinner with me. It was around 5 o'clock; I was ill; no one was home. The two of us sat down to eat, the phone rang, it was for An.

13 Punin is referring to the jubilee celebration of the academy's founding in 1725. "Academy of Sciences" is written in another hand.

After two–three minutes she returns with her slippers in hand and a glowing look on her face and says that she is leaving to go visit the Zamyatins immediately. There was still soup she hadn't eaten in her bowl.

I realized that she was going to dinner and was terribly offended. (Lately our dinners have been poor due to the general poverty.)

An. went to get dressed, I went after her and said that I didn't want her to go. An. began to ask me to let her and produced various arguments, although she couldn't explain why she had to go precisely now (to dinner). We quarreled.

We argued for a long time. I don't have the words to express the pain, but now An. is sleeping here in the study, and we still haven't made up. How can she sleep when we haven't made up? . . .

She didn't go to the Zamyatins.[14]

22 November

Today I said to An.: "I often think now, what else has yet to happen, what kind of change must there be within, so that the thought of suicide becomes completely real and inescapable?"

"And I often think," says An., "how has it happened that I haven't already had the opportunity to resist suicide?"

"There, that's the way, that's it" . . . and we, smiling, moved on to another subject . . .

*14 February
1926*

I was at the Hermitage with An. We looked at the Italians, Flemish, and French drawings (an exhibition).

We went to "bow" to the Litta Madonna. We met Gaik Adonets (the editor of "Life of Art")—he said in a Georgian accent, "What an outrage the way everything is hung here. They don't understand a thing . . ."

18 February

Today An. didn't come to visit—this hasn't happened in a long time,[1] I didn't see her all day. I'm sitting alone, it is cold in the study (50 degrees) "and it is sad and painful."

---

1) Shileyko arrived from Moscow and is living with An., so I cannot go see her, and she is sick, she sent a note. [Punin's own note]

14 Akhmatova's note in the margin: "What kind of guy starts to complain when he himself is to blame?—Anna."

I have not held her hands today, nor seen her gray eyes . . .

All winter An. has helped me work, has read and translated French books . . .

It is thawing, the trees have turned black. This winter was persistent and severe. An. felt better because of the freezing cold, probably, she is sick today because of the thawing. How attractive and wondrous she is . . .

Miscalculations, discussions, exile of the Zinovevites—this has all been lived through, and there is more to come. Months and years of endurance. We thought up a good prison, one for everyone at once, and without bars.

Twelve o'clock; I'm still waiting, maybe she'll come.

19 Feb.

All night in my sleep I sensed that I hadn't seen her yesterday.

13 March

I returned today with An. from Moscow. Galya has found a new place, she is completely lost and joyless.

In Moscow I learned that Aseev, Pasternak, Selvinsky,* and Brik went to Trotsky to complain about how there is nowhere to get published. They're only publishing popular literature, and experimenters, they said, don't get published.

Trotsky had a conference with Voronsky,* Polonsky,* Osinsky,* Lezhnev, and the aforementioned on the matter.[15]

LETTER FROM GALYA AHRENS TO ANNA AKHMATOVA

Dear Anna Andreevna,

Forgive me for the thoughtless phrase I uttered, I don't think anything more than what I said, and don't be embarrassed to come because you thought that of our long acquaintance. You know me well enough. I realized that you were hurt when you refused to come to tea and then N. N. confirmed my supposition. If you believe me, then forget it, and come as always.

Greetings, Anna Ahrens [Galya]

20/V/26

15 All of these men tried to strike a middle ground in the debates of the 1920's on literature, arguing for a literature that was neither mere propaganda nor simply "the sum of its devices."

2 July 1926
on the little
boat

We are returning from the islands. Peace and quiet . . .
and what will be?—Anna

3 July 1926
on the little
boat

I swam behind the yacht club. Nikolay took a picture
of me in the water. All day together, in *windy* weather.
(Provincial architecture.) We are close!—Anna

the same day
and the same
place

An. is a wild sprite, God, she knows what she says,
and demands that I write like both Goncourts.—
K[oty] M[alchik]

Program minimum. Today is our first meeting with
the sun this year. [Akhmatova]

I watched how An. lay on a bench wondrous under
the sun with arms like bows. [Punin]

"That you bring song to the war
A flute sweet as a bullfinch"

(DERZHAVIN TO SUVOROV) [AKHMATOVA]
14 JULY 1926. MARBLE PALACE

NOTE

Nikolay!
You repeat to me every day that I keep you from working and obviously you don't wait to hear my reply that you, too, keep me from
working. This obviously is not worthy of your attention, and every
time I am so ashamed for you that I cannot say these words.
    Akhm.
21 July
Marble Palace

CONVERSATION BOOK

[no date]

Akuma, forgive me—I spoke poorly—but I cannot
agree for you to go abroad. [Punin]

We will not speak of it. I *want* to *believe* that you did
not want to hurt me so badly. Departures are neither
here nor there. A[khmatova]

Not true—I meant something else—not to hurt you, but that you secretly want to leave me—we must speak of this. M. [Zimmerman] is also in love with you. [Punin]

Twice today you said to me in front of others that I am a do-nothing and that I pretend to be sick when I should work. It is true and since you both work it is unpleasant for you to see me. It is a completely natural feeling. That's why I immediately forgave you this afternoon. But it pains me that you again repeated it in front of Luknitsky,* who, as you know, makes note of everything. We already made up this afternoon, yet in 2 hours you repeated the same words. [Akhmatova]

NOTE ON PLAIN PAPER FROM AKHMATOVA TO PUNIN

I went to Lyudmila's. If you don't have an evil heart, call me. You'd be amazed at it all. And you know, how hard it is to make it right. I feel dark and frightened.—A.

4 November 1931 [16]

I stoked the stove.

---

16 The year 1931 is written in with a different pencil, presumably at a later date.

NOTEBOOK TEN
1936

Introduction Punin's second imprisonment and release. Stalinist terror begins.
Akhmatova leaves Punin. Akhmatova's relationship with Vladimir
Garshin.[1]

29 July '36
Sheremetev House

I haven't written for about three years. What I did write has not been
preserved.

I am old. Today I took Irina and Galya to Astrakhan. Alone. For
a month I lived with Irina in Razliv—we became friends.

An. is not here. At the end of June she left Moscow to see
Shervinsky*—and since then I haven't heard anything about her.

I was in prison. An. wrote Stalin; Stalin ordered me released. That
was in the fall.

1   Notebook Ten is the last diary in the collection held at the Harry Ransom Humanities
Center at the University of Texas at Austin. It contains very few entries; considering that
the year was 1936, this relative silence makes what is written all the more ominous. Eleven
years had passed since the entries in Notebook Nine. During these years Anna Akhmatova
moved into Sheremetev House to live with Punin. Punin's wife, Galya Ahrens, and Irina
also lived in the apartment in the rooms next to them. This is usually attributed to the
lack of housing, but it is apparent from Punin's later diaries that his wife remained a very
important part of his life and that she never really left him. As Akhmatova maintained
their relationship until his death, so Punin's relationship with his wife did not end until
her death in 1943.

By 1936, Joseph Stalin's power had been consolidated and the Five Year Plans, which
called for rapid industrialization, collectivization of agriculture, and the liquidation of
kulaks (farmers who had flourished in the relative freedom of the years of the New Economic Policy), were in full swing. Purges of the Party ranks and arrests and repression of
"fellow travelers" (those who sympathized with the Party, but were not members) began.
Collectivization was fiercely resisted: peasants burned their crops and slaughtered their
animals rather than giving them up to the government. The result was famine. For many
artists and writers life had become unbearable. The preeminent poet of the revolution,
Vladimir Mayakovsky, committed suicide in 1930. Akhmatova's friend and fellow poet
Osip Mandelshtam was arrested in 1934, while Akhmatova was visiting. Akhmatova's son,
Lev Gumilev, was arrested briefly in 1933 and then again in October 1935. Nikolay Punin
was also arrested at this time. Gumilev said that students from families of the intelligentsia were being arrested and accused of being part of anti-Soviet organizations. Punin
was also accused of being the head of one of these organizations.

Love has abated, become dull, but hasn't gone. Lately I miss An. with the same familiar pain. I convinced myself it was not out of love, but from spite. I lied. It is her, still the same. I looked over her pictures again—no, they don't look like her. She's not here, she's not here with me.

30 July '36

I simply awoke and realized that An. had taken away all the letters and telegrams she had written me in all these years, I also determined that Lev secretly (from me), obviously by her instruction, took the leather notebook in which An. wrote poems from my wardrobe, and, leaving on business, took them to An., so I wouldn't know.

I want to tear out all my ribs from the pain.

An. has won this fifteen-year war.

30th— afternoon

There is a physical quality to this pain. Each time I smoke it gets worse.

31 July (last day of July) "Razliv"

People look like old stage props put up in the shed of a provincial theater.

Yesterday I sent her a second telegram return receipt requested: "Anya, please telegraph me, tell me how you are, I sent money" (I sent money); I also sent the letter: "Anya, it is frightening that you are silent. I don't want anything from you. I love you."

When you suffer, all things seem different.

Hamletism.

Evening, wind, dacha. There is little desire for activity because of this, and you become a graphomaniac.

12 o'clock at night; dacha, wind, night.

> *"I drink for my destroyed home,*
> *For this, my evil life . . ."*[2]

5 August

On the first I decided to go after her to Moscow. I should have left on the evening of the second; on the morning of the second she arrived. Now we are living together at the dacha in Razliv. She was so happy and thankful that I waited for her.

(She had received neither the telegram nor the money.)

2 September

Evil days. Everyone has already returned to the city. "Winter" has begun.

2 Lines from Akhmatova's poem "The Last Toast" (1934).

6 October	This year there is an early cold autumn. Today it is thirty-seven degrees above freezing, like all the days before. I am sitting alone—this so rarely happens.

I don't know anything about friends or enemies. They have scattered around the world; each on his own road, as it probably always happens in old age.

I know many live with the desire to guard against life: some shrink away into invisibility, others, not expecting the blows, are hit themselves. No one is friends with life. And nothing has come of it for me. So the result will come. Death is terrible. |
| *1 August.*
Fontanka | It's as it was in prison: in turn there was extreme despair, then baseless hope. |
| *30 November* | Yesterday I humbly celebrated my forty-eighth birthday. Sasha wasn't there.[3] He is in Murmansk; he left to work a bit.

The 8th Special Congress is in session; a new constitution.

They shot Largo Cabalero's son.

Today I saw the film "Chapaev" with Genya [Evgeny] Ahrens.*
Liked it.

Today snow fell and lies in a thin layer; it isn't cold.

All day I worked on a lecture, "Spanish Art."

I am writing a history of the Academy's 20 years. |
| *16 February* | Anya!

"Cult of the weak."

I love you. |
| *10 September*
1937 | I was in Moscow (after the Volga)—only frightened eyes. I have never seen it that way. In one department we were sitting and talking about various things, like art, and suddenly one of us dreamily says: "Olga Konstantinovna, someone should organize a wintering for ten years in Africa."

What was he thinking?

Irina Shchegoleva, the wife of Altman, herself says:

"Ilyushka Zilbershtein hates me so much that he promised to send a man to me who would infect me with syphilis."

She said this to Altman while he was lying ill and she was feeding him orange compote. |

3   Punin's brother Aleksandr.

12 Sept.	How, in what way, do people know that one or another person is a genius?
	Doesn't the ability to recognize this justify mankind?
	Out of a hundred million people—a million are party members. Why not everyone?
20 Sept.	An unusually long summer (warm). April was hot. We are still sleeping with the windows open.

—(on a completely different subject)

As soon as I arrived home, I learned that Professor Garshin had been to see Anya. A while later Anya tells me a not completely decent anecdote.

I say suspiciously:

"Did Garshin tell you that?"

Anya, quick-wittedly:

"No, a stranger on the tram."

—(on another completely different subject)

Soon our two lives will add up to a century.

ENCLOSURE [NO DATE]

"Agreement" written by Igor Ahrens*[4]

Agreement

I, the undersigned, pledge that for every "excellent" grade I will pay Igor Ahrens 5 rubles. For a grade of "good" in history, zoology, geography Igor will pay me 2 rubles, and for the other subjects, I will pay him 2 rubles for a "good" grade. For anything so-so Igor pays me 50 kopecks. For any grade of "poor," I will take half of the money earned by him in the week, for the pay paid out in the course of 5 school days. For a grade of "very poor" *all* will be liquidated.

Signature: Ahrens:

Signature of Punin: [not signed]

See the Glossary.

LATE MATERIALS FROM THE PUNIN DIARIES

1941–1952

Introduction   *After five years, the diary again. The siege of Leningrad. Punin's*
third wife, Martha Golubeva. Evacuation with Galya, Irina, and
granddaughter Anna to Tashkent. Life in Tashkent. Return to
Leningrad. Punin's third arrest and exile to the Siberian labor camp
in Abez. Correspondence from camp. Death of Punin.

DIARY—1941[1]

August 26   For more than two months there has been war. I had forgotten that I
could keep a journal. Today Tika reminded me of this and said that I
had forgotten because I am not living on the edge.[2] She is constantly
saying that I, like many, am on the tail end of time; the war goes straight
through my head. "Write," she said, "even so-so writing vindicates time.
What is happening is so great that there is no sense in trying to rise
above it, it is simply not possible; either you *are* above it, and then your
efforts are unnecessary, or they are fruitless." And I said: "Yes." And now
I am sorry that I didn't keep a diary from the first day of the war. So
much has passed that it isn't possible to resurrect it or even to discern
what was real from that which was so-called "smoldering trash." "Smoldering trash" is that nervous gossip, simply "hysterics," which reigned
and still reigns around us. Everyone, for example, calculates five times
a day—because the sums are always different—how much more macaroni they can receive, or meat, or kielbasa, according to their ration.

1   The Non-Aggression Pact of August 1939 between the Soviet Union and Nazi Germany
unleashed the war. According to the pact, Russia acquired parts of Poland and the Car-
pathian Ukraine. Stalin was much criticized later by Western historians for trusting
Hitler and not using the time between the pact and Hitler's invasion of Russia in 1941
wisely. The Great Purges of 1936–1938 had decimated the officers' corps and probably
contributed to Russian losses when Hitler violated the pact and invaded Russia on
June 22, 1941. Leningrad was completely encircled by the German army by September
of the same year except for a single lifeline across Lake Ladoga which was kept open
throughout the siege. It was this passageway to safety that the Punins took when they
were evacuated to Samarkand.

2   "Tika" is the nickname for Martha Golubeva.

All that this calculation can in general tell us is that the ration system is stupidly set up. But what are these rations to us, who have lived through the starvation of the revolution, through the starvation of collectivization, through the starvation of the provinces, what is this macaroni and this meat? Today one man said equitably: "In reality they've been inviting us to die quickly for the past twenty-five years." Many have died, death draws near, as near as it can. Why should we think of it, since it is thinking of us so earnestly? And still the "smoldering trash" suffocates our souls. And the war goes on, turning the world inside out. The war doesn't interest me; war is a boring thing, but still it goes on, and like the world, it turns me inside out. And so I shake all over from trepidation, from curiosity, from fear of being killed.

So here I sit at my writing table. The windows are pasted with black paper, the lamp burns. It is fall, but it is still warm in the apartment. Beyond the windows it is quiet. From 10 o'clock on you can't go out, and this silence beyond the windows is audible. Tika is in the kitchen ironing under the blue light of a lampshade made from wallpaper, and she is bathed in the soft rays of this blue light. Today they announced that our troops abandoned Novgorod. We knew about this three days ago. Today we learned that our troops abandoned Vyborg.[3] The ring is closing. But beyond the windows it is quiet. There were two air raids; one just before evening. Three days ago we could hear the cannonade, but now it's quiet. Flies buzz around the lamp, and it is completely quiet at home, in this our "slightly crazy" home.

I sit and think, "How many souls have gone to heaven in these two months?" True, it's not a very fruitful thought, but I often think about it, especially as night falls, gazing at the greenish light of the sky between gray autumn clouds. And what else does a silent man have to think about under this thunder of war? Once, in my youth, I had wanted at some time to enumerate in my diary each thing that was standing on my writing table, so that I would remember it later. When I read that entry, I don't remember anything. And now, too, I want to recount everything that surrounds me, but not from a desire to "remember it later" (there isn't going to be any "later"), but from a sense that we are perishing. A large majority of us will perish, and that means each of us, each one of us thinks, "But maybe not me." True, the morose think, "It will be me." But some here and some there will perish; precisely who, we don't know. There is something in all this

---

3   The losses at Novgorod, south of Leningrad, and Vyborg, to the north on the Karelian Isthmus, meant that the city was surrounded.

that resembles the way we lived in the "days of Ezhovshchina," when each person thought, "Tomorrow, maybe it'll be me." And for so very many it was.

Today I also went to the Academy. There is confusion and chaos. They are evacuating. They strongly tried to convince me to go. I would go; it's to Samarkand. But that would mean to get drawn into the war. No, I'm not going. It is better to "chase windmills" while it's still possible. The lamp burns. It is quiet. Lord, comfort the souls ascending to heaven.

Not long ago I said to someone, "Now there are two frightening things: war and evacuation. But of the two, evacuation is the more frightening." It's true, this is just a saying. But without a doubt evacuation is "smoldering trash." Why didn't anyone evacuate us in the "days of the Ezhovshchina"? It was just as frightening then.

Much has passed since the beginning of the war. Passion rushed through the city like a river overflowing its banks. People ran and fell. Now starvation is setting in. Soon the time will come when no one will feed us. No one is thinking of God yet; they have just begun to talk of the church bells. Much is yet to come.

28 August,
morning

It's raining. Fall. The evacuation has been halted for eight days, and it is quiet. We remember the first impressions of the war. Well, of course the radio: Molotov's speech, about which A. A. (Anya), who ran in with disheveled hair (graying) in a black silk Chinese robe, told us.[4] And the first feeling of minor terror at home. And then the paper strips, mostly crisscrossed, pasted to the windows. The house became lighter from these pastings, decorative, as if the whole was built with trellises. Now we no longer notice this. Much has turned topsy-turvy.

6 September

Yet another day has passed. Yesterday lectures at the Academy began. The audience is sitting on beds, because the cots for some kind of military section have been set up in the auditorium . . . Yesterday all day the cannonade was audible. By evening shooting had begun around the city. Shooting today too, until evening, so that every 15–20 minutes you'd hear a shot. They say that somewhere, on Glazovaya St., two stories were demolished. It was long-range, but from where, no one knows. One also hears that there are landings everywhere in the suburbs. The circle is fragile and therefore the mood, mainly among those

---

4 On Sunday, June 22, 1941, at noon Foreign Commissar Vyacheslav Molotov made a radio speech to all Russians informing them that the war had started.

being evacuated, wavers. They still hope to break through the ring. Everything from the front is the same: innumerable symptoms of break-down. Yesterday I saw two of our students near Gatchina—sponges; they praise the marine units and "curse" the command. There is much hysteria. But now it is so calm, as if nothing were happening.

12 September Well, so this is how life goes! I haven't written in so many days because there was nowhere to write. The first air raid was on the evening of the 8th. It began around 11 P.M. Malayka, Galya, Tika, and I were at home.[5] We didn't leave the apartment. It still didn't seem terrifying. It began right after the alarm. We put out the lights and stood at the open window. The bomber droned with a high pitch intermittently, the search-lights swept past, red rocket flares burned here, then there—in a word, just as it's supposed to be. But then the whistle came, loud and piercing, at first it grew stronger, as if getting closer to us, then began to get quieter, and suddenly a terrible crash, thunder, in a few seconds—the second whistle and again crash and rumble, then a little further the third time it crashed, thundered, and rumbled. The explosions of the anti-aircraft guns came from further off, heading toward the north. All of this in the course of a few minutes. We were silent. It became clear, that this was not simply a warning, like the dozens before, but a raid, and these were the first bombs. The anti-aircraft guns fell silent around 12 o'clock, about 1 A.M. there was an all-clear signal. The moon shone. It was quiet in the garden.

The next morning Ira returned from duty at the civil defense and announced that one of the bombs had fallen on Fontanka 22. This was Tika's house, but I called Tika at the station (that day she was on duty at the civil defense) from the Academy (our phone had been taken away). "Yes," she said, "the ceilings fell in, and the building will proba-bly collapse. Papa asked us to come help him move things out."

That day there were endless warnings, and I only made it to Fontanka by 6 o'clock. In front of the entrance opposite Tika's window was a crater. Asphalt in huge cracks, both floors had come off the foun-dation, the corners were slanting, and the central section stuck out. Cracks were everywhere. I went into the apartment. Andrey Andreevich (Tika's father) closed his trunks and carried them onto a truck. Every-thing inside was destroyed. The cupboards lay on the floor, and every-where there were shards of dishes and glass among pieces of the fallen ceiling and cornices. The clock had stopped at a quarter to twelve.

5 Malayka is a nickname for Punin's granddaughter, Anna Kaminskaya.

The sirens rang . . .

I interrupted this entry yesterday because of the warnings. In a word, home has ceased to exist here. "My home is now on the horizon," Tika said later.

Since that day we have spent all our free hours dragging Tika's remaining things to my apartment. What can I say, darkly remembering my life, but that it pleased me now that few possessions had come my way. With each item, her past arrived here.

Last night was comparatively calm, a few bombs fell relatively far off. 10 to 11 at night was the most (so far!) terrible. Now after the warning the anti-aircraft guns over our heads thundered so strongly that we didn't stay in the apartment and went down below into the stairwell— Tika, Ira, Malayka, and I. There were terrible blasts. The bombs fell one right after another close to our house. When the third fell, I was upstairs. I had gone up to turn out the light in the corridor. I had just shut the door when I heard that whistle and then the thunder. It seemed to me that the whole apartment shook. They thought the same downstairs and discussed what had fallen in the rooms.

I write, but my hands are shaking; around the city they are shooting long-range. Today they took Duderhof, Taytsi, and Krasnoe Selo.[6] It is now 5:55. The rumble and falling shells in our region can be heard. Just now, I think, one fell on Liteyny Boulevard. I am alone at home, waiting for Tika.

16 September. Night.

Quiet. I am alone. Ira is sleeping. Galya and Tika are on civil defense duty. I went to the Academy. There on Vasilevsky Island it is alarming. Smaller ships have entered the Neva and have moored on the bank across from the Academy. During the afternoon there was a warning siren, the students saw how a downed German plane fell into the Neva. In the region of the Finland Station they dropped pamphlets and called for us to surrender the city. This place was surrounded by a strong detail of militia. That's how afraid they are.

I went by the Hermitage to get a permit for me, Ira, and Tika to go to the bomb shelter during street fighting. I don't really believe that it will be intense. As far as I can make out, the army is divided and almost cut off from the city. There would be no one to fight in the city. The communists won't fight. But it is possible there might be shooting and fires. Besides, much is still possible.

And so in the face of all this I can't "be myself," and just can't get it

---

6   Duderhof, Taytsi, and Krasnoe Selo are small towns just beyond the Leningrad city limits.

together. It's not that I have lost my head, but I am living in the fuss of life, not creatively or on the heights. I don't have the strength for that. And if they kill me now, or in a few days, I will not rise into the ether to love and peace. I will stand there, such as I was in my everyday life: greedy and aimless, even a little sensation-prone and gossipy. I have not grown tired of life, yet I have not grown wiser; and I have not grasped it, have not learned to view it with that unboundedness, which alone can give the true sense of relationships . . .

I just thought: if the churches were open, and thousands prayed, most likely, with tears, in the twinkling twilight, how much less palpable this cold iron matter in which we live would be.

25 September

After that terrible daytime bombing raid of the 19th the city was again shot up with shrapnel. There were many victims. There had been a lineup waiting for graves since evening. They go by number, like at the ticket counters during the season when everyone leaves town in the spring. The bodies are taken in carts to the graveyard. The ration of bread is 500 grams a day; there is nothing in the markets. Some people I hardly recognize, they have grown so thin. Many have aged: having grown withered and gray. It will soon be a month since we were surrounded. What are "they" hoping for, why don't they surrender the city? The Germans repeatedly dropped fliers, announcing that the Soviet Army was no longer near Leningrad, that the city was surrounded, and they are calling on the inhabitants to demand that the command surrender the city.

Evening,
11 o'clock

An hour ago there was a short "air raid"; now it is calm. Sasha (my brother) came by and told us that there was a new ultimatum with the threat that in the event of refusal they would renew bombing on the 26th, that is, tomorrow. It is terrible and one doesn't want to believe it. In the afternoon Garshin came by and announced that An. is leaving Leningrad the day after tomorrow. An. had already left here long ago, and lately lived with Tomashevsky* in the Writers' Union building, where there is a bomb shelter. She is very frightened of the bombing raids, in general of it all. Having announced this, Garshin put his hand on my shoulder, began to cry, and said: "Well, there it is, N. N., so yet another period of our life is ending." He was depressed. Through him I gave a note to An.: "Hello, Anya, will we see each other again or not? Forgive me. Just be calm.—the former K. M." When I learned of An.'s departure, I didn't give it any meaning, just as I don't give meaning to anything that is happening now, but it still seems to me that this is all by chance and temporary. But because of Garshin's words it's as if I woke up; perhaps we really will never see each other again, absolutely never, and this is not by chance or temporary. It's strange to me that Anya is so afraid: I am so used to hearing about death from her, about her desire for death. But now, when it is so easy and simple to die? Well, let her fly off, then! If only she gets there.

Suddenly and quickly all that existed before the war is coming to an end.

Already the eleventh! Again I was wrong. The city stands, and there is even the feeling that it won't be taken in the coming weeks. Something happened at the front. In particular, I no longer see the same number of deserters, who had flooded the city two weeks ago. If it weren't for the daily air raids, primarily in the evenings immediately after sunset, it would be possible to live and work. We are starving a little, but that can be endured.

I have become afraid of the evening raids. Around 7 P.M. a light nervous trembling comes over me. I wait, and I wait in such a way that I can't do anything or even think. Usually in these cases I play solitaire and get nervous if it doesn't come out. I listen closely, notice every sound, sometimes I shudder from some kind of incidental noise which has nothing to do with the sounds of bombing and air raids. There it is finally, the siren. And I become more relaxed; then again there is great tension. It flies, buzzes for a long time or intermittently, then falls silent—it is probably diving. Then the pilot—a man with a German face, perhaps has already pressed the pedal. At this moment the anti-aircraft guns begin to rumble and now there will be the whistle, and the bomb is flying and falling—it never seems to be falling directly on you, but right by you, or into the apartment where you live—and you are surprised that there is no whistle, but the plane again buzzes with its slow, assuredly calm sound and dies out somewhere in the distance. It flew past. It's quiet; then again it buzzes, and again the same. Usually during the evening raids we go out into the "trench" in the garden, but there it is the same, only the building in which you are living doesn't shake. Lately I have begun to go to the bomb shelter at the Hermitage (Winter Palace). There it is almost inaudible. The anti-aircraft guns are barely audible and only if a bomb lands close by can the explosion be heard, and then the floor shakes. There I can catch a bit of sleep, for some reason more secure that there's no danger, although no one knows whether the Rastrelli arches will hold.

15 October | Snow fell. How early. I saw it in the morning through the little window of the lavatory at the Academy where I spent the night. It fell and is staying; 28 degrees and clear. There was no bombing last night and we slept in turns of two and a half hours each. And now it is quiet. Just this minute two fighters noisily went over the garden, and again it is quiet. They stoked the fire, in the room it is 52 degrees. Cozy. Ira is making dinner. All of this against the background of the war. Mariopol has been abandoned, the battle is heading in the direction of Tver. They have gone around Moscow.

This snow is so beautiful, this day is so beautiful in its fragility. "This is time," says Tika, "but war is space, which becomes time only in the past." "Space which becomes time immediately is beautiful," she said. Today I have been praying all morning; I am not speaking, I am praying silently, in my heart. And it is just as silent as the snow.

Every evening, gathering up food for the bomb shelter and leaving, I think: will I see these things and these rooms again? Perhaps they will no longer exist, perhaps I won't.

Yesterday a postcard came from Pavlovich in Moscow in A. A.'s name, with the news that Marina Tsvetaeva ended her life.

22 October | And now old age is approaching. I go to meet it in the fantastic space of war. I am alone in the world and yet at the same time not alone. She is near—the strict guard of my life. Before her steadfastness I often feel like a false little boy and I remember, I see, how impurely I live. If I weren't so insignificant, I would right much in my life through her. But I am traitorous, weak, and fickle. She often cries bloody tears that I am imperfect to such an extent.

I love the world and I still want to live, I love the world as it is. I sense it and these spaces of the air, and the souls and this dust on the things on my table. I love you and I sense you so clearly in myself and myself in your boundlessness. Happiness, and it is happiness to such an imperfect, such an empty and criminally shallow person. In what peace the universe still lives.

20 November | Another month has passed. There isn't enough time to write. On the 6th a bomb fell across from us, into the theater. We are left without glass in the windows. We replaced the glass with plywood. There is still firewood. Temperatures in the 40s and 50s. It is tolerable. Starvation. In essence there aren't words to describe it, there aren't enough words. They bomb us every night. The raids were especially heavy at night from the 6th to the 8th. They can't bury them all. Torn-up bodies lay waiting to be buried at the cemeteries for 8 days. For the digging of the graves they are demanding bread—200–400 grams. The ration now is: 1st category—250, 2nd—125 grams. My body is weakening. I see poorly. I am forgetting things. I forget names, the most well-known facts. I am still eating a good dinner at the "House of Scholars." It is terrible for Ira and Anka. There is nothing left for them to eat. There is no grain. There hasn't been meat for over ten days.

Sasha came by. Paralyzed by fear and confusion. Yes, there are no words to describe it. But all the same I want to say something, to find the words for this. Nothing expresses things as they are. Gunfire. And we have become accustomed to it; we don't even think about it. If there was just a little respite, perhaps I could express this state of being, this starving body. I would describe the day, such as it is. How Ira goes from line to line during the shooting, how shrapnel bursts overhead in the streets, how she returns, not having gotten anything, and quietly says: "Papa, nothing was handed out, there is nothing." And how I answer her: "Well, that's O.K., we'll make it somehow." And so on.

My light, my world, that is what you are.

It's O.K., we'll make it somehow!

26 November   It's all the same; all the worse. Yesterday I became weak, and was so hungry that at night I took some bread and a piece of ham from Tika's box and ate, but even so I didn't sleep until morning and I couldn't drive away the recurring thought: how to get something to eat. I survived like this until this evening, until dinner at the "House of Scholars." They gave us soup made from oats and stewed cabbage. In the afternoon from twelve-thirty until four there was bombing; two high-explosive bombs fell not far off, that means that the apartment (in particular, the floor) shook. Later we learned that they fell near the Field of Mars.

In the evening there was another air raid warning. I waited it out at my brother Lev's. They live significantly better than us. They are still feeding them, they have some kind of provisions, for example, tomatoes and rice. I sat with them, looked hungrily at the bread and the steaming bowl. Soon they will be flying out and I hope to move into their apartment. They have a large store of firewood, are on the first floor, and are closer to the "House of Scholars" and the Hermitage.

When the bombing is over the firing of grapeshot begins and there are many casualties from grapeshot. One acquaintance, the historian Rosenberg, told me during dinner that one of his worst impressions of the war is a puddle of blood and not far off in the snow a hand in a bloody white glove and a fur cuff. The shell had fallen on a line of people waiting for bread.

But maybe the starvation is even more terrible. Many are already falling in the streets and dying. Those who are responsible for elderly people and children are mainly the ones perishing. It is good to be on your own at such a time. One person can make it somehow. For the third day I stood for 7 hours to get "pastries" for Anichka (Malayka). You can get them at "Nord." They are not very sweet, but all the same they have flour, jam, cream, and, probably, eggs. Generally we aren't able to get what they give for ration cards, there isn't enough time in the day.

At night when I wake up, it is terrifying to think of what will be, mainly because I can't imagine anything. It seems it's too late to surrender the city, and it is so terribly difficult to fight. How many should have to die for the city to capitulate?

They are still giving us electricity, although with interruptions. There is not enough fuel to bring products to the stores.

To the north the cannonade rumbles. It is quiet at home. Ira is sleeping although it isn't very warm. If I could only get a good sleep. It would be easier in the morning. But you still await the bombing; there is something mystical in nighttime bombings. How terrible they are!

There, as the gunfire rumbles, the building and earth shake. 10 o'clock. Today I am relatively full. Because we got a little lard and I fried myself a piece of bread.

I am no longer giving lectures, I can't any longer. There could be some trouble as a result, but I can't.

13 December
For a long time I have wanted to write De profundis—tonight, starving, I thought about this topic.

De profundis clamavi: Lord, save us . . . We are perishing. But His Greatness is as implacable as the Soviet power is unbending. It is not so important to it, having 150 million [people], to lose 3 of them. His Greatness, resting in the heavens, does not value earthly life as we do. We are perishing. I am writing with a cold numb hand. Some ten days ago, in the morning, I felt a coldness in my body; it wasn't that my body was cold, because it was still warm in the room. It was the first touch of death. We are living in the frozen and starving city, ourselves abandoned and starving. I can't recall the snows ever falling in such abundance. The whole city is completely covered in snowdrifts like a shroud. It is pure, because the factories aren't operating, and it is rare that smoke rises from the chimneys over the houses. The days are clear, and travel might be easy, but the city is buried like the provinces, white and crackling.

The trams haven't run for five days. In a huge majority of the regions there is no electricity. In many buildings the plumbing has frozen. They carry the bodies in plain caskets on sleighs and bury them in mass graves. The courtyards of the hospitals are heaped with bodies, and there's no one to bury them. It has been over a week since there was an air raid, but there are gaping holes in every building on every street — a reminder of the most terrible events. For a long time there hung an arm up to the elbow, attached by someone to the fence of the garden of one of the destroyed buildings. Dark crowds of people walk past with faces swollen and earthlike.

And everything is simple, no one says anything particular. They don't talk about anything besides ration cards, and also about how they are being evacuated. They simply suffer and probably think like I do: maybe it's not my turn yet.

At night I feel the loneliness most of all and the senselessness of petitions and prayers, and sometimes I cry quietly. I think that each of us quietly cries if only once every twenty-four hours; some at night, like me, others, perhaps, during the day. And there is no salvation. And one can't even be imagined, unless you give in to daydreams. "We turned our backs on Him," I think, "and He on us." And I know that this means to give in to dreams. "Miserere," I mumble, and add — there it is, "dies irae."

Lord, save us.

LETTER FROM N. N. PUNIN TO A. AKHMATOVA[7]

14 April '42

Greetings, Anichka,

I am endlessly grateful for your attention and I am touched; and it is undeserved. I am still in the hospital, not so much because I am ill, but because it is better here than on my own: there is a soft bed, and

---

7   Punin wrote to Akhmatova from a hospital in Samarkand after he had been evacuated from Leningrad along with his wife Galya, daughter Irina, and granddaughter Anna. Akhmatova, who had been evacuated a year earlier, came from Tashkent to visit him. Martha "Tika" Golubeva was not able to join them until much later. Akhmatova was apparently very touched by this letter and showed it to many people. Family friends Emma Gershtein and Nina Olshevskaya-Ardova discussed Punin and Akhmatova; Gershtein notes in her memoirs that Nina felt Akhmatova loved Punin most of all: "Nina continued: 'Punin was very much in love with her. I'm not even speaking about his letter from Samarkand, the one she was so proud of and showed to so many people. But what happened to the note he sent her from prison camp? I saw it myself. Anna Andreevna showed it to me. It was on a scrap of wrapping paper. He wrote that she was his greatest love. I remember one sentence especially: "We had the same opinion about everything"'" (from Konstantin Polivanov, ed., and Patricia Beriozkina, trans., *Anna Akhmatova and Her Circle* [Fayetteville: University of Arkansas Press, 1994], pp. 151–152).

they feed me; although it is not great, it is free. And peaceful. I am still not completely strong, but all the same I feel alive and I rejoice in the sunny days and the quietly unfolding spring. I look and I think: I am alive. The understanding that I have remained alive brings me to a state of ecstasy, and I call it the feeling of happiness. Moreover, when I was dying, that is, when I knew for sure that I was going to die (this was on Petrovsky Island at the Golubevs', where we had moved for a time because it seemed that the only warm room in Leningrad was there), I also felt ecstasy and happiness. And it was precisely then that I thought a lot about you. I thought about you because the spiritual tension I was experiencing then (as I already mentioned to you in my note) was something like the feeling I had in the '20's when I was with you. It seems to me that for the first time I understood you so completely and clearly, precisely because it was absolutely unselfishly; that is, I did not count on seeing you ever again; it was really my meeting with and farewell before death. And it seemed to me then that there was no one whose life could be so whole and complete as yours. From your first poems of youth (the glove with the left hand) to your prophetic murmuring along with the rumble of your poem.[8] Then I thought, this whole, in its volition—and this seemed particularly valuable to me— was still involuntary; that is, inevitable, and didn't seem to depend on you at all. I can't put into words now everything that I thought then, but a lot of what I didn't forgive in you rose before me as not just forgiven, but even, perhaps, as the most beautiful. You know that many judge you because of Lev, but then it was so clear to me that you made the clearest and doubtless best choice that you had. (I am speaking of Bezhetsk.)[9] And Lev would not be what he is now, if he had not had that Bezhetsk childhood. (I thought a lot about Lev, but I'll tell you about that some other time—I am guilty before him.) In your life there is a strength, as if it had been carved into stone, in one stroke, by a very experienced hand. I remember that all this filled me with joy and with a completely extraordinary meditative feeling, not a sentimental emotion, but as if I were standing at Heaven's gate; a lot of what I was feeling seemed straight out of the "Divine Comedy." And I rejoiced not so much for you, as for the universe, because I sensed that from all of this there wasn't necessarily personal immortality, but there was immortal-

8   "The glove with the left hand" refers to Akhmatova's 1911 poem "The Song of the Last Meeting" from her first collection *Evening*, and "the rumble of your poem" undoubtedly refers to Akhmatova's great later work *Poem without a Hero,* which she began in the forties and continued to work on into the 1960's.

9   Akhmatova and Gumilev's son Lev was raised by his paternal grandmother on the family estate in Bezhetsk.

ity. This feeling was especially strong. It was not so terrible to die; that is, I didn't have any aspirations personally to live, or to be preserved after death. For some reason I wasn't at all interested in this, as I was in the fact that the Immortal exists, and I am part of it, and that was so beautiful and so majestic. You seemed to me then, and now too, to be the highest expression of the Immortal that I had come upon in life. In the hospital I managed to reread Dostoevsky's *Devils*. As always, I found it difficult and didn't like it, but at the end of the novel, like a golden dawn amidst the terrible and improbable darkness, are these words: "A single everlasting thought, that something endlessly fairer and happier than myself exists, completely filled me with a boundless emotion—and glory—oh, no matter who I am, or what I have done, it is much more necessary than personal happiness for a man to know and to believe every moment that somewhere there is already complete and peaceful happiness, for all and for everything . . ." and so on. These words are almost a perfect expression of what I was feeling then. Precisely "glory"—precisely "peaceful happiness." And you were the expression of the "peaceful happiness of glory." But I have remained alive and I have preserved this feeling itself and a memory of it. I am so afraid of losing it and forgetting it now that I force myself not to, not to let that which has happened to so much of my life happen. You know how I am shallow, not making any effort, even worse, when destiny summoned, I lost the best of what she gave me. The sun, which I so love, supports me after that frozen hell and it is easy for me to keep that feeling of immortality before its sunny glory. And I am happy.

I am doing well here and it is nice in the hospital, my hand has almost come back to life. As you can see, I am already writing as I used to. True, there is a lot to worry about, how to get settled, how to feed oneself, but these things don't swallow me up as they did before. And I don't miss the things I left behind, except for a few, which I simply forgot to take out of haste.

On the train when I fell ill, I remembered Khlebnikov for some reason and I understood him as the most pure sound, the most pure voice of my time, and as a synthesis of that time, in relation to which Mayakovsky was something one-sided, just an incident. You are no single incident but for some reason I cannot correlate you with Khlebnikov and I still don't understand it.

Coming into Tashkent, I didn't expect to see you and I rejoiced to the point of tears, when you came, and even more, when I learned that the other day you were at the station again. Your attention to me is endless. In the telegram that Ira gave to me yesterday, you asked if there was anything you could send. I really want to come see you; but that won't be soon. I will stay here another week and then I'll have to find a room and get settled. If by then we haven't received any more evacuation money I will ask you to send some for the trip. But I also heard that you are getting ready to come to Samarkand and this would be wonderful. True, I would rather come see you, but one won't interfere with the other. Thank you for the telegram.

Anya, there is sun and clear sky and last night there were so many big stars, I can still see them, but in the north I couldn't see them for your eyes.

I am a little tired from writing. My letter has turned out long, and perhaps a little confused. Forgive me. I kiss your hands and again thank you for everything.

b. KM.[10]

DIARY — 1942

23 September

Again a diary, but for how long? And precisely now, when nothing is happening. We are sitting in Samarkand, time flies, but one day does not differ from another. In those last weeks of starvation in Leningrad I didn't write in my diary; yet just then it would have become interesting. My brother was dying and died; a dozen people with whom we were connected were dying and died. But I could not write—I was a starving dystrophic. And the ink froze and I could barely move from the bed to the chair. I wouldn't have survived if it hadn't been for the evacuation. So we have traveled thousands of kilometers. My memories of it are dim. I don't remember well how they began to feed us or how we kept going, traveling for more than a month. My memories of the last days of my stay in the Samarkand hospital and of my first day after leaving it are clearer. It was spring; the fruit trees had already bloomed and everything quickly became green.

I wrote two letters to An. from the hospital. She was in Tashkent and came to the train when we stopped there. She was kind and tender, as she never had been before, and I remember how I was drawn to her and thought a lot about her, and I forgave everything, and confessed everything, and how all this was connected to that feeling of immortality, which came and stayed with me when I was dying of starvation.

During the last weeks of starvation and on the road, and when I left the hospital, I was in a kind of ecstatic state and I was constantly emotional and in a state of constant joy that I was alive. I don't know if this was because of the spring and the sun, or because of starvation. When

10   "b. K.M." is probably "byvshii Koty Malchik," "your former pussycat."

we left Leningrad, spring was beginning. I don't remember Leningrad ever being so beautiful as during that fatal winter and that spring. It was silver-white, silent under the green sky, really like under a shroud. And the dead, most often wrapped (probably by their loved ones) in sheets, lay on the streets, and the soldiers of the air defense took them away on sheets of plywood. They hadn't buried anyone in graves or in cemeteries since November. The deceased were light and seemed like little children; the soldiers easily lifted them from the snow and placed them on the plywood, and they didn't bend, because they were frozen. They lay everywhere, especially in the morning. Probably people brought them out from their apartments at night, and put them wherever possible.

On the day of the evacuation, the morning of the 19th of February, I stood for a long time on the bank of the river by the Academy, and bade farewell to the cupola of St. Isaac's. They had scraped off the gilding (or painted over it) in the fall, and it darkened blue in the sun through the whitish darkness. The snow crunched underfoot, but in the sun it seemed to begin to melt. On that day, as I recall, they began to clear the snow off the streets for the first time. Groups of people, mostly women, wrapped in whatever they had, just something warm, people who looked like heavy sacks scraped the snow with shovels and carried it to the banks of the Neva on the same pieces of plywood that had carried the deceased. I remember well their sluggish and heavy movements, the way they walked, as we all walked along the Leningrad streets that winter—they were the movements of the exhausted.

Close to dusk we left in buses for the Finland Station. I carried Irina's daughter, Malaychka. There weren't enough cars in the train which they had gotten for us, in particular, there wasn't an 11th car, which was the one I was to ride. They packed us onto the train, and we stood waiting until the next day. In the evening there was an air raid; the first one after the long winter break. They had already begun to feed us there. I began to feel poorly from eating so much bread (they had given us enough for a few days). I remembered that a starving person can't eat a lot, and had already started to try to eat less, especially less bread. And then I remember our slow movement to Ladozhky (to Borisovaya Griva), the frozen trip in buses across the lake, and the terrible Khikharevka.

Our bus broke down within 5 kilometers of Khikharevka, and we began to freeze. 3 A.M., barracks in Khikharevka, wheat porridge, pain in the stomach, stool every hour, going wherever you can, soiled pants, dulled consciousness, bombing, fire in the barracks, things abandoned on the way, boarding the international train at night by the light of the glow of burning oil, a samovar and electric light.

Then it was all over; at dawn the train left. Lying on a soft seat semi-conscious, I heard the names of those who had died in Khikharevka. And from then on, day after day, week after week, we went and kept going, and it became warmer and warmer, and I rejoiced at the first flowers—they were irises—somewhere in Kazakhstan, and near Tashkent they brought a branch of blooming apricot in to me on the train and that is all I remember. Tika is in that other world, with the snow and the dead, and we, having been saved, are here on the platform in Samarkand.

The thing I remember most clearly from this trip, is how in Khikharevka I covered Malaychka's head with my hand as she cried when bombs fell all around, and I felt a joy, similar to happiness, that I was with her, and that I could protect her with my body. And then there was one night, somewhere near Novosibirsk, an unbearable pain, and how she became quiet after that, and how Galya gave me medicine. Beyond that, I also remember various bits: my first cup of sweet tea . . .

7 October

I thought about one of my mistakes. In the book about Lebedev, I used the "Wedding" by Picasso as a contrast and I asserted that Picasso was formalistic.[11] True, this is from Lebedev's own words, but it is still not a justification. All of Picasso's art is precisely from within, from the soul, precisely not formalistic. The fact that I could be so mistaken indicates insufficient understanding, shallowness, and impudence.

Picasso is time itself and life itself.

16 October

Tika isn't coming; there has been no more news from her. And if she does come, with what will I feed her? With what will I feed Irochka and Malayka in the coming year? The payment of wages is two liters of kerosene.

There are now quiet autumn days of incomparable beauty. The afternoons are so quiet that it's as if your eardrums had burst. The leaves are slowly yellowing or, more precisely, turning red; the earth is resting, warmed by the sun. At times it is wonderfully clear. Only in the mornings and evenings is there haze: a pearly haze in morning, just before sunset and immediately after the sun it is a stormy haze, similar to smoke.

11 N. N. Punin, *Russkii plakat 1917–1922: V. V. Lebedev* (Petrograd, 1922). The question of Picasso's influence on and place within Cubism and the history of art in general plagued Punin all his life. He wrote extensively on Picasso in articles on Tatlin and Cubism, often contrasting Picasso with Cézanne.

LETTER FROM N. N. PUNIN TO M. A. PUNINA[12]

26 October '42

Samarkand

Greetings, dear Miichka,

I am sorry that you didn't get the letter I sent you in August. It is so nice to read your letters; in them I can hear your happy ringing voice. Your move to Shuya and your description of your rooms delighted us. You write that "We're well fed," but we'd like to know what you're fed with. This interests us, first of all because before you glimmers the probability of all of us moving to your area, and second because the problems of food are looming large before us. We are also well fed, but only at the price of selling everything that we have. We smiled sadly at your account of the napkins, linens, and even coarse cloth on the table, because we haven't had those things for a long time, and we no longer have either Galya's winter coat, or mine, or Irina's good dress, and so on.

But we don't despair, we are satisfied with the warmth and the many wonders of our region. Yesterday was the first rain since May. It has gotten colder. The trees are red and the leaves are falling. They have covered the grape vines with earth for the winter, but the third harvest is still ripening. There are a lot of tomatoes and there are still potatoes yet to come. A lot of people began coming here only after the events in the south, and the prices have come close to European prices. Today we put on warm clothes for the first time, but three days ago it was hot and I didn't wear anything but a shirt, underpants, and pants. Now it is evening, and we are sitting around the oil lamp. Beyond the windows it looks just like snow—it is the moon. Our windows are small and square and set deep into the adobe walls. Anka is sleeping. It can't be said that she is exceedingly fat, but as before she loves bread and eats it constantly. She remembers you often, but it's hard to say exactly what she remembers. In any case, there is Mara and there is Miichka, and it appears they are two different people. She loves Miichka more, and she is waiting for her to come here. The classes at the Academy haven't begun yet, since the students are picking cotton, so I cheerfully bargain at the market and look at the mountains; they are still deep blue, they haven't yet been covered with snow. The winter will probably be diffi-

12   Marina Aleksandrovna (Mara) Punina (1923–1979) was Punin's niece. Lev Punin was Punin's brother, and Sarra was his wife. See the Glossary for a full account of the Punin family.

cult for us: there will be no free time, and nothing left to sell. We had wanted a reserve of flour for the winter, but this isn't going so well, Ira bakes something every day: and it is good, and it is eaten up, and our reserves are dwindling.

But no matter; we will probably make it until February and then "the little boy will come down from the mountain and will blow his horn 'du-du-du' and will bring everything" as Anya tells it.

Not long ago I received a letter from Lev Punin. It wasn't happy. Sarra often writes. As always they are barely making ends meet: but now there isn't anyone to send them money, they are out on their own. In general news comes to us from all ends of the earth, but there is no news from Leningrad. Martha Andreevna [Golubeva] hasn't come yet and it's been more than a month since we've heard a thing from her. Is everything working out well there?

I am reading a delightful book: André Antoine. "The Diaries of a Theater Director." [13] Recommend it to mama; it is rare to find such a simple, decent, and accurate book. Such is life.

I kiss you warmly, my dear little friend, live as you are, and everything will be wonderful.

Kiss mama and don't ever forget us. Your Kolenka.

DIARY—1943

There exist troubled secrets, and they come to pass. The soul has weight, like a flower. Now it is lighter on earth, the earth is lighter, but it's not at its normal weight.

When people who have had a difficult and arduous life are dying, it is easier for the people around them.

Space and time are the divine casing in which matter lives. Neither space nor time was created by God. They were within him. They are Him, they are His form. Space and time are the medium in which matter lives. It is not the soul that lives in the body; the body lives in the soul, that is, in space and time; the body is dying, but the soul remains immortal; the world is finite, like matter, but it is infinite in space and time.

Space has neither measure nor limit; however, it gains both measure

13 André Antoine (1858–1943) was a French theater director who revolutionized French staging and discovered most of the first generation of twentieth-century French playwrights. Antoine's great successes included the plays of such native dramatists as Eugène Brieux, Georges de Porto-Riche, and François de Curel and such foreign contemporaries as Gerhart Hauptmann, Henrik Ibsen, and Lev Tolstoy. Antoine was a film director in the early 1920's and remained a prominent literary figure and critic until his death.

and limit through matter; matter is commensurable, but time and space are not.

Space and time become known to the soul through rhythm. The soul hears the rhythm. The soul is everything, and everything is also the soul. The sense of rhythm, harmony, beauty, fairness, as well as many other feelings are characteristic of the soul . . .

The universe is open, revealed, and addressed, as something opened, to every living thing. It is time and space, the soul, the immortal; that is, the divine, or God . . .

It is impossible not to feel the soul, but it "realizes" itself in the body, through matter, that is, it senses itself in matter. It "realizes" itself within the bounds of matter, with the clarity and tangibility inherent in matter. But this "realization" is limited by matter itself, which is why the soul realizes the measure of matter and matter itself more than it does itself. It is because of this that its "realization" is so fragile and confused; because matter exposes itself, it, matter, "is realized" more intensely than the soul itself.

The soul, as a part of the universe, as a part of the divine that possesses time, space, intellect, feelings, and many other qualities, is by its nature a creative energy, creating, eternally creating. This is one of the basic characteristics of the divine. Life as applied to the soul implies creativity; for it to live means to create. The greater the capacity of matter to create, the more soul there exists in it and the more concentrated the solution of the soul in this piece of matter. By creating, the soul perfects matter. And thus the universe is perfected . . .

The soul, as such, cannot suffer in our ordinary sense of the word; it feels everything that accompanies creation. Its basic state is exultation. The soul suffers only in and from the imperfection of matter, which it strives to overcome, which it struggles with, which it surrounds, saturating it. This, however, is only one particular example of its existence . . .

LETTER FROM A. A. AKHMATOVA
TO IRINA NIKOLAEVNA PUNINA

22 August [1943]

Dear Irochka, there are still no shoes (there will be), but look at what a doll I got for your Anyuta.

Today it is exactly two years since we learned of the blockade of Leningrad and were even part of it, remember?

Don't get sick, study, read books (it's easy to give advice), and don't forget me. I am still in Tashkent.

Kisses. Akuma.

Cigarettes and greetings to your parents.

LETTER FROM A. A. AKHMATOVA TO N. N. PUNIN

Dear Nikolay Nikolaevich, this is Rafa Taktash. Talk to him and impart your wisdom to him. He wants to attend your Academy.

I have been fairly seriously ill since the 15th of Aug.

Eros—S/Zummer again beckons you to Tashkent.

Write me. Congratulations on our victories.

A.

1 Sept. 1943. Tashkent.

The boots will be coming any day.

DIARY—1943

1 September

At the end of August she came, and it became clear that I don't love her.[14] Everything I wrote a year ago was illusory feelings . . . Illusory feelings are common enough; many people live through them. She came with such a grudge against me and with bitterness at the death of Toshka that there was nothing to be saved. It seemed to me that she considered me to blame for his death.

It is difficult to determine which feelings are illusory and when. Death does this best of all.

On Saturday, the 28th, Galya died. She died quietly, I can say, in my arms.

Emptiness; it is possible to think that I lived for her, but it hasn't been so for a long time. A month ago I was in Tashkent, with Anya.[15] I quietly spent eight days in her home.

14 "She" refers to Martha Andreevna Golubeva (Tika). "Toshka" is Valentin Kazimirov, Martha's first husband.

15 Leonid Zykov suggests that this meeting may be referred to in Akhmatova's poem "Vstrecha," written on October 16, 1943, in Tashkent:

> *Like a fearful song's*
> *Cheerful refrain—*
> *His climbing the shaky stairs,*
> *Bridging the separation.*
> *Not I to him, but he to me—*
> *And there are doves at the window . . .*
> *And the yard is in ivy and you're in the raincoat*
> *   I told you to wear.*
> *Not he to me, but I to him—*
> *   Into the dark,*
> *   into the dark,*
> *   into the dark.*

(TRANSLATION FROM ROBERTA REEDER, ED.,
AND JUDITH HEMSCHEMEYER, TRANS.,
The Complete Poems of Anna Akhmatova, 2:214)

It would be good if life ended, but it isn't ending, because I still think about the future, about what I *will* do.

LETTER FROM N. N. PUNIN TO M. A. PUNINA

6 October '43

Samarkand

Miichka my light, we returned from the cemetery not long ago, today is the fortieth day [since Galya's death]. The days have become wondrously summerlike. It is already not so hot, and there still hasn't been any rain, and that's since May.

Galochka lies on a high dry hill, almost at the precipice, below flows the winding Siab—a small stream with bright green banks. There isn't any water in the cemetery itself, so nothing grows there. There is just yellowish sand, and you can't plant flowers. We had a requiem and decorated the grave site with thuya, zinnias, dahlias, and asters. The wind blew. It was lonely, but peaceful, and you could see far all around. There were the three of us and also a student, who had respected Galya. The majority have already begun to forget her.

And life goes on quickly and inexorably . . .

I was in Tashkent with Anna Andreevna. I spent 8 days with her in peace. She is O.K., she's holding up, and is still preparing to fly to Moscow, and yet never does. She was very tender and attentive. She promised Anya some shoes and underclothes. She'll probably send them in the near future. In reality, we are all almost naked; we have sold everything we could, and are taking advantage of the long warm season. What does a man need under the sun? Underwear, and a light shirt.

When I returned from Tashkent, Galya had already fallen ill. I arrived from the train around evening. She was ironing beyond the gates and nearby a large ram that she had just bought was tied. She was healthier before her illness than she ever had been in Leningrad, and she faded away in a month. On the eve of her death, she was emaciated, like death itself. Perhaps in Leningrad she could have been saved. But not here. Her heart was exhausted by night duty, by caffeine, and by the weight of the Samarkand work. Tell mama that lately, in spite of her great activity, she gave the impression of someone who was very tired of life and who was done with it. She was full of short-term wishes for today and the next day, but she didn't have any wishes for the future. She pined for Igor and for the two days before her death it was as if she saw him near her, as if he had come into the room. On the last night I sat in the chair by her until about 4 A.M.; she was weak, but didn't complain of anything. In the evening M. A. came in, and she smoked a cigarette with her and then said: "What bliss." [16] At four I lay down and fell asleep, exhausted after two nights. When I went to her at 8 A.M. she was unconscious and in agony. We injected her with everything that we could, camphor and caffeine, but it didn't help. Ira ran for the doctor; soon she returned with him, and M. A. came. Around 9 A.M. she stopped breathing. Soon she herself closed her eyes. There was fear for her life, but no one expected such a rapid end.

On the 9th day Olga Vasileva (now Schwede) was at the requiem with her daughter Tanya, and some of the ladies from the Academy. After the requiem, they drank tea with us and ate sweet rolls, baked by Ira, and pies, brought by Olga, with a lot of fruit. On the table, as today, there stood roses. Everyone got a rose as a memento. All of this is the Samarkand way, and it is probably amazing to you. Nevertheless, it is difficult to live.

Noisily, never tiring of chattering, Anka takes part in all of this. "Galya is sleeping, until the prince wakes her." We had made up this legend together, and she eagerly goes to the cemetery and then sings to the whole kishlak: [17] "Lord, have mercy . . ."

Three days ago, we got Zoya [Punina's] letter full of premonitions. Soon, probably, your answer to my postcard will come. Kiss mama and comfort her. Tell her that it is a warm starry night above the earth, and that as the priest said today, they are all looking down upon us, they rejoice, if things are well with us, and they are sad if things are poorly. I kiss you, my happy little flower (once Anya called you a strawberry) and I await your letters. Give mama a warm kiss and sit quietly with her and talk about Galochka.

Your uncle and friend N.

DIARY — 1944

24 February

I will not do anything else. On the 16th we got on the train. For four days and nights we sat in Samarkand due to every kind of problem. In Tashkent we stopped again; Anya (An.) came in a car. In a fur hat. Gray hair; kind. She gave Anichka a little dog, gave Ira soap, gave me cigarettes. As before (in the summer), she called Garshin "my husband." I don't really understand what that means. It was still a "comedee," as little Nika says. She says that she was "moved by Galya's death." I would like to know what kind of thoughts accompanied this feeling. "My hus-

16 "M. A." is Martha Andreevna Golubeva.
17 "Kishlak" is the name for a small village in Central Asia.

band," apparently so that I wouldn't count on anything. And I am not counting on anything. I remember her, like a "star." And that's all. "A dot," Nagel said.[18]

In "Anna's sphere" everything is in good form and everything is finished. There were no moans or gnawing finalities.

With Tika everything is difficult and complicated. She did not want to ride with me in a soft coupe and had our director completely confused. I don't know what she said to him. I explained it to him like this: "My wife? That's all in the Leningrad past," that's how I responded to his phrase: "I thought she was your . . ."—he didn't finish. This affair, moreover, has a past. It is our conversations, and they can't be written down. It was painful for me for the whole trip, and it was in pain that I returned to the snow.

As soon as I got into this snow, into Russia, melancholy enveloped me. The past arose: ice, death, loneliness, and emptiness; I thought about Galya. Now I remember Samarkand with longing, at times to the point of deep suffering. There I didn't feel the past so much.

I was in Moscow, met with Bruni, then with Shklovsky and Pasternak. Both Pasternak and Shklovsky still want to do something and evaluate everything that has happened from the point of view of what they are doing. And that's why I wrote: "I will not do anything." Shklovsky is a wit beyond measure. Pasternak drones on as before; he's gotten gray, but he's childlike in his soul. Bruni is living more seriously, more responsibly, and more quietly. I want to write down a lot of what was said by him. He rejects the 19th century, the French. There is no scale to it (to the 19th century). Everything was based on personal response. He spoke about Theophanis the Greek as if about something toward which he himself was striving.[19] I saw his Kazakh watercolors. They are good, but heavy, or else I don't understand anything. They don't evoke any purifying feelings in me. There, at his place, I saw Chekrygin. That is very powerful art. I feel him. He contradicts life. Gradually, when you stop looking at his art, the feelings evoked by it expand, and then it becomes clearer: art is one thing, and it isn't that which is life, and life is something else. Art isn't something that flows out of life, but it lies across life, like a shadow, but it is a shadow of a different quality; because of the shadow, life is perceived as something other. Basically you forgive it everything, specifically, you don't forgive it, but you can look at it, admitting its existence.

18 Nagel is the main hero in J.-K. Huysmans's novel.
19 Theophanis the Greek was a twelfth-century master icon painter.

I know, however, that you simply can't live only by the feeling that is evoked by art, like the art of Chekrygin. It is passing, because the feeling of life is stronger and more concentrated. All this is very simple. There is no kind of philosophy here; it is all simple experience.

Bruni also said that Dostoevsky's *Adolescent* is a Parthenon from the point of view of form. I can't understand that at all. Form is something internal, spiritual, and of the soul. It is the limit which the artist places on his "I." I will return to this again.

Bruni, it appears, understands form as matter, as something material.

Bruni also said that when he was ill with dystrophy last year and thought that he was dying, he thought, "I am ashamed and horrified that I have done so little." I recalled that for me it was easy. Tika said, "You're not an artist. An artist must act and could not have felt otherwise than Bruni did."

DIARY — 1944

8 April

On the question of realism.

It is essentially important to place the emphasis on the goal, that is, tirelessly to pose the question of the meaning of art, of its purposefulness. For what, and from what kind of impetus, is one or another work of art created? That which the ancients called "catharsis" is the thing close to which we must seek the goal. Purification, liberation, enlightenment, esthetic satisfaction. In the broadest sense it is possible simply to speak of good art.

In our contemporary art, so-called realism has become the goal. They have elevated a method to the level of a principle and have substituted the method for it. Nothing, except the ruin of art, can come from it.

Make good art with any means you like, but just make good art.

10 April

Yesterday I was at Lazarev's.* This is the first time I have seen him for a more or less extended period. He is energetic, completely together, intelligent, irreproachable in his positions. He was polite and even affectionate, as is characteristic of him.

I felt like a losing gambler in front of him. And I think he sensed this. He displayed respect for me, not just as someone of the same profession, but also as a man who had professional abilities and who even had some uses in this profession, in a word as someone who understood how the game was played. But I couldn't play with him, not for anything. I could only shuffle the cards a bit, as if I were showing with what I might have played.

"It's nothing," I thought, sitting in the train. "Don't let this embitter or depress you. Of course, you have lost your scholarship, as you have lost much else. But you know yourself how you are compensated. You have only to understand well by what you are compensated."

21 May

Shadows dance on my window . . .

Diaries are written:

either out of a vain wish, that someone in future generations would read them;

or from a desire to show them to someone close to them (a witness?);

or because there is no one to talk to;

or in order to formulate and, consequently, to understand one's confused feelings and thought;

or from graphomania and a lack of anything else to do.

I write, probably, for all five reasons at once.

6 June

There is a "war melancholy." It is a specific feeling. One of its peculiarities is that everything in the world seems doomed to perish, the whole visible world is perceived with the melancholy of death. Perhaps it is only our affliction, of the people of Leningrad. Here in Zagorsk it is stronger than it was in Samarkand, and perhaps it will be even stronger in Leningrad. For some reason stability was not so necessary in Samarkand: "I drink to my ruined home . . ." [20] In this there is contact with suffering. Her "persona" depends upon intonation, voice, mainly upon the voice, upon the structure of everyday life, even upon stray ends, but the large form [of poetry] is not characteristic of her. It isn't given to her, since neither love nor suffering was given to her.

The great form is the trace of a great spirit.

"I am free, it's all a game to me . . ."—She herself gave it away.

Once Tika said: "You, like Raskolnikov, accustom yourself to everything, as if it were going to kill you."

*24 June
(three years)
1944.
Zagorsk*

Sometimes there are such beautiful states of being. You hear, you distinctly sense the spiritual quality of the world. I want to say: there exists a color quality to things, well, like red for instance, in a dress; you always see and sense this, but sometimes you enter into some kind of deeper relationship with this color. You like or dislike this color for what it expresses: . . . the various . . . characteristics of the women who

---

20 | A quote from the first line of Anna Akhmatova's poem "The Last Toast," dated June 27, 1934.

are wearing it; the place it occupies in the surroundings, and so forth. In short, you sense not only the physical-material quality of the color, but also its meaning, its soul, if you wish.

I consider the state of being in which these spiritual qualities are accessible to the senses to be usually elevated and characteristic of genius. Forms of great perfection.

Well, this notebook is everything.

24 July 1944. Leningrad

We returned to Leningrad on the 19th. I was overcome by curiosity on the way. Through the windows I saw destroyed bridges, leveled forests, smashed-up vehicles, crashed planes, and so forth. At Volkhov-Chudovo and Popovka the earth was trenched, and there were craters here and there. Many places where there used to be villages or dachas were overgrown with tall weeds.

30 July

E. A. Tyrsa told us about the very horrible death of N. L. His wife died before him, in spite of the fact that she was a predator; even before the war and during the war we saw her at the LOSKh cafeteria in constant efforts to get various rations and occupied with various schemes.[21] Her death made a horrible impression on him. From that moment on, he went around unshaven (in the end with a long beard), he wore her fur hat, he was completely passive; then he began to forget about everything and was virtually irresponsible.

Not long before his death he really didn't go out anywhere and didn't undress; he slept in that same woman's hat. They brought him kasha, and he heated it right on the stove (without a pan). He gave his things to someone to sell them. A man came to see him, an artist it seems. When L. fell asleep, sitting in front of the stove, he simply took his watch off him, took the money out of his pocket, took his books and coat out of the closet. [. . .] Either L. didn't notice this at all, or, when his rare friends would bug him about it, he would simply say: probably . . . he took it. Then he died.

We brought a cat with us, knowing that in Leningrad all the cats had been eaten and thinking that there wouldn't be any. We were amazed when we heard the feline concert in our garden. There truly aren't any dogs. I have seen only one dog in the whole time since our return.

The longer you look at Leningrad, the more terrible it is. The holes for windows, the boards. It is empty, but they say that even a month ago it was completely empty.

21   "LOSKh" is the Leningrad Section of Soviet Artists.

In our apartment, much has remained the same as it was when we left. There are traces of our numb, dying hands. Galya tied that rope over the stove to dry her stockings. Her death lies on many things. Many can't even see all this. Today Tika said: the souls of the dystrophic are held in the leaves of these gardens.

There are such conversations between those who remained behind and those who are returning: "What, did you sit it out at the rear?" and they answer: "And you were still waiting for the Germans?"

Anya comes by almost daily. Of Garshin she said: "He has his own course in life."[22]

An attempt on Hitler's life; we are marching on Berlin.

It is nice by the window. The sky is covered by slow clouds and the huge lime trees quietly rustle. Neither Galya nor Sasha and many others can hear or see. Soon, I think, neither will I. It is nice at this window. A man should be alone . . . from time to time.

7 September   Lately I have heard more than once of an interest in "Art Nouveau." This theme has become engaging for some reason. Of course, our generation, which came out of "Art Nouveau" and, it seems to us, completely overcame it, has every basis for being interested in its origin. But to answer the question "What is modernism?" is even more difficult, it appears, than answering the same question about "romanticism."

It has always seemed to me that "modernism," like any other cultural phenomenon, including art, is first and foremost a feeling. And to understand this feeling means to understand the very essence of the phenomenon. Formal signs of "the modernist style" can be easily defined. But what is the feeling, hidden in Nietzsche and Hamsun, in Van der Welde and Munch, in Van Gogh and Gauguin, in Vrubel, Serov, Annensky, Blok, and so forth? All of them are modern and there are hundreds more!

In essence, it is a feeling of languor. It is a feeling that is sometimes full of energy (as with Nietzsche), sometimes sleepily dreamlike (Gauguin). It is a feeling, dependent on the conflict between the internal and what we ordinarily call the external. Of course, it is exhaustion and, of course, it is a morbid reaction to events, to the passage of history. It is

---

22   Akhmatova's relationship with Garshin ended when she returned to Leningrad after the war. During the war they corresponded, and he asked her to marry him and to take his name. She agreed, but when she arrived on the train in Leningrad he picked her up and asked her where she would be staying (he had married another woman during the war). This hurt her deeply, and she destroyed all her correspondence to and from him and removed his name from her dedication to the *Poem without a Hero*.

a braking rhythm, drawn out or nervously broken, overcoming excessive resistance or extraordinary pressure. It is not a feeling of a religious character, and not atheistically pagan. It is more like a feeling that is resting upon personal responsibility and therefore it is to a great measure historically isolated. Hence its historical brevity, the fact that it wasn't long lasting. It is a socially limited feeling, and therefore not at a universal level, in contrast, for instance, with the feeling of the baroque. (It differs from romanticism to a great extent in its spiritual exhaustion, and therefore the demonic beginning, the "self-destructive demon," is almost absent in it.)

Of course, there is the characteristic association of "Art Nouveau" with symbolism, and for an understanding of the feeling lying at the basis of "Art Nouveau," it is essential to discover the peculiarities of the history of this stage in the history of the symbol.

The genesis of Art Nouveau is in the north, and there it has a healthier character, that of folk art. Then there is the superficial interpretation of China and Japan. (There is something Buddhist about Art Nouveau.)

In short, it isn't melancholy, or despair, or passion, or uneasiness, although all these feelings enter into the makeup of "Art Nouveau sensibility" (in particular with Nietzsche). It is primarily languor, that is, something passive in relation to "urgent historical problems." There is something that is always a rejection of today in the name of the individual day. The world is only symbol, or event, or a play of light.

"Life is a terrible thing," repeated poor Cézanne.

8 September

Suffering is a simple and concrete thing. There is nothing relieving in it, even despair, which in another sense is not suffering.

DIARY — 1945

23 February

Yesterday Ioganson* and Osmerkin* came to see Anya. They brought a bottle of champagne, some wine, and some crab. Anya drank two bowls[23] and was the way she is when she's a little drunk; she read poetry, and I left to do the housework.

When everyone had left (at one A.M.) I returned to help her clean up the dishes, and she covered her face with her hands and began to cry. It seems that Osmerkin had said in passing that there was a rumor (with him it's always in passing and always a rumor), that Leva [Gumilev] was in the penal battalion. She sat on the bed and began bitterly to

23   "Pial" is the type of bowl used in Central Asia and Asia for drinking tea, etc.

lament her fate. I had not seen her in such grief in a long time. "What do they want from me, from me, and from Leva . . . they won't be happy until they kill him and me. The penal battalion is execution, for the second time he has been sentenced to execution . . . What did my boy see? He was never a counterrevolutionary . . . He is capable, young, full of strength. They envy him, and now they're using the fact that he is the son of Gumilev . . . As they made me Gumilev's widow . . ."

24 February

People are amazed at my relationship to Galya. Galya was the only one who didn't betray me, didn't abandon me. She fell out of love with me just enough to stay with me in the conditions of my life. All the rest abandoned me, like something useless. "You won't get on with him." Of course, they are right, I am that way and need to be dumped. But Galya didn't leave me and died in my arms. So is it so amazing that I can't forget her? That without her I am empty?

3 March

They had the Yalta meeting. The Government of the Earthly Sphere was founded. Khlebnikov has returned to our home.[24]

It is the twilight of national governments. And as is understandable Germany has been left out. The last (and also Japan, which didn't succeed in escaping the boundaries of national governments in time) national government. Neither America, nor England, nor our Soviet Union is a national government. They are unions, states, dominions, whatever you like.

All this has brought me to a state of great excitement today. If only it were possible to give a paper on Khlebnikov.

There they are, the ribs of the new world.

13 April

I turn on the radio and hear: ". . . the all-powerful wisdom of God was pleased to take the immortal spirit of Franklin . . . Roosevelt from us . . ."

10 May

All the same, this is how it was:

The 8th of May I gave a lecture; at a quarter to one, as soon as I had finished, a female student came in and announced something in a voice that was drowned by applause. I guessed that it was the end of the war. Since the evening of the day before some rumors had been circulating,

---

24 | In 1921, the Futurist poet Velemir Khlebnikov developed his ideas about the laws of time and founded what he called the Government of the Earthly Sphere, which would one day supersede the petty national governments of the present; in other words, he projected a vision of world government, with himself as secretary-general.

based on the overseas radio. I went to the administration; in the hallway they were congratulating each other, and some people, the women, of course, were exchanging kisses. From the administration I went into the cafeteria; in the furthest room about 20 students were sitting, the majority were painters. They greeted me noisily and made me drink vodka which they produced from under the table. Rumors were going around that between 3 and 5 there would be a citywide demonstration. I went to the Oreshkovs; they have a radio. On the radio there wasn't any kind of special programming. I stopped by the administration again. They said that someone must have called from TASS . . .[25] No one knew anything for sure.

Then when I was with Tika we met Dobroklonsky (a professor) in the hall, and he suggested that we go have a drink. There weren't any more lectures. We went. There was nothing particular going on outside. Then I went to Petrovsky, to Tika's. On the radio there were the usual programs, but we still waited and from time to time we gathered at the loudspeaker. I returned home and went to bed at about 11:30, having turned off the radio. There was nothing except the usual orders. I woke up at 7; around 8 we turned on the radio. The congratulations from the regional committee of the party. It all became clear. Soon we learned that they gave us the day off. Ira ran down to the store. Then we drank champagne; I went to see Leva . . . there we also drank champagne; no one was visiting them. I got home around 5. We had a lot of guests, and we drank cognac and vodka. I went to see Tika, at Petrovsky. I spent the night there, and from their window I saw the fireworks.

(July)

I haven't written in so long that the ink dried up in the inkwell.

The white nights have passed. It is worth it to live on earth for the sake of the white nights. Not for long, but you do live, and it seems you are a man . . . They make me and Tika calm, confident, and free.

For the sake of them I read *The Idiot* for the first time. It is a light and true book. Tolstoy seems like a shrew and a "journeyman of the novel." There is no earthly confusion of life. When I finished it, I lay there for a long time feeling light and a little sad; well, like an angel.

At first Dostoevsky isn't overfond of Nastasya Filippovna, the "lady with the eyelashes," as I accidentally called her in a conversation, but then, by the end of the novel, he laid everything at her feet. That's composition. Amazing.

---

25 TASS (Telegraph Agency of the Soviet Union) is the central news bureau.

28 August   I went to Türiseva, to the Rabis resort.[26] On the evening of the 20th I was sitting in a room, playing chess. Someone in the corner pronounced the name "Akhmatova"; I eavesdropped, it was something bad; they were reading the paper. Having finished my game, I went to get a paper.

I slept poorly that night. I woke up at 6, my heart pounding, and this lasted until 12. I went to the doctor, and he gave me valerian with lily. I felt better. At first I thought "in general"; about art, that is. By morning I began to think about Akuma. I felt sorry for her: she loved it . . .

That same day we left. I came home, and she was alone; she had gotten thinner . . . Well, I had known her state for a long time. I was afraid that things were worse with her. Never mind, she'll hold out.

DOCUMENTS

N. N. Punin. Declaration [1947]

To the board of the Leningrad Section of the Union of Soviet Artists

I ask the board of LOSKh to no longer consider me a member of the Union of Soviet Artists. My decision to leave the ranks of the Union is motivated by the following considerations.

At a discussion of a closed exhibit of a group of Leningrad artists [. . .] in connection with my speech regarding the work of the artist Sokolov, accusations were made against me, [. . .] which in the majority of cases were either unfounded, or evoked, as it seems me, by the tendentious desire not to understand me, and sometimes, especially in the case of the speech of the chairman of LOSKh, by direct misinterpretation of the thoughts I expressed.

In general I am plunged into some confusion by the shielding of the artists of LOSKh from serious criticism, which is sometimes displayed by the chairman of LOSKh in his speeches. I don't consider artists, even if they are members of LOSKh, infallible gods, who cannot be touched and if I defined some works as fit for the drawing room and others as an encroachment on art, then I have my bases for that, and I am prepared to defend my opinion before any competent arbitration. [. . .]

You came down on me because I didn't touch upon the ideological level of the works under discussion in my speech, but [. . .] the ideo-

26   Türiseva is a Finnish resort town.

logical content of the majority of the works was so low that there was nothing to say.

I cannot, unfortunately, pass over one other circumstance. Lately in his speeches against me, the chairman of LOSKh has adopted such an unbridled and rude tone, close to that in which hawkers at the market converse. I never thought that it was possible to speak in such a tone from the tribunal of a public union organization. No matter what I have said, or how mistaken my judgments may have been at times, I never gave anyone cause to think that any interests besides the interests of art were directing me. Therefore, I do not want to and should not endure rude insults or all kinds of tendentious fabrications directed at me any longer.

In view of all the above mentioned, I ask the Board of LOSKh to grant my request and no longer consider me among the members of LOSKh.

25 February 1947. N. Punin.[27]

Order of the Main Administration of Universities of the Ministry of Higher Education of the USSR

No 29/4K. Moscow. 15 April 1949.

To support order No 398 from 7 March 1949 of the rector of Leningrad State University of the Order of Lenin in the name of A. A. Zhdanov on the release of Punin, N. N., professor of the Art History Department, from the university, as someone who could not ensure the ideological-political education of the student body.

Head of the main administration of universities, member of the collegiate of the ministry of higher education of the USSR, Professor K. Zhigach.

LETTER FROM A. G. KAMINSKAYA TO A. A. AKHMATOVA

8 Aug. [1949]

Dear Akuma. I am happy. I found two white mushrooms. I had a hedgehog, he lived with us for two days and crawled away under the bushes. I have been swimming in the sea and I am learning the poem:

---

27 When Punin was first criticized for "Formalism" (which was the patent formula for denouncing any artist or scholar who was deemed insufficiently "Soviet"), he received an outpouring of letters from current and former students who wished to give him their personal support, but who were afraid to openly support him for fear of causing him greater suffering.

"To become that seaside girl again,
To wear sandals on my feet,
And to put my braids up in a crown
And to sing in an anxious voice."[28]

Kisses, Anya.

[Addendum by I. N. Punina]: 8 August. Hello, Akuma, hello, Lev! Don't scrub the floor! Hello from R. A. Irina.

LETTER FROM N. N. PUNIN TO A. G. KAMINSKAYA

14 August '49

Anya, hello, I send you my greetings. You would like it here. There is the sea and pine trees. You haven't ever seen such a big sea. And there's so much sand you could bury our whole house, and there'd still be some left . . .

Kisses, Papa.

LETTER FROM N. N. PUNIN TO V. M. ZUMMER

31 January '49

Most-respected Vsevolod Mikhailovich,

Recalling your friendly relations with me in Tashkent, allow me to write you a few words.

Invoking the fates, I have had to study Al. Ivanov. With great difficulty, after almost a year of searching, I finally managed to acquire most of your work. I have, besides "Systems" and "On Faith and the Church," "Eschatology," "Problematics," and "Unpublished letters to Gogol," but I can't find "Botkin as a Source" or "Al. Ivanov on Turgenev" anywhere. I also know that there are some of your works which were published by lithographic methods, but only know what I've heard about them.

But this isn't what I wanted to write to you about. I wanted to express my admiration for your work. There is so much scholarly responsibility, precision, ability to limit oneself, and along with this, a kind of intellectual courage in them. I have already reread them many times and still find new valuable observations and disciplined thoughts which I hadn't noticed immediately. In notorious polemics you gained a shining victory, and with such magnanimity! I consider the problem

---

28 From Akhmatova, "I see a faded flag above the customhouse" (1913), in *Rosary,* in Reeder and Hemschemeyer, *The Complete Poems of Anna Akhmatova,* 1:337.

of the interaction of "Systems" with the book by Strauss forever solved. But I would like to go a little further, and I allowed myself to assert in my own work that to a well-known degree Strauss' book "became the driving factor in the spiritual development of Ivanov." In particular I am completely convinced that Ivanov came under the strongest influence of Hegelianism. (Probably through Chizhov, who, if I'm not mistaken, translated Hegel's *Encyclopedia* into Russian.) Why didn't you mention anything about this? . . .

You have a wonderful understanding; there's so much I'd like to talk to you about. There is no one to talk to here. My co-workers at the Russian Museum simply don't know your works, even "Systems." It's so sad! What loneliness!

[. . .] I showed "Eschatology" to A. A. Akhmatova, who is a little afraid of you for some reason. She was very interested. In general I propagandize you as much as I can. Thus the introduction to one of the chapters of my work consists of full citations from Zummer. And this is natural, since your work has solidly entered into the historiography of Russian art.

Well, forgive me my too ecstatic letter.

How are you doing there in blessed Tashkent? They say you had a very harsh winter there, yet we still don't have snow.

I warmly shake your hand in friendship and with all my heart.

N. Punin.

DOCUMENT

D Ministry of Higher Education

Enclosing, with this, all the documents that support my right to receive a pension, I ask you to submit a petition for me for such.

N. Punin. 1949, 5 July. Leningrad Fontanka 34 Apt. 44

LETTER FROM G. GLAGOLEVA TO N. N. PUNIN

Nikolay Nikolaevich! I beg your forgiveness in advance for my note, but things are so difficult now because of everything that is happening that I wanted to say a few words to you.

I will not talk about what we, the students, are losing with your leaving the Academy. You were for us truly the best, most valued professor, because of whom alone it was worth continuing our studies, especially in the past few years! And for many, very many, your lectures will remain for our whole lives the most wonderful, deep, and "real" of any that were given at the Academy. Only you taught us to really understand and love art! I want to tell you that we will always remember, value, and love you, as a pedagogue, as a scholar, as a person. It is very difficult now to see and hear all these unfair accusations directed against the innocent and best people. I would like to announce this loudly, to make a change . . . Only fear of harming you holds all of us back from "decisive" action.

But be comforted with the fact that all this is doubtless temporary and everything will soon return to normal. Forgive me again for this stupid letter, but it was difficult to refrain from writing it.

I wish you health and happiness with all my heart.

With deep admiration, Glagoleva.

NOTE FROM N. N. PUNIN

I kiss you, I kiss all three of you. I am not losing hope. Papa.[29]

MATERIALS FROM INVESTIGATION PROCEEDINGS N 3746

Archive of the All-Russian Special Commission for Combating Counterrevolution, Sabotage, and Speculation—the Unified State Political Directorate—the People's Commissariat of Internal Affairs

I
Resolution / Decree for Arrest

Leningrad, 1949, August 11, I, the senior operational plenipotentiary of the UMGB—LO, Lieutenant Prusakov, having reviewed the materials on the criminal activity of Punin, Nikolay Nikolaevich, born 1889 in Helsinki (Finland), Russian, Citizen of the USSR, from the family of a military doctor, former professor, twice subject of arrest: in 1921 for counterrevolutionary activities (released 5.II.1921 for insufficient evi-

29. *Over this cradle*
I am bending like a black fir.
   Bye, bye, bye, bye!
   Aye, aye, aye, aye . . .

I don't spy a falcon
Neither far nor near.
   Bye, bye, bye, bye!
   Aye, aye, aye, aye.

AUGUST 26, 1949 (AFTERNOON)
FOUNTAIN HOUSE

dence of crime) and in 1935, as a participant in a counterrevolutionary terrorist group (released 4.XI.1935 by order of the enemy of the people Yagoda), art historian by profession, former professor at the Leningrad State University named in honor of A. A. Zhdanov and the Academy of Arts in Leningrad. [. . .] I found:

Punin is hostile to the existing government structures of the USSR. In 1935 he expressed terrorist sentiments toward the leaders of the All-Union Communist Party (Bolsheviks).

In the first years of the existence of Soviet power Punin N. N. propagated idealistic views in his articles.

At the beginning of 1921 criminal proceedings were instituted against Punin N. N. for counterrevolutionary crimes, however, by resolution of the OOVChK of February 5, 1921, the investigation in relation to him was discontinued due to insufficient evidence.

In 1935 Punin was arrested for the second time as a participant in an anti-Soviet terroristic group together with students of the Leningrad State University A. P. Borin, L. N. Gumilev (son of the poetess), and others.

Moreover, Punin expressed terroristic sentiments toward the leaders of the Bolshevik Party and the Soviet government. [. . .]

Being an apologist for Formalism, Punin defended formalistic principles in art in his lectures, in his seminar classes, and also in his scholarly work over the course of many years, bowed down before bourgeois art of the West, and announced that "Russian, even more so Soviet fine art, is only a pitiful reflection of the art of European countries." [. . .]

On the basis of the above-mentioned, we have decreed that Nikolay Nikolaevich Punin be subject to arrest and investigation.

> Senior operational plenipotentiary . . . Prusakov
> Head of the Dept. UMGB Leningrad Region Major Grigorev
> "Agreed"—
> Head of the Dept. of Administration of MGB of the Leningrad
> Region Colonel Minichev.

The actual decree announced to me on August 27, 1949.

> Signature of the arrested: N. Punin.

Questionnaire of the Arrested Party

Physical Description: 1. Height: Tall (171–180). Build: average. Shoulders: stooped. Neck: long. Hair color: dark auburn. Eye color: light blue. Face: oval. Forehead: high. Eyebrows: arched, thin. Nose: big, narrow, shape of nose: straight. Mouth: small, drooping. Lips: thin. Chin: tapering. Ears: small.

Testimony of N. N. Punin

(From the interrogation of 14 September 1949)

[. . .] Undoubtedly the struggle with proponents of "true art" and the position on the artistic front of that time caused me to make generalizations that gradually acquired a political slant. In my public appearances and in print I declared that it is becoming more and more apparent that in our Soviet conditions there are almost no people for whom art could live and that there is nothing by which and no one for whom Russian art and artists can live.

And furthermore, reviving the subject, we are not reviving art itself with it; we don't even need to see pictures with "new subjects" from Soviet life, in order to understand the senselessness of all attempts to revive art. However, I am convinced that these attempts are made officially, that they are made in the name of "new culture," and that only proves, as I have said many times, how far Russian artistic life has declined. I have often asked myself whether the artists themselves feel a creative passion of any kind in all of this. And I have quickly given myself the answer: in my opinion, they (the artists) are too demoralized, too estranged from their conscience, to talk about art, about quality, and one hears only complaints that no one values them or buys their works, that they've "nothing to live on."

In culture itself, I am convinced, there is occurring something which makes the works of artists, of even those who are recognized and respected by everyone, lifeless and defeated.

Thus, by 1935 my political views had become such as to make me a vehement opponent of the politics of the Party and Government in the area of art. [. . .]

(From the interrogation of 19 September 1949)

[. . .] I have not rejected the role of the great Russian heritage and of Russian realistic art as a whole; and I have always highly valued and talked about the work of Surikov,* about F. Vasilev,* about most of Repin's* work, and about the Russian "wanderers" in my lectures. I also highly valued realists such as P. Sokolov, Fedotov, and others. I was also especially taken with the study of the brilliant Russian artist Aleksandr Ivanov. [. . .] I worked in the Russian Museum for 19 years and could not fail to appreciate the heritage of Russian realistic art, and I also reject the statement that I worship the formalistic art of the contemporary West. [. . .] In principle, I think that an artist shouldn't blindly worship anything, but should go his own way, studying with the masters who can teach him to make good paintings.

FROM THE INTERROGATION OF V. A. SEROV,
BORN 1910, [. . .] CONCERNING CASE N735-49

November 21,
1949

Question: How long have you known and what is your relationship with him?

Answer: I have known Nikolay Punin since 1930 as a teacher at the Leningrad Academy of Art, but I have never had a personal relationship with him. From about 1945 to 1946 I encountered him at the Artists Union. Punin spoke at meetings and conferences . . . I did not agree with him. I didn't have any other relationship with him.

Question: What relationship do you have with Dzhakov?

Answer: I have a good relationship with Dzhakov. We sometimes see each other privately.

Question: What kind of relationship does Dzhakov have with Punin?

Answer: It is difficult for me to say whether they are acquainted, but Dzhakov does not share his views and has demonstrated this in the pages of the newspapers.

Question: Whom does Punin associate with?

Answer: I don't know. I have heard rumors that his closest relations are with the artist Traugot.

Question: What do you know about N. N. Punin's speeches on art?

Answer: In the fall of 1946 at the Union of Artists Punin said: "Whether or not the government likes it, our art has to take Western European art into account." All his speeches, including this one, were taken down by a stenographer, and they gave Punin the stenograph copy of his speeches for corrections. Punin returned the stenograph copy with corrections, and I noticed that the phrase I just noted was published without correction. At that moment, Professor S. K. Isakov was in the office of the Union of Artists. I showed him this phrase from Punin's speech, and Isakov turned to Punin, who was in the next room, and told him that it was inappropriate to leave such a phrase in the stenographic copy. N. N. Punin read this phrase, crossed out the word "government," and wrote "governing board." I told Punin that at the meeting he had talked about the government, and that everyone heard it, and the meaning of the phrase refuted the substitution of the under-standing of "governing board," since the Board of the Leningrad Union of Artists cannot be accountable for the art of the whole country. [. . .]

Question: Did you write an article in the newspaper *Evening Leningrad* entitled "For the Further Flourishing of Art"?

Answer: Yes, I wrote that article in the beginning of 1949.

Question: In this article, you call N. N. Punin an "ideologue of new art" and an "advocate of the reactionary idea of art for art's sake." On the basis of what evidence did you draw this conclusion?

Answer: Around 1918–1919, the "Lectures on Art," which he also publicly gave in courses for artists, were published by Punin. Moreover in the same year Punin also published a series of articles in the papers on art. I myself read in Punin's essays that in his opinion old Russian art, which he called realistic, had already become obsolete and that the young art of the left had come to take its place. He said: "Futurism is an improvement on communism. Realism and its lack of talent are one and the same. Futurism and Cubism are an expression of the future of art. Form is in itself already enough of a subject of art."

On the basis of these statements by Punin, I came to the conclusion that he is an ideologue of "left reactionary art" and an advocate of the reactionary idea of "art for art's sake" and a theoretician of Formalism in art.

Question: In this same article you wrote that N. N. Punin criticized the best works of Soviet artists and scoffed at the method of Socialist Realism. How do you know this?

Answer: In April of 1945 Punin gave a paper at the Union of Artists on the topic of "Impressionism and Painting," and in it he asserted that "Soviet art is a backward art, while contemporary Western European art, like the art of Picasso, and also the art of Western Europe at the beginning of the 20th century, like the art of Cézanne and Van Gogh, is the highest achievement of contemporary culture." As I recall, Punin then said that he doesn't understand what Socialist Realism is, since it, he says, is an indefinite concept. [. . .]

Question: How do you evaluate the art of Cézanne, Van Gogh, Picasso?

Answer: The art of Cézanne and Van Gogh is an expression of the decadent movement and is evaluated by Soviet society as formalistic. Picasso is also related to the Formalists, in spite of his useful activity for the cause of peace. [. . .]

CERTIFICATE

Akhmatova, Anna Andreevna, born 1892, city of birth Leningrad, works in the 5th Dept. of UIGBLO in recordkeeping, and in connection with this she was not interrogated as a witness to the activities of N. N. Punin.

Gumilev, Lev Nikolaevich, was arrested on 6 November 1949 and was sent by command of the investigative section on especially important activities of the MGB of the USSR.

Head of the 2nd Dept. of the Investigative Dept. of UMGB LO Lieutenant Kovalev.

24 November 1949

CERTIFICATE

The textbook on the history of Western European art, published under the editorship and personal participation of N. N. Punin in 1940, by "Iskusstvo" publishers, contains major mistakes of a formalistic and cosmopolitan character and is permeated with bourgeois subjectivism. By command of the Presidium of the Academy of Artists, and the Director of the Repin Institute, since the 1st of September this book is no longer recommended as a textbook and has simultaneously been removed from the archives of the libraries of the Academy.

LETTER FROM N. N. PUNIN TO M. A. GOLUBEVA

7 September '50

Dear Tika! Finally . . . I am writing you from Vologda on the wall (on the way to the camp).

I can't tell you anything definite now. I have endured the year by your love and by love for you. And I am still holding on by it. That's all.

My health is good. My treatment was impeccable. The most difficult stage is now. I think that soon I'll write you about everything. Oh, Tika! I kiss all of you. Sin.

LETTER FROM N. N. PUNIN TO M. A. GOLUBEVA

15 September '50

Dear Tika, I am writing to your address on the Fontanka, since I don't know whether you are living at the Academy. I won't write you about my case, there's nothing you don't already know [. . .]

My address is: Komi ASSR. Kozhvinsky region, town of Abez, post box 388/16-g. Don't expect any letters from me in the near future. You can write to me in an unlimited quantity; so write me as much as you can. I can also receive "printed matter," so send me the most interesting papers ("socialist realism," too) and books you think are worth it. I have the right to receive 100 rubles a month; ask Leva P. to help with money for me. I am allowed to receive a package a week. I am placed in the 4th category, that is, I have been freed of all work, and I don't know what to do with myself. Perhaps by spring you can send me a box of paints, and I'll take up painting again. I need energetic and longstanding help. You're going to have a lot of worries now.

But look, don't despair! As I wrote you from Vologda, your love and my love for you supported me like a wondrous image. I never loved anyone with such passionate respect, and so simply. But about that another time.

It is still warm here, and on clear days the sun warms us well.

I kiss you tenderly, and I also send kisses to all. I am waiting, oh, how I await, your letters.

Your Sin.

LETTER FROM N. N. PUNIN TO M. A. GOLUBEVA

17 November '50

Tika, my dove, my quiet light and my comfort. I am using my right to send you a second letter this year. In jail I still hoped to write you a lot, but that, too, has passed. Probably, this is all vengeance for the pain I caused you: the sleighs, Perm, the Black road, Zagorsk, etc. (How I cried, as I was going through Zagorsk on the 4th of September, over your unrealized life!) But in any case, you are always in my heart and I am never and nowhere without you. So, if it is fated for me to die here, I will not die alone. Only it's strange that I cannot see you or hear you or touch your hand. All the rest is just hardship that is more or less trivial.

For a month and a half I was in the hospital; I rested and got my bearings pretty well. Your medicine happened to arrive on the day of my discharge, so there had been nothing to treat me with, but I got well on my own . . .

The first "ecstatic" package made everyone around me happy. I know that you can't feed me without borrowing money from relatives, so don't go to any expense. I understand that you rejoiced that I was alive, and of course "extra quality" tea is wondrous to the taste, but still . . .

I hear each of your words and every intonation, and there's nothing dry about your letter. I can't write Irochka anymore but she knows that I love her and am grateful to her.

Anyuta! I kiss you for each C you got in school this year. Thanks and greetings to Roma. I send a kiss on the forehead to Nika and Lyulli; I also send kisses to Irochka's slender fingers.

I want to wish you, my dove and savior, and Irochka happy birthday again. May Irochka pass on to everyone my commandment: "Take care of Tika" [. . .]

They are very interested in art here. There is a history professor; he speaks very well about the works of Picasso, and about space and time in art. He knows the history of art as well as I do, and he lived in Paris for a long time.

Well, good-bye; perhaps tomorrow I'll get a letter from you (they come on Saturdays) . . .

LETTER FROM N. N. PUNIN TO M. A. GOLUBEVA

19 February 1951

Tika, dear, I wish you happy holiday, my Dove, and only hope that you will keep the light in your heart and overcome your sorrow. I don't know when this letter will get to you, since everyone is writing letters with the New Year and they, naturally, only trickle through the censor [. . .]

I would still like to receive Wölfflin, and more books on art (Alpatov has had huge success in the camp, but not with me. What, is the first volume impossible to get?) If you could also get illustrations for clarification of Cubism (from the icons and Negroes to Picasso's "violin"). Irochka is writing me about the paints; oil paints are cumbersome and expensive to send, but if you could get a box of pastels, paper for them, and obtain colored reproductions of still-lifes and landscapes, I could, by interpreting them, do something for the cafeteria and club. As it is, I'm a useless person! Well, that's all there is about our daily life.

[. . .] Thank you for the Chinese jugglers. I read that part of the letter aloud to a few people; it is so wonderful and precise. I never thought that during my lifetime you'd be alone at the performance; it's cruel! But I'm not bitter, after all, can one be bitter if there is love? Bitterness is illuminated suffering, fruitless suffering, strictly speaking. Oh, Tika, spread your wings wider; both the world and life are a miracle, literally, and both are unique and inexplicable. You want a novella: when Raphael was finishing his self-portrait, death came for his soul, but since the portrait looked so much like him, death couldn't tell which was the real Raphael and was about to take the soul from the portrait. "Signora," Raphael said, "take my soul; that one is immortal." Perhaps this will show you exultation, that is, an as yet incomplete feeling. No matter, it will be completed. But you called my letter sweet, and I was insulted? Really, "sweet"? Oh, Tika! My dove, patience, patience . . .

Irochka's letters (there are 17 of them, 13 of yours, not counting the telegrams) give me a lively description of everyday life at Fountain House, but I just don't understand what happened to my room, did they really just leave it? It pains me that I can't write to her, but what

can I do but endure? And I go along, still feeling my way with a walking stick when it's dark. I got a postcard from Irochka from Moscow.
How's her dissertation?

10 March. I had to interrupt the letter: they took away my pen; it
wasn't allowed. They also took our checked blanket, since they took it
for a woman's scarf; I had to tear off the fringe and hem it, then it was
considered bedding. Lots has changed during this time; the sun heats
the temperatures up to 50–60 degrees, and the days are full. I read
"The Gods' Desire." But then in the evenings I feel a melancholy that
saps my strength, and it is terrible to wait for the future. I play chess to
the point of stupidity (perhaps somewhere you could find a pocket set
with pieces that stay put?). You say that I ask for too much, but really
it's wise that you don't send anything I've requested. It's been a long
time, more than a month, since I've received any letters from you. I
have gotten Irochka's and Anyuta's letters, although one a week later
than the other. The packages have also started coming late; the fifth
one took 20 days; I am exhausted with anticipation. But soon this could
all end. Kiss all the children with my tender love, and greetings to all
the beasts. Everything will be fine, if you stay the way I imagine you,
strong and beautiful . . .

Irochka! I send kisses, papa.

LETTER FROM N. N. PUNIN TO I. N. PUNINA

[no date]

Greetings, Irochka, my daughter. Finally, I made it to my chance to
write you a note. Ivan Andreevich Petrenko will send it to you; he is a
noble fellow. He served his time and now is released on unsupervised
exile. He helped me a lot, and so if he turns to you for help, help him,
as much as you are able. You'll receive several letters from him and
will learn about me in detail. I wasn't judged by a tribunal, since there
wasn't any material for a trial, but by a special meeting. My case is based
on 1935 and cosmopolitanism. For a long time they found difficulties
dealing with my release in 1935, and they disregarded it. Gumilev dam-
aged me without wanting to; they connected me to his case, although
obviously he didn't contribute to this. He himself was arrested on the
basis of the old case. Akuma hung by a thread. Probably her poems in
"Ogonek" saved her.[30]

---

30 Punin is referring to Akhmatova's poetic cycle "In Praise of Peace," printed in *Ogonek* in
1950. This cycle represents Akhmatova's attempt to save her son's (and perhaps Punin's)
life after his arrest in 1949. The poems praise the country and inadvertently Stalin.
Akhmatova never really considered them part of her body of work and requested that
they not be included in her collected works.

I am healthy and feeling vigorous enough. Only from time to time I am overwhelmed by gloom, as you could tell from my letter to Tika in DVS, but don't be sad.[31] Thank you for your concern and love. I often reread your letters, they are wonderfully written. Each memory of Anyuta brings a lump to my throat. The story about her exams was delightful. That's her style. I don't need any underclothes, we can only wear prison issue. The only thing I need is galoshes on felt boots and one foot binding. I really need packages and a little bit of money for the canteen.

[. . .] There is just one more thing, send this note to the address and announce the address of my camp. That's all. Forgive me, dear, this disorganized note. They are rushing me. I am worrying and waiting for your help. Describe everything to me in detail. Write every Saturday, I am waiting. I send you a kiss, my little angel, and a kiss for Anyuta's eyes. I don't have the words for Tika, she is amazing. I often dream about all of you. I send greetings to everyone, everyone, and tell Miichka not to forget me. I send you kisses and I believe that we'll see each other soon.

Papa. And special thanks to Roma.

LETTER FROM N. N. PUNIN TO A. G. KAMINSKAYA

17 April '52

Greetings, Anyutochka, my little light and angel. I found out your address and rushed to write you: congratulations to you and all who remember me, for all the holidays both past and future. My health is good; not long ago, it's true, I fell ill with the flu, but I'm better, although I didn't have any medicine that would help. The medicine that Tika sent is gone, and she hasn't sent any more, as with the other things I asked for. I have two requests for mama; could she possibly get a milligram of penicillin? It costs 18 rubles; is that expensive? Well, if she can. And then galoshes. That's the last thing, when mama has a little money, although now maybe you could wait until you come?! Somehow she managed to send me a knitted shirt; I was very pleased. It is long, and that's a lot warmer . . .

Now I can read a little, but during the winter I couldn't: we had one lamp for 200 people. And it hung from the ceiling at a height of 7 meters. And you know that here the moon sometimes doesn't rise at all in the winter; it circles the sky, and there's a lot of sky. There aren't any houses or towns, and so it circles around. If Tika is getting ready to

---

31   "DVS" stands for Dom Veteranov Stseny, the House of Retired Stage Artists.

send books, then have her send only Shakespeare, Goethe, Dante, and so forth, but I wouldn't be able to read anything else; like cod-liver oil it won't go down . . . I am reading a little Delacroix; it's good: haughty sadness. Well, good-bye, my little angel, I kiss your brave eyes. Kiss mama, Roma, Tika, and Mashka (thank her for sending a kiss to Tika) and everyone for me. It's a good thing that you left there; only I wonder what happened to Akuma; did they throw her out? Or did she go to Moscow? Don't forget me and love me! I look forward to your letters.

I love to read your mama's letters very much. And as for her work, she shouldn't be afraid to tell me, she'll get it written.

LETTER FROM N. N. PUNIN TO M. A. GOLUBEVA

13 June '52, Abez

Dearest Tikanka, my dove, don't despair so; you'll lose me because of it: I know it myself; the longing is darkening your "bright face." All I have to do is wish to see you right now, and you retreat into the distance, diminishing to a single point. Only by living above time and space can I feel you near. Lately I have been somewhat disturbed, I haven't gotten a letter in more than two months, the last postcard, "Again no letter . . ." was from the tenth of April. And that's also when I received the package with Shakespeare (thank you!). You described Yudina's concert wonderfully. But I wanted to say that Beethoven is a restless person (dynamic), and yet the world lies in almost complete peace; it just contracts and expands (it breathes). And Bach understood this. Moreover, suffering is still imperfection; the world does not suffer, even when it is in a tragic state, and Bach knew this, too. Kiss Nika's forehead for me. I bow at the feet of angels you live among; unparalleled nobility. I am terribly looking forward to letters. Kiss Irochka, Anya, Mashka for me. The future is opening up and everything is becoming bright. Oh, Tika. I kiss your heart; you make the world shine. Sin.

LETTER FROM N. N. PUNIN TO A. G. KAMINSKAYA

11 May '53

Greetings, Anichka, my dove, my little steppe bell! They have allowed us to write our letter for the second half of the year; this is also a good sign; we are waiting, like everyone. I have received very few letters from you. The last postcard I got from Tika was from the 7th of February. I was hurt that I didn't get a long letter in answer which she had promised me. She should write it again. Also, I didn't get the Wölfflin, although mama said that she saw it sealed up in a package a year ago. But it's O.K., times have changed! There is nothing to read, and no one is going to send papers, but sometimes we'd really like to know what's going on; you see, here we imagine a lot of things.

Give Akuma my gratitude and thanks for the Easter package. Everything was very tasty, but a letter would have been more interesting, and besides, you don't have to have just one or the other! Your handwriting is very good now; good girl! But as usual you didn't pay enough attention: "Congatulations"! . . .

Well, so long for now, my little light. Don't forget me or stop loving me. Give mama and Tika a big kiss for me, and one to papa, and Darochka, and Mashuka, and Nika, and everyone, and say hello to everyone. I miss the tree and columns; if only I could touch them! I look forward to your letters. I kiss your little hand! Danya!

LETTER FROM N. N. PUNIN TO M. A. GOLUBEVA

29 June '53

I got the package; I didn't notice any changes; they picked on the Academy a little; the candidates are still the same brotherhood; neither Tatlin, nor Favorsky, nor S. Lebedeva, etc., is there. I thought, "I will sit here in Abez as long as A. Gerasimov is sitting where he is." Am I right? But really none of this is important. I have been reading your old letters; you hold me up on a pedestal very well. And that's important. Don't pride yourself in me, so I won't become proud. I myself sense that I live radiantly, but that hardly depends on me. You are a light, and everything around you is radiant. . . . Everyday life has gotten somewhat better; people are being moved around; I don't even need my razor or books anymore, since the people for whom they were meant have gone to other camps. It could happen to me, but I doubt it. I am fine here with you. And we'll see each other soon enough anyway. I am completely provided with warm things for winter, except for my hat, which the authorities equitably threw in the trash with disgust, since it was dirty, torn, and scorched from the heater. So absolutely send me a hat, the cheapest you can find.

This year we had a wonderful spring; by May there wasn't any snow left, and by the end of May the temperatures were over 40 degrees. June was bad, and now we are having gray days, much like you are probably having. A weak west wind blows constantly. But this spring I got so sunburnt, you would have been amazed. I looked like I had just come back from the south.

I just looked at your photograph: you don't resemble at all the one that I dream of and whom I remember very well. I remember you, I even remember your wrinkles, and as for your narrow nostrils, you won't understand this at all, but they are narrow nevertheless. Just remember how the very tip of your nose goes down when you talk. It is simply incomprehensible to me why all this has happened. Besides, this isn't the most important thing; there is another beauty, and it is better to keep quietly silent about it . . .

As far as the boots are concerned; they were meant for Gorbatenko. He should be thanked for all the services he has performed for me. The only thing that bothers me is their cost. Let Ira figure that out herself.

If only you could see how they fuss about events here; there's both gossip and idle conjecture. It's a good thing that I can be completely at peace. As if it had nothing to do with me.

My quiet light, I send you kisses.

LETTER FROM I. P. GORBATENKO TO M. A. GOLUBEVA[32]

Lady Maria, I am writing you about your husband Nekolay Nekolaevich. He died on the 21st of August at 11:45, not having been ill. On the 20th he got money and had came to me to pay debt and I look at him and say where're you going. That he brought money to pay the debt he said he'd never be able to repay me and you always find an answer and he left. In the morning I went to work and he stood by the dormitory. I said hello to him and say why are you up so early and he said he couldn't sleep and thinks that they promised him that he would go home and they wrote that they even sent his suit out to the cleaners and his wife was getting his room ready and for some reason he doesn't get any packages and probably they are waiting and says when I took money from you I bought 20 apples from the Ukrainian who delivers packages and yesterday took a liter bottle of milk . . . needed to go eat breakfast and left. Two and half hours later they come tell me they take Nekolay Nekolaevich Punin to hospital on stretcher I dropped everything and ran to the hospital and as soon as I went in he says, do you see? this morning I was standing talking to you and now I'm in the hospital and when I ask he says come see me at 12 there'll be a doctor. I shall ask him what to buy and since I left from him at 11 exactly and I had come back at 12 they tell me Nekolay Nekolaevich died at quater to 12 that he was no longer and I don't remember how I stood there

---

32 This letter was written by one of the men in camp with Punin, who apparently had little education. I have left the letter in its ungrammatical state to preserve the mood and tone of the letter.

and still didn't believe and went to the bed and he lay there like alive and I asked the ones nearby how did it happen and they said he said he was cold and called the orderly who looked after the patients and asked them to give him a hot-water bottle at his feet. The orderly left and he held out his hand and they said it was his pain in the heart that he had all his life, but he never felt pain in his heart anytime in his life and he tanned well and I always said he looked like a Negro, and he laughed. But let's imagine that I feel very well, and we read letters that you didn't go to vacation in the country and that you were waiting for Nekolay Nekolaevich to come. Then good-bye and hello to Anya and her mother.

POEM BY ANNA AKHMATOVA

In memory of N. P.

And that heart will no longer respond
To my voice, exulting and grieving.
Everything is over . . . And my song drifts
Into the empty night, where you no longer exist.

1953[33]

---

33 Translation from Reeder and Hemschemeyer, *The Complete Poems of Anna Akhmatova*, 2:258.

GLOSSARY

Ahrens Family (also often trans-literated as Arens)	Evgeny Ivanovich (1856–1931), Punin's father-in-law, was married to Evdokia Semenovna (1856–1917), father of Punin's first wife, Anna "Galya" Ahrens (1892–1943). Evgeny Ivanovich and Evdokia Seme-novna had two other daughters, Vera (Ahrens-Gakkel, 1883–1962) and Zoya (1886–1969). Zoya married Punin's younger brother Aleksandr, "Sasha" (1890–1942). The Ahrens also had a son, Lev (1890–1967), who was a biologist and married Sarra Yosifovna (born Sauskan, 1900–1982). Lev and Sarra helped the Punin family to take care of Akhma-tova in her last years. The couple had three children, Evgeny (Genya, born 1921), Igor (1923–1942), and Yury (Yura, 1921–1942). Punin men-tions them in his later entries.
Aland Islands	A series of islands off the coast of Finland in the bay of Bothnia. In 1920, the League of Nations settled a dispute over the islands between Sweden and Finland.
Aleksandr III (1881–1894)	Tsar who came to the throne after the assassination of his liberal father, Aleksandr II, who had emancipated the serfs. His reign marked a return of reactionary repression in matters of censorship, education, and national autonomy. Under the influence of Sergey Witte, how-ever, Aleksandr III managed to keep Russia out of war and to launch its industrial modernization through the building of a vast railroad network.
Altman, Nathan Isaevich (1898–1970)	Painter and graphic artist, whose portrait of Akhmatova may be one of the most famous done of her. He worked in the Department of Fine Arts and taught at the Petrograd State Free Art Studios from 1918 to 1920.
Alyansky, Samuel (1891–1974)	Owner of the Alkonost publishing house, which printed Akhmatova's *White Flock* and the third edition of her *Rosary* in 1922. By 1924, he had ceased to publish her work, and by 1925, after a secret government edict, she was not published at all.
Annensky, Innokenty (1856–1909)	A poet, playwright, and director of Nikolaevsky gymnasium in Tsarskoe Selo from 1896 to 1905. He also translated all of Euripides into Russian and wrote several plays based on Greek myth. Annensky had a great influence on Punin's generation, not just those who attended the gymnasium, but also several of the great poets of Russia's

Silver Age, such as Anna Akhmatova. Akhmatova called Annensky her "teacher" and also considered him the teacher of Pasternak, Mandelshtam, Gumilev, and even the Futurist poet Khlebnikov. Annensky's strong support of his students in spite of their demonstrations and strikes may have cost him his job. He was relieved of his post at the gymnasium in November 1905.

Anrep, Boris Vasilevich (1883–1969)

Artist and mosaicist, Akhmatova's lover in the early 1910's. Anrep emigrated in 1917. Akhmatova dedicated many poems from *Belaya staya* and *Podorozhnik* to him. Anrep himself wrote several poems dedicated to Akhmatova and immortalized her image in his mosaics, most notably the panel *Compassion* in the National Gallery, London (1952).

Arakcheevshchina

Period named after General Aleksey Arakcheev, a rather simple-minded, extremely loyal Russian soldier, whom Aleksandr I (1801–1825) used as his "man Friday." Arakcheev was put in charge of the military colonies which Aleksandr I founded in 1810. These were peasant villages under rigid military discipline that were supposed to provision themselves and provide soldiers in time of need. The peasants regarded the colonies as the equivalent of prisons. In 1832, there was widespread revolt in these colonies, after which Nicholas I abolished them. Some scholars have seen their establishment as Russia's first experiment in state socialism. Arakcheev was not personally in charge of the oppressive censorship laws and restrictions on education that were instituted around 1820, but the entire period from 1815 until 1825 is known as the Arakcheevshchina.

Aseev, Nikolay Nikolaevich (1889–1963)

Poet and writer. He began his writing career in 1911 and was originally associated with the Centrifuge group of Futurists. After living in the East for five years, Aseev returned to Moscow in 1921. In 1922, he joined the Lef group and began publishing in its journal, *Lef.* He was a proponent of "factography," and much of his work was versified journalism and propaganda. In 1939, he was one of a group of writers who attempted to get Akhmatova a special pension after her expulsion from the Writers' Union.

Auslender, Sergey Abramovich (1886–1943)

Writer and literary critic important to the literary movements of the early twentieth century in Russia such as Acmeism. Close friend of Nikolay Gumilev. After the revolution, Auslender became a well-known writer of Soviet youth literature.

Balmont, Nikolay Konstantinovich (1890–1924)

Poet and musician, son of Konstantin Dmitrievich Balmont (1867–1942), whose own poetry inspired two generations of Symbolists. He was most famous for his cycles of sonnets and for the exotic strain in his poetry inspired by his many travels. Konstantin Balmont was exiled to France in 1920 and remained there until his death.

Bebel, August (1840–1915)	Writer who mingled trade-union with national electoral politics and helped make the German Social Democratic Party the largest Marxist political party in the world and the most successful.
Belinsky, Vissarion Grigorevich (1811–1848)	The first professional critic in Russia. He was famous for being a well-educated member of the intelligentsia with radical political views and a "raznochinets" or man of other than gentry or noble origins. He was heavily influenced by German philosophy and created "revolutionary-democratic criticism." His short career and life were intense, earning him the nickname "furious Vissarion." The future critic Nikolay Punin would obviously have been flattered to be called "furious Nikolay."
Bely, Andrey (pseud. of Boris Niko-laevich Bugaev) (1880–1934)	Poet and leading representative of Russian Symbolism. He was also a novelist, literary critic, polemicist, and theorist.
Benois, Alexandre Nikolaevich (1870–1960)	Painter, critic, art historian, and memoirist. Benois was a key figure in the World of Art movement and wrote many articles in the journal *Rech'* against the new currents in Russian art such as Futurism and Cubism. After 1915, he began writing his memoirs. A volume of his letters has been published recently.
Blok, Aleksandr Aleksandrovich (1880–1921)	Poet and playwright. Considered a Symbolist and decadent poet, Blok at first embraced the revolution, becoming active in Soviet institutions such as the World Literature publishing house, the Free Philosophical Society, and the Bolshoy Dramatic Theater. In 1918, he wrote the verse epic "The Twelve," which was controversial in both form and content. The critics immediately saw it as a justification for and acceptance of bolshevism. In form, it was seen as radically experimental, using polyphony, street language, and revolutionary slogans as a vehicle for the poetry. Punin apparently has a different opinion, seeing Blok as the end of an era, rather than the beginning of a new one. Blok's last two years of life were indeed filled with despair and disillusionment with the revolution.
Bloody Sunday	January 9, 1905, when military troops opened fire on demonstrators, with an unnecessary and publicly dramatic loss of life.
	Several events loomed large in the life of Punin and Russia in the years before the First World War. First was the war with Japan and the disastrous naval battle in the Straits of Tsushima, in which virtually the entire Russian Baltic Fleet was lost, after the epic farce of its global

journey; it skirted England but became embroiled in a scandalous incident with the British fishing fleet off the Dogger Bank and, having reached the straits that separated Russia's Far Eastern ports from Japan, found itself outmaneuvered and outgunned by the much better trained and equipped Japanese fleet. Sergey Witte, Aleksandr III's shrewd, competent finance minister of the early 1890's, had launched a policy that resulted in the rapid industrialization of Russia at about the same time that Japan was also rapidly industrializing. Although it was central to Witte's policy that Russia remain at peace, key aspects of his policy—the rapid construction of railroads (including the trans-Siberian), the large-scale importation of foreign capital (which depended in turn on fiscal stability), the rapid increase of agricultural exports (with strong pressure on the peasantry to bring more grain to market)—created more social and political turbulence than the tsarist regime thought it could control. Nicholas II, who succeeded to the throne in 1894, tended to distrust Witte and proved all too vulnerable to the political temptation of engaging in a quick, successful war in the Far East against a presumably backward Asiatic power in order to bolster his regime's political prestige at home. It was a fatal mistake.

Meanwhile, there was increasing pressure at home for expanded democratization and some form of representative government on a national scale. The wartime disasters gave considerable impetus to the political movement and intensified social discontent. On January 9, 1905, a large group of workers who had been organized into a "police union"—that is, a trade union approved by and to some degree sponsored by the police (the tsar wanted to show his "fatherly" concern for working conditions)—marched on the Winter Palace to present the tsar with a petition of their grievances. They were led by an Orthodox priest, Father Gapon. The military opened fire on the peaceful demonstration, killing many. "Bloody Sunday" was followed by a series of protests and strikes that became the "Revolution of 1905," which was in turn marked by the activity of spontaneously formed Workers' Councils or Soviets, in which, in Petersburg, Leon Trotsky played a prominent role. Nicholas II brought Witte back into the government and issued a manifesto granting Russia its first constitution and first elected representative body, the Duma, albeit on the basis of limited suffrage. As order was restored, the tsar dismissed Witte, dissolved the Duma, and called for new elections based on even more limited suffrage. The period between 1905 and the outbreak of the First World War was one of great political and social turmoil in Russia—a curious period of attempted political repression from above accompanied by continued democratic expansion from below. Paradoxically, during this period

Russian universities were among the freest in the world and some segments of even the legally permissible Russian press were among the boldest and most radical anywhere. The entire situation was extremely volatile.

Boguslav-skaya, Ksenya

See Puni, Ksenya Leonidovna

Borodin, Aleksandr Aleksandrovich (1885–1925)

Son of an engineer and classmate of Punin's. His mother, Anna Vladimirovna Borodina, was a friend and relative of and frequently corresponded with Innokenty Annensky, then director of the Tsarskoe Selo gymnasium. Borodin would go on to become the teacher of Russian there.

Brik, Lilya (1891–1978)

Wife of Osip Brik, literary theorist and playwright. She was also the lover of the poet Vladimir Mayakovsky and inspired many of his poems. Anna Akhmatova had a low opinion of this ménage-à-trois: "Literature was put aside, all that remained was the Briks' salon, where writers used to meet Cheka agents . . . It was his [Mayakovsky's] home, his love, his friendship; he liked everything there. That was his level of education, of his sense of camaraderie and of all his interests. He never left them, you see, he never broke with them, he loved them to the end" (*The Akhmatova Journals,* ed. Lydia Chukovskaya, 1:93–94).

Bruni, Lev Aleksandrovich (1894–1948)

Painter, designer, and close friend of both Tatlin and Punin.

Bruni, Nikolay Aleksandrovich (1890–1937)

Poet, musician, sculptor, and brother of Lev Bruni.

Bryusov, Valery Yakovlevich (1873–1924)

Symbolist poet, novelist, and critic. His life and love affairs became the subject of his art and of the art of others. Punin mentions him in his diary entry from January 2, 1920 (Notebook Two), because he feels a conflict between his personal life and work and does not want affairs to interfere with his work.

Burlyuk, David Davidovich (1882–1967)

Poet and artist, one of the founders and theoreticians of Russian Futurism. Burlyuk emigrated in 1920 and lived in America from 1922 until his death.

Cabalero, *Largo* *(1869–1946)*	Spanish socialist trade union leader. The Spanish Civil War began with a military uprising led by Gen. Francisco Franco on July 17–18, 1936, in response to a left-wing electoral victory. Franco represented the Nationalist conservative faction, which successfully controlled the western provinces of Spain. The Republican or Loyalist faction, which included republicans, socialists, communists, and anarchists, controlled the industrial areas of the country and defended Madrid against the nationalists. Largo Cabalero served as prime minister and minister of war between September 1936 and May 1937. By the winter of 1936–1937, the fighting had turned to a stalemate. Fascist Italy and Nazi Germany sent weapons and aid to the Nationalists, while the USSR aided the Republicans. The Comintern organized thousands of liberals and leftists from fifty-three countries into volunteer brigades to fight fascism. The war ended in victory for Franco and the Nationalists in 1939.
Chekhonin, *Sergey* *Vasilevich* *(1878–1936)*	Artist and sculptor. He was a member of the board of the Department of Fine Arts along with Punin and also worked for the State Porcelain Factory.
Chekrygin, *Vasily* *Nikolaevich* *(1878–1922)*	Painter and member of the Makovets society of artists, named after the hill on which Sergius of Radonezh built the Trinity-Sergius monastery. This reflected the group's emphasis.
Chukovsky, *Korney* *Ivanovich* *(pen-name of* *Nikolay Vasi-* *levich Kor-* *neychukov)* *(1882–1969)*	Writer, literary scholar, children's poet, and translator. Chukovsky's children's poetry is known by heart by most Russians to this day. In 1916, Maksim Gorky invited Chukovsky to head the children's section of the publishing house *Parus,* and at that time he began to write for children himself. He was also quite famous as a translator and translation theoretician. Anna Akhmatova had a close friendship with both Korney Chukovsky and his daughter, Lydia Chukovskaya.
Danko- *Alekseenko,* *Natalya* *Yakovlevna* *(1892–1942)*	Sculptor who did a famous porcelain statuette of Akhmatova.
Department *of Fine Arts* *of the Nar-* *kompros* *(IZO)*	Formed in 1918. Punin was vice-chair and a member of its board for the Petrograd section. The department had the task of organizing exhibits, establishing cultural policy, and engaging in political agitation. The State Free Art Studios were organized in 1917 after the revolution and eventually developed into Vkhutemas. Free government workshops

offering classes and lectures were first introduced in France in 1848 by Louis Blanc during the high tide of the revolution of 1848. In 1918, Punin joined the Department of Fine Arts of the People's Commissariat of Education and became deputy head and then head of the Petrograd section. He was also on the editorial board of the department's journals *Art of the Commune* and *Fine Art.* He wrote many articles on contemporary art and was one of the few to embrace this art and write about it in a systematic and critical way. During this time, he also organized art studios for workers and in 1919 gave lectures to workers on art, which were later published as *The First Series of Lectures (Pervyi tsikl lektsii).*

Domestic theater

Had a long tradition in Russia. In fact, before public secular theater was condoned and popularized by Empress Elizabeth in the mid-eighteenth century, domestic drama produced at court and in the homes of the aristocracy was very popular. Some members of the nobility retained their own acting and ballet troupes. By the late nineteenth century, Russian drama was flourishing, although the age of the "well-made play" of the 1850–1860's was coming to a close. By this time, the popularity of domestic drama had spread to families of the intelligentsia and upper-class. In fact, Anton Chekhov's famous 1896 play, *The Seagull (Chayka),* contains a homegrown play within the play. It must also be noted that Innokenty Annensky, the director of the gymnasium at Tsarskoe Selo, which Punin attended, was a playwright himself and encouraged his students' interest in drama.

Druzhinin, Aleksandr Vasilevich (1824–1864)

Novelist and critic.

Dymshits-Tolstaya, Sofya (1889–1963)

Artist who worked in Vladimir Tatlin's studio. She is best known for her work with stained glass.

Eikhenbaum, Boris Mikhailovich (1886–1959)

Literary critic, somewhat associated with Formalist criticism. Although he wrote on all eras of Russian literature, from Gavrila Derzhavin to Akhmatova, the book referenced here is *Anna Akhmatova,* written in 1922. It was the first book dedicated to the poet; along with insightful analysis of her poetry and its role in the future of Russian literature, he also coined the unfortunate phrase that Akhmatova's lyrical heroine was "half-harlot . . . half-nun." This phrase was later snatched up by Stalinist and other Soviet critics as a weapon against the poet and her work. Korney Chukovsky, another critic and friend of Akhmatova's, also noted the poet's dismay at Eikhenbaum's work: "Saw Akhmatova. She was very kind to me. She complained about Eikhenbaum: 'Since he wrote his book about me, we no longer know each other'" (from Konstantin Polivanov, ed., *Anna Akhmatova and Her Circle* [Fayetteville: University of Arkansas Press, 1994], p. 86).

Ezhovshchina   The period between 1936 and 1938, the worst years of Stalin's purges and the great "show trials" when "old bolsheviks" from Grigory Zinovev to Nikolay Bukharin confessed publicly to the most improbable crimes constituting high treason. (Bukharin's confession in particular was so improbable as to clearly parody the whole procedure.) The entire ranks of the officer corps of the Red Army above the rank of field officer were decimated, to the Soviet Union's grief once war began. Marshal Mikhail Tukhachevsky was shot. General (later Marshal) Georgy Zhukov had to be released from the gulag in late 1941 to be put in charge of an army! The period was named after Nikolay Ivanovich Ezhov (1894–1939), who succeeded Genrikh Yagoda as commissar of internal affairs (NKVD) in 1936. Ezhov was in turn succeeded by Lavrenty Beriya in 1938, under whom arrests and executions were at first slowed down and then after the war (1946–1952) reintensified. After a year as commissar of river transport, Ezhov was himself executed in 1939. Beriya was dispatched by Stalin's successors in 1953.

Akhmatova wrote a cycle of poems about this period entitled *Requiem* (1935–1940). Although *Requiem* could not be published within the Soviet Union until many years later, the cycle was well-known abroad and brought Akhmatova world fame. In the introductory piece to the cycle Akhmatova writes about the "Ezhovshchina" and waiting in the prison line to see her son Lev:

> *In the terrible years of the Ezhov terror, I spent seventeen months in the prison lines of Leningrad. Once, someone "recognized" me. Then a woman with bluish lips standing behind me, who, of course, had never heard me called by name before, woke up from the stupor to which everyone had succumbed and whispered in my ear (everyone spoke in whispers there): "Can you describe this?" And I answered: "Yes, I can." Then something that looked like a smile passed over what had once been her face. (Judith Hemschemeyer, trans., and Roberta Reeder, ed.,* **The Complete Poems of Anna Akhmatova,** *2:95)*

Favorsky, Vladimir Andreevich (1886–1963)   Artist and religious thinker.

Fedin, Konstantin Aleksandrovich (1892–1977)	Novelist, short story writer, and essayist. Fedin's first novel, *Cities and Years,* was one of the first novels of the Soviet era. Its use of different kinds of speech and disjointed time sequences captured the upheaval of the revolutionary era. The novel's theme is the struggle of the intelligentsia to embrace and be accepted by the revolution; the intelligentsia's representative fails (perhaps a reason, among others, for Punin's lukewarm review of it).
Fedotov, Pavel Andreevich (1815–1853)	Russian realist painter whose works, like Aleksandr Ivanov's, reflected Russian life and the attitude that art should uplift and improve humanity. Fedotov's works satirized the mores of the rising middle class in Russia, and his paintings had a great influence on the realistic painters of the late nineteenth century who loosely formed a group called the Wanderers. Ivanov attempted to bring the gospels directly to the people through his art and was a fanatic believer in Russia's destiny.
Filonov, Pavel Nikolaevich (1882–1941)	Artist, one of the founders of the Union of Youth (1910). He also founded a school called Masters of Analytical Art (1920's) and was head of the section for communal ideology at the Museum of Artistic Culture established in 1922 by Tatlin.
France, Anatole (pseud. of Jacques Anatole François Thibault) (1844–1924)	French novelist, poet, and critic, whose political satire and critical essays had a profound influence during his time. He held a friendly attitude toward Russia and its political experimentation. France won the Nobel Prize for literature in 1921.
Garshin, Vladimir Georgevich (1887–1956)	Anatomical pathologist, professor at the Military Academy of Medicine. He met Akhmatova while she was a patient at the Kuibyshev Hospital. Garshin was married at the time (his wife died during World War II). Their relationship lasted until 1945, when Akhmatova returned to Leningrad from evacuation in Tashkent only to find he had married another woman.
Gessen, Arnold Ilych	Joint-owner of the Petrograd publishing house. He had planned to publish a two-volume collection of Akhmatova's poems, but was unable to because of the 1925 ban against her.
Gippius, Zinaida Nikolaevna (1869–1945)	Poet, fiction writer, playwright, and critic, married to writer Dmitry Sergeevich Merezhkovsky (1865–1941). Both were famous in St. Petersburg for their writings and for their participation in religious and philosophical groups. Gippius wrote under several pseudonyms. She initially embraced the revolution, but in 1919 emigrated to Europe with her husband. Although Akhmatova quotes Gippius' poetry here, she

generally had a poor opinion of both writers. She told Lydia Chukovskaya, "They kept trying to get me to visit, but I avoided it because they were nasty—in the simplest, most elementary sense of the word" (*The Akhmatova Journals,* 1:62).

Glebova-Sudeykina, Olga (1886–1945)

An actress, dancer, and renowned St. Petersburg beauty, very close to Akhmatova from 1913 to the time of her emigration in 1924. For a while, they even lived together. She appears as the goat-footed nymph in Akhmatova's *Poem without a Hero* and was a frequent habitué of the Stray Dog cabaret. Half of the Petersburg avant-garde was in love with her, including Velemir Khlebnikov. Her blonde hair and striking, pale, gray-blue eyes were a marked contrast to Akhmatova's dark, aquiline beauty. In 1907 she had married avant-garde artist Sergey Sudeykin, but the marriage was brief. (Sudeykin's second wife, Vera, later married Igor Stravinsky. See John Bowlt, ed., *The Salon Album of Vera Sudeikin-Stravinsky* [Princeton, N.J.: Princeton University Press, 1995].)

Golubeva, Martha Andreevna (1906–1963)

Art historian, collaborator, and friend of Punin in his last decades. She was nicknamed "Tika." His relationship with her lasted until his death in the Abez prison camp in 1953. Her sister, Darya Golubeva, and daughter Masha (Mashuk) are also mentioned in the diaries. Her first husband, Valentin Kazimirov, is referred to as "Toshka" in the diaries. He perished during the siege of Leningrad.

Goncharova, Natalya Sergeevna (1881–1962)

Painter, graphic artist, and theatrical artist. Goncharova was influenced by Cubism, Futurism, and Rayonism. From 1915 she lived in Paris with her husband, Mikhail Larionov. The stage sets she created for the Ballets Russes were both beautiful and innovative.

Gostiny Dvor

A large department store on Nevsky Prospect in St. Petersburg.

Gumilev, Lev Nikolaevich (1912–1992)

Son of Akhmatova and Nikolay Gumilev, raised by Gumilev's mother at their family estate in Slepnevo. Akhmatova visited him during the summers and at Christmas, and as an adult the two were close. Lev was arrested in 1933 and 1935 for short periods and then again in 1938. This time he was exiled and spent several years in Siberia before going to the front to fight in World War II. Gumilev was again arrested in 1949, freed in 1956, and exonerated that same year. In later life he became a distinguished Orientalist and something of an ideologue. Some Neo-Eurasians regard him as a founder of their movement.

Gumilev, Nikolay Stepanovich (1886–1921)

Poet and literary critic. One of the founders of the Acmeist movement, to which Anna Akhmatova belonged. Also Anna Akhmatova's husband from 1910 to 1918. Gumilev was executed in 1921 for alleged counter-revolutionary activities.

Huysmans, *Joris-Karl* *(1848–1907)*	French novelist and art critic, considered a decadent writer. His novels are steeped in mysticism and hostile to the scientific orientation of late-nineteenth-century naturalism.
Ioganson, *Boris Vladi-* *mirovich* *(1893–1973)*	Socialist Realist painter and administrator. He was the vice-president and then president of the USSR Academy of Arts in the 1950's and later was first secretary of the Artists' Union.
Ivanov, *Aleksandr* *Andreevich* *(1806–1858)*	Russian realist painter whose works, like those of Pavel Fedotov, reflected Russian life and the attitude that art should uplift and improve humanity. Ivanov attempted to bring the gospels directly to the people through his art and was a fanatic believer in Russia's destiny. He spent most of his adult life in Italy, never knew success in his lifetime, and left many works unfinished, including his *magnum opus,* a cycle of biblical studies. He is perhaps best known for his painting *The Appearance of Christ to the People* (1837–1858) and for his landscapes. He is often compared with the Impressionists and Cézanne, especially in his rejection of the lyrical element in nature which reflects the inner state of an individual. Nikolay Punin devoted three chapters to Ivanov in his textbook on Russian and Soviet art.
Ivanov, *Vyacheslav* *Ivanovich* *(1866–1949)*	Poet, critic, and scholar. "High priest" of the Russian Symbolist movement. He emigrated in 1924 and lived in Rome until his death in 1949.
IZO	See Department of Fine Arts of the Narkompros
Kamensky, *Vasily* *Vasilevich* *(1884–1961)*	Artist, Futurist poet and pilot, friend of Velemir Khlebnikov. Khlebnikov dedicated his poem "Zhuravl'" to Kamensky.
Khlebnikov, *Velemir* *(Viktor Vla-* *dimirovich,* *1885–1922)*	Futurist poet whose prose work "Razin: Two Trinities" (1921–1922) had a strong impact on Punin. In this work, the poet identifies himself with the peasant rebel leader Stenka Razin, who began a Cossack-led revolt against the institution of a secular state. The hero had a resurgence of popularity during the years of revolution. In Khlebnikov's piece, the poet is not Razin, but a Razin minus one, an anti-Razin. He wishes to "choose as my Volga *his* destiny, which ended on the scaffold as an eagle ends in cruel beak, but giving my life a direction running counter to his . . ." (from *Collected Works of Velemir Khlebnikov,* ed. Ronald Vroon [Cambridge, Mass.: Harvard University Press, 1987], 2:146). If Razin is a hero whose actions became a source of myth and poetry, then

Khlebnikov's poetry and art would become action. Khlebnikov believed that destiny is written, but might be rewritten by a poet-prophet. Like Tatlin's art, Khlebnikov's poetry was meant to change the world, to play an active role in creating a new society. (See also the entry on "Zangezi" below.)

Kluev, Nikolay Alekseevich (1887–1937)

One of the most famous of the "peasant poets." Kluev's early work described idyllic nature scenes and was influenced by the Symbolist movement. Later he consciously moved toward civic poetry, dressing as a peasant and writing long poems combining nationalism and religiosity. His name is often mentioned in conjunction with the other great "peasant poet," Sergey Esenin.

Klun, Ivan Vasilevich (1873–1942)

Painter.

Komarovsky, Count Vasily Alekseevich (1881–1914)

Russian poet and literary figure, famous among all who lived in Tsarskoe Selo and influential in the Acmeist movement. Akhmatova considered Komarovsky one of the last poets in the line of "Tsarskoe Selo Mythology," which included Pushkin, Fedor Tyutchev, and Annensky, among others.

Komsomol

The Union of Communist Youth. During the mid-twenties, there was a great push by the Soviet government to raise the cultural awareness of youth, in particular the politically aware youth of the Komsomol. After Trotsky's 1923 book *Literature and Revolution,* in which he declared that the proletariat was not culturally aware enough to produce world-class literature, many reacted strongly by pressuring the current cultural institutions to become not just revolutionary but "Soviet" and to promote and include the Soviet youth.

Kornilov, General Lavr Georgievich (1870–1918)

Commander-in-chief in the Provisional Government. After the February Revolution a Provisional Government was set up and Nicholas II abdicated, effectively putting an end to tsarist rule. The Provisional Government was to share power with the Soviets of Workers' and Soldiers' Deputies, but refused to pull out of the First World War. By July, the dire economic situation and antiwar sentiment had sparked mass demonstrations by workers, soldiers, and sailors in Moscow and Petrograd. A. F. Kerensky, minister-president of the Provisional Government, placed Petrograd under martial law and appointed General Kornilov commander-in-chief. Kornilov had just returned from the front, where he had participated in the abortive Russian offensive against the Germans in Galicia.

Conflicts arose between Kerensky and Kornilov, and at the end of August Kornilov sent troops toward Petrograd. Kerensky interpreted this as a military coup d'état. What happened next is somewhat anticlimactic and has been interpreted differently by various sources. According to Soviet sources, the "Kornilov Revolt" was crushed by the Red Guard and revolutionary sailors and soldiers led by the bolsheviks. Others cite lack of support for Kornilov among his own troops and a railway strike as the main reasons for the failure of the coup. Whatever the causes for the coup's failure, there was little fighting; on September 1, Kornilov surrendered and was imprisoned.

Korsakova-Galston, Aleksandra

A graphic artist, nicknamed "Yuksi." Korsakova was Punin's lifelong friend, whose correspondence was often a comfort. She emigrated to Germany, where she married an American pianist and eventually moved to St. Louis, Missouri.

Krasin, Leonid Borisovich (1870–1926)

Engineer, early fundraiser for the Social Democratic Party, and a member of the Bolshevik Central Committee. He aided both Lenin and Trotsky at times and wanted to unite the bolshevik and menshevik factions. Later he became the Soviet expert on foreign trade who prepared trade agreements with Austria, Italy, Great Britain, and Germany in 1921.

Kronstadt, John of (Ioann Ilych Sergiev, 1829–1908)

Famous religious figure of the time. He was the *proto* of the Andreev Cathedral in Kronstadt. Stories of his miracles drew many believers to his church.

Lapshin, Nikolay Fedorovich (1888–1942)

Graphic artist who worked at the Porcelain Factory with Punin.

Larionov, Mikhail Fedorovich (1881–1964)

Painter, graphic artist, and theatrical artist. Larionov's early work was influenced by late Impressionism and Fauvism. Along with his wife, Natalya Goncharova, Larionov was one of the major artists in the Rayonist movement. From 1915, the couple lived and worked in Paris, where their costumes and stage designs garnered fame at the Ballets Russes.

Lassalle, Ferdinand (1825–1864)

One of the founders of the German Social Democratic Party. Like Marx, Lassalle was a German intellectual of Jewish descent, but with much more of a flair for adventurous politics. He was opportunist enough to flirt with Prussian statism and Bismarckian politics.

Lazarev, Petr Petrovich (1878–1942)	Russian physicist and art historian whose research included the study of color perception.
Lebedev, Vladimir Vasilevich (1891–1967)	Painter and graphic artist.
Lef	A journal between 1923 and 1925. It grew out of a loose group of Constructivist artists, Futurist poets, and Formalist critics. The journal's contributors represented the Institute for Artistic Culture, Department of Fine Arts, and Meyerhold's State Theatrical Institute. The covers of *Lef* are now considered some of the best examples of Constructivist art and in particular of the montage technique.
Lentulov, Aristarkh Vasilevich (1891–1967)	Painter active in Futurism, Cubism, and Orphism.
Leonteva, Lydia Sergeevna (Lida)	Punin's first love. She is later referred to as "Dama Luni" in the diaries and her image as his first love and also first awakening of his inner life continued to surface throughout his life.
Lezhnev, A. (pseudonym of Abram Zakharovich Gorelik) (1893–1938)	Marxist literary critic and theorist. Regular contributor to *Krasnaia nov'*.
Life of Art	Magazine of the Department of Fine Arts.
Lossky, Nikolay Onufrievich (1870–1965)	Philosopher and translator who, through his translations of Immanuel Kant and Nietzsche among others, introduced much of German philosophy to a Russian audience. In 1922, he emigrated; in the 1950's, he published a history of Russian philosophy as well as critical works on Tolstoy and Dostoevsky. He contributed to the field of epistemology with his own philosophical system called "intuitivism."
Lourie, Arthur Sergeevich (1892–1966)	Composer and friend of both Punin and Akhmatova. Akhmatova lived with Lourie and Olga Sudeykina from 1921 to 1922. Lourie was commissar of music from 1918 to 1920, but left for Berlin in 1922 and eventually emigrated to the United States.

Luknitsky, Pavel Nikolaevich (1900–1973)	Poet, literary critic, and biographer of Akhmatova's first husband, Nikolay Gumilev. Luknitsky, according to General Kalugin (Oleg Kalugin, *Delo KGB na Annu Akhmatovu,* in "Gosbezopasnost' i literatura na opyte Rossii i Germanii") was an agent of the GPU-NKVD-KGB. Kalugin even quotes samples of Luknitsky's dispatches to the GPU on Akhmatova's contacts and opinions. [contributed by Leonid Zykov]
Lunacharsky, Anatoly Vasilevich (1875–1933)	Critic, playwright, and first communist director of culture. He was a member of the bolsheviks from 1903 and was appointed people's commissar of enlightenment by Lenin in 1917. He did a great deal to keep culture alive during the civil war and after by patronizing poets and Constructivist artists and allowing pluralism and freedom in the arts. He was removed from his post by Stalin in 1929.
Malevich, Kazimir Severinovich (1878–1935)	Painter, graphic artist, designer, and art theoretician. Malevich was one of the most famous artists to paint in the Constructivist and Suprematist styles. He also painted a portrait of Punin in Renaissance dress.
Mandelshtam, Osip Emilevich (1891–1938)	Poet. He and his wife, Nadezhda, were Akhmatova's very close friends. Gumilev, Akhmatova, and Mandelshtam were the most gifted of the Acmeist poets. Although Mandelshtam was at first rather critical of Akhmatova's verse, he soon recognized her as one of the really authentic voices of her generation. Her physical voice itself he considered memorable. Both suffered the disfavor of the bolshevik regime. When Osip and Nadezhda were forced into administrative exile by the regime in the provincial town of Voronezh, Akhmatova was a frequent visitor. Osip was arrested and sent to Siberia in 1938, where he died in a transit camp. Akhmatova and Nadezhda remained close friends until Akhmatova's death.
Marr, Nikolay Yakovlevich (1864–1934)	Linguist and author of several books on language. According to his "new teaching on language," the strict division of languages into families is a false construct. His more "organic" approach to language factored in a community's collective instinct, material life, and economy in the evolution of language. Marr argued that pure, homogeneous language formations did not exist. For more on Marr's role in Soviet scientific thought, see Boris Gasparov's article on philosophy and the avant-garde in *Laboratory of Dreams,* ed. John Bowlt and Olga Matich (Stanford: Stanford University Press, 1996), pp. 133–150. See also Katerina Clark, *Petersburg, Crucible of Cultural Revolution* (Cambridge, Mass.: Harvard University Press, 1995), pp. 212–223. Marr later became, under Stalin, virtual dictator of language-study in the multilingual society of the USSR. Long after Marr's death, persuaded largely by the

arguments of the very courageous Georgian linguist A. Chikobave, Stalin turned against Marr and denounced him and his teaching in his famous *Essay on Linguistics* (1952), rumored to have actually been written by Chikobave.

Marx, Karl (1818–1883)

Along with his close friend Friedrich Engels, the founder of so-called scientific socialism. His self-assumed role was to bring the modern (Hegelian) philosophical project of "understanding" the world into the revolutionary, political, working-class project of "changing" it. In this sense, he was the "mind" of the First International Workingmen's Association (1853–1868) and the inspiration of the Second (1871–1914).

Matyushin, Mikhail Vasilevich (1861–1934)

Russian artist associated with Cubists and Futurists and husband of artist and writer Elena Guro. Matyushin became interested in art in 1889 and worked with the World of Art painters from 1906 to 1908. Later Matyushin and Guro's apartment became an important meeting place for avant-garde artists, and Matyushin translated and edited the 1913 Russian edition of Albert Gleizes and Jean Metzinger's *Du Cubisme*. Matyushin produced works of nonobjective art which investigated the interrelationship of form and color and its effects on the viewer, while continuing to write music for Futurist operas. From 1918, Matyushin taught art and directed the Department of Organic Culture at the Petrograd GINKhUK. His research into form and color was published in 1932.

Mayakovsky, Vladimir Vladimirovich (1893–1930)

Often called the "poet of the revolution." Mayakovsky later came under constant criticism for his poetry and lost his initial fervor for the revolution. Unfortunately, he ended his own life in 1930.

Meerson, Yosif (1900–1941)

Constructivist artist who worked closely with Vladimir Tatlin on the model for the Monument to the Third International.

Mitrokhin, Dmitry Isidorovich (1883–1973)

Graphic artist.

Miturich, Petr Vasilevich (1887–1956)

Artist and close friend of Vladimir Tatlin. Miturich was one of the last people to be with the poet Velemir Khlebnikov before he died. Miturich's letters to Punin asking for money and describing Khlebnikov's plight are heart-wrenching. Although Punin was able to send money, nothing could have saved Khlebnikov from the paralysis and gangrene which killed him.

nepman	The nickname for the new businessperson who took advantage of the relative economic freedom under the New Economic Policy initiated by Lenin in 1921 and lasting until the First Five Year Plan in 1928.
Nicholas I (1825–1855)	Tsar who began his reign with the thorough suppression of the Decembrist revolt that refused to recognize his legitimacy. He made the political police and the corps of gendarmes key instruments of his administration and introduced a censorship so rigid that it could scarcely be enforced and made the more intelligent censors extremely uncomfortable. He was known to many as "Nicholas the Stick."
Nietzsche, Friedrich (1844–1900)	Philosopher, author of *The Birth of Tragedy from the Spirit of Music* (1872), his first published work. It was inspired by Richard Wagner, whom he later turned against, but with whom he had a lifelong love/envy relationship. The book had and still has an enormous influence (for its influence in Russia, see Bernice Glatzer Rosenthal, *Nietzsche in Russia* [Princeton, N.J.: Princeton University Press, 1986]), being the most powerful account of the origins of tragedy, and by implication of art in general, since Aristotle. For Nietzsche, the origins of tragedy lie in pastoral ritual (etymologically, "tragedy" means "goat-song") and are closely connected with the cult of Dionysus. Greek tragedy, however, involved a delicate balance between Dionysus, a night-time god of the unconscious forces and energies, of overflowing and the erasure and overcoming of self and of all boundaries and definitions, and Apollo, the god of sunlight, clarity, precision, boundaries, and definitions. Ulrich von Wilamowitz-Moellendorff, the doyen of classical scholarship at the time, declared: "This work has nothing to do with science!" But classical scholarship was never the same again.
"Old Petersburg"	The Society for Old Petersburg, founded in 1921, when the city of Petrograd organized celebrations in honor of the death of the poet Aleksandr Pushkin. During the relative economic and cultural freedom of NEP, the members of this society began a "Preservationist" movement, which soon gained popularity. Along with this movement to preserve the cultural heritage of Petrograd/St. Petersburg, there was also an initiative within the government to refurbish the cities of the new Soviet Union. Thus, in 1925, the Society for Old Petersburg undertook the repainting of the city's buildings with their original colors.
Osinsky, Valerian Andreevich (1887–1938)	A leading figure in the Bolshevik Party and literary critic.

Osmerkin, Aleksander Aleksandrovich (1892–1953)	Artist who painted the 1939 portrait of Akhmatova entitled "The White Night." Although he and Ioganson were friends, Ioganson officially criticized him in the late forties for his "Formalism."
The Passage	A large, glass-roofed shopping "mall" on Nevsky Prospekt, across from Gostiny Dvor.
Pavlovsk Railroad Station Hall	Hall where many influential artists and writers of Punin's generation who grew up in Tsarskoe Selo listened to great classical music. The poet Osip Mandelshtam (1891–1938) dedicated a section of his auto-biographical work of literary prose, *The Noise of Time* (1923), to the hall as well as a long, dense, complicated, ironic poem, "Music at Pavlovsk," which rang all the changes and implications of classical musical concerts at a railroad station. To Punin and his contemporaries, this charmed childhood in the tsar's "toy city" would always hold a special place in their hearts after all the revolutions and war.
Péguy, Charles (1873–1914)	French poet who believed in socialism and had a lifelong obsession with Joan of Arc. Much of his poetry combined religious faith with patriotism. He was a lieutenant in the First World War and died in battle.
Pestel, Vera Efimovna (1886–1952)	Painter.
Petrov-Vodkin, Kuzma Sergeevich (1878–1939)	Artist and member of the board of the House of Arts. Petrov-Vodkin did several portraits of Akhmatova, most notably a 1922 portrait with a mysterious shadowy figure behind her.
Plekhanov's prognosis	Prediction by Georgy Plekhanov, the father of Russian Marxism, that if the bolsheviks seized power, they would find themselves in the hapless situation of a small minority in control of a vast country. Lenin died in January 1924. Trotsky, after an initial struggle for power in which he proved himself surprisingly inept, lost influence. He was exiled to Siberia by 1927 and banned from the USSR by 1929. The mood here is of impending, ominous change. These changes and the attitude of the intelligentsia toward them are hinted at in Punin's description of the Party that took place on January 18. The proletariat itself was a relatively small minority, and the bolsheviks were having trouble enough recruiting genuine proletarians as Party members. The bolsheviks would either be overthrown or would be forced to rule by tyranny. In

either case, the democratic ideals of socialism would be seen as betrayed and the revolution discredited. This view was shared by many non-bolshevik Marxists, who tended to see the "elemental" (*stikhiinii*) aspect of the revolutionary movement as most vital and the "conscious" (*soznanyi*) element as inevitably subordinate to it. Lenin's whole idea of Party organization (see his pamphlet *What Is to Be Done?*) stressed the importance of the "conscious" element provided by professional revolutionaries.

Poletaev, Evgeny Alexeevich (1880–1937)

Writer, philologist, and head of the Department of the Secondary School of the Petrograd Section of Narkompros in 1918–1919, with whom Punin wrote *Against Civilization* in 1918. He was arrested in 1937 and died in a camp.

Polonsky, Vyacheslav Pavlovich (originally Gusin) (1886–1932)

Literary critic, editor, and historian. Editor of *Pechat' i revoliutsiia* from 1921 to 1929 and *Novyi mir* from 1926 to 1931.

Popova, Lyubov Sergeevna (1889–1924)

Painter, set designer, and textile designer.

Puni, Ivan Albertovich (Jean Pougny, 1892–1956)

Finnish-born painter and graphic artist involved in Cubist and Constructivist movements. He later exhibited Suprematist works and issued a Suprematist declaration in which he stated that "a picture is a new conception of abstract, real elements, independent of meaning." Puni exhibited in Russia, France, and Italy, and in 1919 he taught in Vitebsk with Marc Chagall. After emigrating in 1920, he lived in Berlin and exhibited at Der Sturm gallery before settling in Paris, where he lived until his death.

Puni, Ksenya Leonidovna (née Boguslavskaya, 1892–1972)

Painter, wife of Ivan Puni.

Punin Family

Nikolay Mikhailovich, Nikolay Nikolaevich Punin's father, and Anna Nikolaevna (1865–1898) had four children, Nikolay (1888–1953), Aleksandr (Sasha, 1890–1942), Leonid (Lenya, 1893–1916), and Zinaida (Zina, 1892–1980). Nikolay Mikhailovich remarried to Elisaveta Antonovna (née Jannine-Perrault, 18??–1928). They had one son, Lev (1897–1962).

Rasputin, Grigory Efimovich (1865–1916)	A Siberian holy man who had a great influence on Tsar Nicholas II and his wife, Aleksandra. She felt he was the only one who could cure the crown prince Aleksey's hemophilia. When Nicholas went to the front in 1914, he left Aleksandra and Rasputin in control. Rasputin proceeded to drink and debauch his way around the capital until a group of nobles including Prince Yusupov and Grand Duke Dmitry poisoned, shot, and drowned him. Rasputin's influence and actions helped to further erode the people's faith in the tsar.
"Razin"	Prose work by Futurist poet Velemir Khlebnikov (see the entry for Khlebnikov above).
Repin, Ilya Efimovich (1844–1930)	One of Russia's most famous nineteenth-century portrait painters. Repin painted a well-known portrait of Tolstoy dressed as a "muzhik." He was a member of the Wanderers or Peredvizhniki, who were artist-members of the Society for Traveling Art Exhibitions, which was formed in 1870. This society grew out of the sense that democratic tendencies were so evident among painters such as the Russian Realists that it needed systematic organization. The society included almost all the best painters of the time, and one of their main obligations was to take their exhibits to towns around the country in order to introduce art to a wider portion of the population. Since it was historically considered one of the few "democratic" societies of tsarist Russia, it was highly valued by the Soviet regime.
Rolland, Romain (1866–1944)	French novelist, dramatist, and essayist who won the Nobel Prize in 1916. His works reveal a commitment to humanism, and his most famous work is the ten-volume novel cycle *Jean Christophe*. Rolland also wrote biographies of famous men such as Tolstoy. During World War I, he was highly praised for his pacifist stand. Later in life he was influenced by Marxism.
ROSTA or Okna ROSTA	The windows of the Russian Telegraph Agency (ROSTA). Vladimir Mayakovsky used the windows after the revolution as a display for propaganda in the form of graphic advertising with short verse captions. Mayakovsky created both art and verse and produced hundreds of cartoons during the short time that the windows were used as display.
Rozanova, Olga Vladimirovna (1886–1918)	Painter and graphic artist.

Russian Contemporary	A private journal (one of about thirty published during the relative freedom of the New Economic Policy), first published in 1924.
The Russian Museum	Originally the Aleksandr III Museum, established in the 1890's. The Russian Museum holds one of the finest collections of Russian art in the country. From 1913, Punin worked at the Russian Museum and organized the icon section there. In the mid-twenties, he organized a section of the museum dedicated to new trends in Russian art.
Selvinsky, Ilya Lvovich (1899–1968)	Poet, playwright, and Constructivist.
Shchegolev, Pavel Eliseevich (1877–1931)	Pushkin scholar and husband of the actress Valentina Shchegoleva.
Sheremetev House	The former palace of the Sheremetev princes, located on the Fontanka embankment in St. Petersburg. Punin lived in an apartment in the annex of the palace from the revolution until he was sent to the labor camp in 1949. Akhmatova lived in a different apartment in the annex with her second husband, Vladimir Shileyko, from 1919 to 1920. She moved into Punin's rooms in the palace in 1926 and stayed there until after World War II. The palace, with its garden and ornate wrought iron gates, is often mentioned in Akhmatova's poetry as the "Fontany dom," the House on the Fontanka or Fountain House.
Shervinsky, Sergey	Poet and translator. Akhmatova sometimes stayed with the Shervinsky family at their dacha in Starki.
Shileyko, Vladimir or Voldemar Kazimirovich (1891–1930)	Anna Akhmatova's second husband. Shileyko was an Oriental scholar and member of the circle that frequented the St. Petersburg cabaret the Stray Dog. He was a friend of both Akhmatova and her first husband, Nikolay Gumilev. Akhmatova asked Gumilev for a divorce in 1918 in order to marry Shileyko in December of that year. In 1919, Shileyko headed the department of Archeology and Ancient Eastern Art at the Russian Academy and through this post was able to obtain a room at the Sheremetev House, where the Punins also lived.
Shklovsky, Viktor Borisovich (1893–1984)	Literary scholar, essayist, and novelist. He co-founded the Formalist movement in literary criticism, to which Punin's art criticism is often compared. His most important work was *On the Theory of Prose* (1925).

Shterenberg, David Petrovich (1881–1948)	Head of the Fine Arts Department of the People's Commissariat from 1918 to 1921. He worked closely with Punin on the organization of an exhibit of Russian art in Germany in 1922.
Smolny Convent	The blue and white, five-domed Smolny Cathedral, built by the famous Russian architect of Italian descent Bartolemeo Rastrelli in the eighteenth century. The convent school for orphans was founded by Empress Elizabeth, and in 1764 it was expanded by Empress Catherine into one of the best schools for girls of noble and bourgeois families. During the revolution, the convent was taken over by the Communist Party and until the fall of the Soviet Union the convent and its surroundings remained an exclusive Party neighborhood.
Sologub, Fedor Kuzmich (1863–1927)	Symbolist poet and novelist, considered to be a representative of the decadent strain in Symbolism. After 1923, Sologub, like many writers, was unable to publish original works, but he did find work under the Soviets; he was chairman of the Leningrad Union of Writers when he died in 1927 (which would account for his nice standard of living).
State Porcelain Factory	Where Punin was head of the artistic department from 1923 to 1925. While he was working there, Tatlin, Malevich, and other Constructivists created some very interesting and avant-garde designs. Most of the artists who worked there however, like Favorsky and Tyrsa, had been associated with World of Art. Akhmatova's close friend Olga Glebova-Sudeykina also designed porcelain dolls and figurines at this time.
St. Pantaleymon's relics	Considered to have healing powers.
Sudeykina, Olga	See Glebova-Sudeykina, Olga
Surikov, Vasily Ivanovich (1848–1916)	Painter, one of the Russian Realists, who was not famous until the end of the 1870's. Surikov tended to paint scenes from Russian history and is best known for *The Morning of the Streltsi Execution* (1881), *Menshikov in Berezovo* (1883), and *Boyarina Morozova* (1887).
Svomas	Acronym for Svobodnye Gosudartsvennye Khudozhestvennye Masterskie, the State Free Art Studios, headed by Osip Brik. Many famous artists and art historians such as Punin taught and worked in these studios.
Tatlin, Vladimir Evgrafovich (1885–1953)	Designer, painter, sculptor, builder of the model for the Monument to the Third International, one of the founders of Constructivism, and friend of Punin, Akhmatova, and poet Velemir Khlebnikov. Tatlin designed just about everything from clothing to dishes in his attempt

to make art useful and a part of everyday life. He was famous for his "counter-reliefs," constructions in mixed media that hung in space, often suspended in the corner between two walls. He was also famous for his model for the Monument to the Third International, which was to represent the new type of monument, which moved away from what Punin called "heads and busts" to interactive, useful monuments to the people. Punin was one of the first critics to embrace and formally analyze Tatlin's work. Like Punin, Tatlin initially supported the revolution, but later distanced himself as he saw the government's repression of artistic freedom. Tatlin was also instrumental in the Department of Fine Arts of the People's Commissariat and in government art schools such as the State Free Art Studios. Punin published several articles on Tatlin in 1919 and 1920 and published the book *On Tatlin* in 1921.

Tikhonov, Aleksandr Nikolaevich (1880–1956)

Writer and collaborator at several publishing houses.

Tolstoy, Aleksey Nikolaevich (1883–1945)

Poet, short story writer, and novelist. Tolstoy's early work was Symbolist; he left Russia after the revolution but returned to the Soviet Union in 1923. His later works were mostly historical novels and he was considered an apologist for the Stalinist regime.

Tomashevsky, Boris Viktorovich (1890–1956)

Literary critic, Pushkin scholar, and friend of Akhmatova.

Trepov, Dmitry Fedorovich (1855–1906)

Chief of police of St. Petersburg. The forces of law and order were under his command. While in charge of repression, General Trepov also tried to establish a line of communication with the working classes and was one of the originators of the idea of "police unionism."

Tsarskoe Selo

Tsars' Village, an aristocratic suburb of St. Petersburg, like Pavlovsk. For Punin and Akhmatova, and indeed for St. Petersburg intellectuals of their generation and social class, it was a place drenched with symbols and allusions, saturated with history and art, with personal reminiscence and much broader emblems of identity. They tended to view it with nostalgia, delight, apprehension, and irony. They were sensitive to the degree that it was a product of imperial will and class oppression; but also of the imperial determination to bring the best achievements of art and civilization (from China as well as Europe) to Russia. Originally the region had a Finnish name that sounded something like Tsarskoe Selo to the Russian ear so that, after Peter the Great's appropriation of it at the very beginning of the eighteenth century, the transition to "Tsar's Village" seemed natural. After the revolution it was called Detskoe Selo (the Children's Village) and still later Pushkin. It consisted of two huge parks, the Summer Palace designed by Rastrelli, aristocratic homes, and a lower-middle-class village whose characteristic smell, according to Akhmatova, was garbage rather than hyacinth. Military victories were celebrated by the erection of new structures in the park. Catherine the Great, who was in love with English gardens, introduced them there, as well as a great deal of chinoiserie. Charles Cameron and Giacomo Quarenghi designed the buildings there. Swans glided over its many ponds, and there were innumerable pathways and a wealth of sculpture, mostly neoclassical. Pushkin had been among the first students at the Tsarskoe Selo Lyceum, early in the nineteenth century, and Innokenty Annensky was headmaster when Punin was a student there. On one of its benches there is a strikingly lifelike statue of Pushkin taking his ease. The statue referred to here is an eighteenth-century work by P. P. Sokolov. It was based on the story of a careless French milkmaid who dropped her pitcher of milk before she could get it home. In one of his most striking and poignant short poems, Pushkin diverted this tale into the theme of the brevity of life and the permanence of art. Akhmatova, Gumilev, and Annensky, among others, also wrote poems inspired by this statue. See Lef Loseff and Barry Scherr, eds., *A Sense of Place: Tsarskoe Selo and Its Poets* (Columbus, Ohio: Slavica Publishers, 1993).

Tsvetaeva, Marina Ivanovna (1892–1941)

Poet: both personally and poetically far more difficult ("tougher") than Akhmatova; ultimately, her great rival in poetic stature. Technically as a poet, she had more in common with Mayakovsky than with Akhmatova. The two great women were quite wary of each other, though ultimately mutually generous. Tsvetaeva's father was the founder of the Pushkin Museum in Moscow. Her husband, Sergey Efron, fought with the White armies during the Civil War. Tsvetaeva was bold enough to defy the Cheka. One of her daughters died of starvation during the Civil War. She followed Efron into emigration in 1922. He became involved in international intrigue and had some role in the murder of Trotsky's son in Paris in the 1930's. When war broke out, Efron returned to the USSR, and Tsvetaeva followed with her son and daughter later. She and her children were evacuated from Moscow to Elabuga, where she hanged herself in 1941. Her son was killed in the war, and her daughter spent years in the gulag.

Turgenev, Ivan Sergeevich (1818–1883)	Novelist and poet, most famous for his 1862 novel *Fathers and Sons*. Turgenev did write quite a bit of poetry, however, most notably his *Poems in Prose* or *Senilia* (1879–1883), which Tsarskoe Selo headmaster and poet Innokenty Annensky played upon in his own *Poems in Prose*.
Tyrsa, Nikolay Andreevich (1887–1942)	Graphic artist who did several drawings of Anna Akhmatova, which the poet liked very much.
Udaltsova, Nadezhda Andreevna (1886–1961)	Painter, graphic artist, and Constructivist.
Vasilev, Fedor Aleksandrovich (1850–1873)	The most talented landscape painter of the 1870's. He liked to paint nature in a state of change and was innovative in his use of color. He is best known for *The Thaw* (1871), *Water Meadow* (1872), and *Marshland in the Forest* (1871–1873).
Verhaeren, Emile (1855–1916)	Belgian Symbolist poet whose poetry was both visionary and socially conscious.
Verkhovsky, Yury (1878–1956)	Poet with ties to the Symbolists.
Vkhutemas	Acronym for the Higher State Artistic and Technical Workshops. Vkhutemas was a specialized school for higher artistic and technical training. The school came into existence in 1920 and was active until 1930, although the name changed to Vkhutein (the Higher State Artistic and Technical Institute) in 1927. Between 1923 and 1926, Vkhutemas was directed by artist V. Favorsky. Both Punin and Tatlin were very active lecturers at the school. Vkhutemas excelled in both experimentation and production linking the arts and industry.
Voinov, Rostislav (1891–1919)	Sculptor.
Volfil	The Volnaya Filosofskaya Assotsiastiya, or Free Philosophical Society, was formed after the revolution by Nikolay Berdyaev and Solomon Frank, who had contributed in 1909 to the anthology *Vekhi* (Landmarks). Both were thinkers who had been Marxists in their youth and

then converted by way of idealism to Russian Orthodoxy. Meetings were often quite extraordinary and involved, among other things, debates on Marxism and Christianity with both sides represented. Russia's most talented philosophers and poets, as well as prominent members of the clergy, sometimes appeared at these meetings. Berdyaev and Frank were forced to leave Russia in 1922.

Volynsky, Akim Lvovich (1863–1926)

Literary critic and art historian who wrote about many things, from Leonardo da Vinci to Dostoevsky. After 1917, he concentrated on the study of dance.

Voronsky, Aleksandr Konstantinovich (1884–1943)

Marxist editor, literary critic, and theorist. Editor of such postrevolutionary journals as *Rabochii krai, Krasnaia nov',* and *Krug.*

Vrubel, Mikhail Aleksandrovich (1856–1910)

An artist of the fin de siècle whose art broke away from the realism of his predecessors. He is perhaps most famous for his portrayal of *The Demon Prostrate* (1902) for a commemorative edition of Lermontov's poem "The Demon." Vrubel was obsessed with the painting, continuing to change the demon's facial expression even after the work was on exhibit. The painting was completed in the same year as Vrubel's mental breakdown.

The Wanderers (Peredvizhniki)

A group of artists who reacted against the current artistic trends in the 1860's and devoted themselves to painting Russian subjects in a realistic style. Their most famous member was Ilya Repin. After the revolution, the Wanderers' portrayal of the Russian people and their suffering took on a more political, populist light that was seen as complementary to the bolsheviks' aims, and interest in their works was renewed.

Windelband, Wilhelm (1848–1915)

German philosopher, historian, and biographer of Nietzsche. Author of *A History of Philosophy* (1901; English translation, 1905).

Witte, Count Sergey Yulevich (1849–1915)

One of the two outstanding statesmen of the last years of Imperial Russia (the other was P. A. Stolypin). To some degree a "liberal" by inclination, he was also aware of the role a stable autocracy could play in the forced, rapid industrialization of Russia, which was his main goal. His support for autocracy was therefore based on rational rather than on mystical-national grounds. He tried to establish fiscal stability based on the gold standard to encourage foreign investment and to increase by all possible means the export of agricultural products and raw materials to help pay for industrialization. Witte had a rare rapport with Aleksandr III, who appointed him minister of finance. Nicholas II distrusted him and called him to office only when he desperately needed him, as, for example, during the dangerous days of 1905. He was replaced in 1906, and Stolypin, a more genuine conservative, became the lynchpin of policy as minister of the interior in 1907. But Nicholas did not trust Stolypin either and seemed to prefer more thoroughly subservient, second-rate ministers. See *The Memoirs of Count Witte,* trans. and ed. Sidney Harcave (Armonk, N.Y.: M. E. Sharpe, 1990), and Theodore von Laue, *Sergey Witte and the Industrialization of Russia* (New York: Columbia University Press, 1963).

World of Art   An artistic group formed in 1898 by Sergey Diaghilev. This group published a magazine under the same name until 1902. It included painters, poets, dramatists, and musicians who looked for inspiration from the West, the Orient, and their own Russian roots. They were at the heart of the Russian renaissance in the arts that led to the formation of the Ballets Russes and the Moscow Art Theater.

Yudenich,
General
Nikolay
Nikolaevich
(1862–1933)

General who fought for the Whites against the Bolshevik Red Army in the civil war of 1917–1921. He took control of Estonia with his army, and on October 21, 1919, he advanced toward Petrograd, entering Pavlovsk and Tsarskoe Selo, coming within twenty miles of the center of the city. Once Trotsky reached the front, the outnumbered White forces fell back to Estonia and disintegrated.

Zamyatin,
Evgeny
Ivanovich
(1884–1937)

Writer and engineer. Zamyatin was a Marxist and embraced the revolution at first. Later he would become critical of Soviet excesses, and in the early 1920's he wrote the antiutopian novel *We.* The novel was not published in its full form in Russian until 1952, and then only abroad, but the English translation by Gregory Zilboorg was published in 1924 and inspired George Orwell's *1984.* Zamyatin soon came under attack by Soviet critics and was banned from publication by 1929. In 1931, with Stalin's permission, he emigrated.

Zamyatina,
Lyudmila

Wife of writer Evgeny Ivanovich Zamyatin.

"Zangezi"   A 1921 dramatic poem, Futurist poet Velemir Khlebnikov's (see entry on Khlebnikov) last major work. The main character of the poem, Zangezi, is a prophet who speaks a universal cosmic language. Vladimir Tatlin staged the poem in 1923, but received poor reviews. Punin wrote an article about Tatlin's "Zangezi," which was published in the May 22

issue of *Life of Art*. In this article he laments that the audiences' inability to understand the poem was based not only on failure to embrace something out of the ordinary but also on the tendency to rationalize and analyze a production rather than to feel it.

Zaum — Transsense or metalogical language first developed by the Futurists.

Ziloti, Aleksandr Ivanovich (or Siloti, 1863–1945) — Famous Russian pianist and composer. He emigrated to the United States in the 1920's, where he remained the rest of his life.

Zinovev, Grigory Evseevich (originally Radomyslsky, 1883–1936) — One of Lenin's closest collaborators, though the collaboration was sometimes a shaky one. In October 1917, he opposed the bolshevik seizure of power. In 1918, when Lenin removed the capital to Moscow, Zinovev was appointed chief of the Petrograd Party organization. In 1919, he was appointed head of the Comintern as well. Along with Lev Kamenev, he supported Trotsky's policy of promoting world revolution, especially in Germany and China. In 1922, Zinovev and Kamenev joined Stalin against Trotsky. Zinovev was replaced as head of the Leningrad Party organization by 1926 by Stalin's friend Sergey Kirov, who became sufficiently popular with the Party rank and file to prompt Stalin's suspicions and, possibly later, in 1934, Kirov's murder, which then became the basis for the great purge. Zinovev was read out of and admitted back into the Party several times. In 1936, along with Kamenev and Aleksey Rykov, he was accused of counterrevolutionary conspiracy and implicated in the murder of Kirov. He was executed. Kirov was replaced by Andrey Zhdanov, who remained head of the Leningrad Party organization until 1948, when he mysteriously disappeared.

Zvucha-shchaya Rakovina (The Sounding Shell) — A cabaret that many in Akhmatova's and Punin's circles frequented.

INDEX